THE PHILOSOPHY OF CRIMINAL LAW

The Philosophy of Criminal Law: An Introduction explores the central [illegible] as intention, complicity and duress, and how they work, both within criminal law practice and in our everyday lives, from legal and philosophical perspectives.

At the heart of the book is the central philosophical concept of responsibility: what does it mean to be responsible for an act, to hold someone responsible for an act, or to give an excuse in order to avoid responsibility for an act? Offering talking points to enrich an ongoing conversation, this unique textbook addresses all of these questions in an accessible way for law and non-law students alike. Real cases are examined in detail and a critical approach to the criminal law is adopted throughout. The focus will be mainly on the criminal law of England and Wales, with occasional cases from other jurisdictions, and occasional examples from other areas of law.

This text will be ideal reading for advanced undergraduate and graduate students of law, philosophy and criminology, as well as political science and sociology.

Christopher Cowley works at the School of Philosophy of University College Dublin, Ireland.

Nicola Padfield is Emeritus Professor of Criminal and Penal Justice at the University of Cambridge.

THE PHILOSOPHY OF CRIMINAL LAW

An Introduction

Christopher Cowley and Nicola Padfield

Routledge
Taylor & Francis Group
LONDON AND NEW YORK

Designed cover image: The Toulouse Judith Beheading Holofernes, by Caravaggio or Louis Finson (c.1606–1607). Oil on canvas, 144 × 173.5 cm (57 × 68.3 in). Collection of J. Tomilson Hill

First published 2024
by Routledge
4 Park Square, Milton Park, Abingdon, Oxon OX14 4RN

and by Routledge
605 Third Avenue, New York, NY 10158

Routledge is an imprint of the Taylor & Francis Group, an informa business

British Library Cataloguing-in-Publication Data
A catalogue record for this book is available from the British Library

Library of Congress Cataloging-in-Publication Data
Names: Cowley, Christopher, 1967- author. | Padfield, Nicola, author.
Title: The philosophy of criminal law: an introduction / Christopher Cowley and Nicola Padfield.
Description: Abingdon, Oxon [UK]; New York, NY: Routledge, 2024. | Includes bibliographical references and index. | Provided by publisher.
Identifiers: LCCN 2023038453 | ISBN 9781032398976 (hardback) | ISBN 9781032398969 (paperback) | ISBN 9781003351887 (ebook)
Subjects: LCSH: Criminal law--Philosophy.
Classification: LCC K5018 .C69 2024 | DDC 345/.001--dc23/eng/20231002
LC record available at https://lccn.loc.gov/2023038453

ISBN: 978-1-032-39897-6 (hbk)
ISBN: 978-1-032-39896-9 (pbk)
ISBN: 978-1-003-35188-7 (ebk)

DOI: 10.4324/9781003351887

Typeset in Baskerville
by Deanta Global Publishing Services, Chennai, India

CONTENTS

AUTHORS AND ACKNOWLEDGEMENTS

Christopher Cowley works at the School of Philosophy of University College Dublin, Ireland. He has been teaching Philosophy of Criminal Law for about ten years. He has a PhD in Philosophy, but also an LLM and MPhil in Law. He is the editor of a volume called *The Philosophy of Autobiography* (Chicago 2015) and the author of a monograph *Moral Responsibility* (Routledge 2013).

Nicola Padfield is Emeritus Professor of Criminal and Penal Justice at the University of Cambridge, where she worked for more than 30 years. She has a broad research lens, engaged in both "hard" law and in socio-legal-criminological research. She is a leading European expert on sentencing law, including the law and practice of release from (and recall to) prison. Her books include *The Criminal Justice Process: Text and Materials* (5th edition, 2016); *Criminal Law* (10th edition, 2016); *Beyond the Tariff: Human Rights and the Release of Life Sentence Prisoners* (2002).

CC wishes to acknowledge the help of Beatrice Krebs, who provided detailed comments on four of the chapters at an early stage of writing. David Prendergast has been helpful throughout. Mark Coen was very generous when I was writing on complicity. NP wishes to thank CC for inviting her to join the project — the vast majority of the labour has been his!

CHAPTER 1

INTRODUCTION

There are lots of textbooks about criminal law on the market, but very few on the *philosophy* of criminal law.[1] What's the difference? Criminal law is a fascinating subject, both as an academic discipline and as a practice. Various other disciplines discuss it too: sociology and psychology, as well as political science and history. But what does philosophy have to offer?

For us, the primary purpose of philosophy is to *analyse concepts*; that is, to examine what the concepts mean, how they are used in various situations, what the user assumes when she deploys the concept, what distinctions she makes in deploying it, and how she might disagree with another in its deployment. The most important concept in the criminal law is "responsibility." Other central concepts are "justice," "harm," "consent," "intention" and "excuse," as well as "complicity" and "attempt" — and of course "punishment." We're going to be looking at all these familiar but complex concepts. Some of them are ethical, and some of our analysis of ethical concepts will lead to ethical criticisms of a particular judgement or statute — this is another purpose of a philosophy of criminal law.[2] Obviously, criminal lawyers and criminal law academics analyse concepts to a certain extent, but philosophers do it to a much greater depth.[3]

In the end the criminal lawyer's task is defined by the law — she has to get the law right, she has to apply it correctly, and she has to understand the latest developments in the law. The philosopher faces no such restriction. The law provides the starting point for her discussions, a set of detailed and often tragic examples, but then she is free to range more broadly within the larger study of human nature, human discourse, and human behaviour. In many parts of this book, we will be discussing quite ordinary situations in order to tease out the relevant ethical intuitions. At the same time, however, the philosopher must respect the internal coherence

1 There are a number of larger works on the philosophy of criminal law. The most impressive is Deigh and Dolinko's (2011) *Handbook on the Philosophy of Criminal Law*. This comprises a series of dense articles on a dozen major criminal concepts. Shute and Simester (2002), Duff and Green (2013), Flanders and Hoskins (2016), and Dolinko (2014) offer edited volumes. Tadros (2007) is a very philosophical work, based more on schematic examples than on real cases. Moore (2010) and Alexander and Ferzan (2009) focus more on the law, and are very detailed and technical. Herring (2020, 4th ed.) offers an interesting "debate" format, but is designed for law students and so skates over some of the more interesting philosophical problems. The closest to our book is Antony Duff's *Intention, Agency, and Criminal Liability* (1990), although its scope is narrower and it is by now inevitably out of date in certain key areas of the law. Finally, the reader should know about the on-line *Stanford Encyclopedia of Philosophy*, which offers many discussions of philosophical issues in the criminal law: see the key words on "theories of criminal law," "moral responsibility," "blame," "legal punishment," "the limits of law," "causation in the law," "informed consent," "moral luck."

In terms of the many criminal law textbooks on the market, we have been drawing mainly from Horder (2022), Child et al. (2022), and the hugely detailed Ormerod and Laird (2021). All three contain excellent detailed discussions that we consider philosophical (and we will be citing some of these), but as comprehensive textbooks they also contain an awful lot of detail.

2 For the purposes of this book, we will be using "ethical" and "moral" synonymously. We are also making three key assumptions: (i) that ethics is at least partly objective, and we therefore reject ethical subjectivism (according to which ethics is no more than a matter of personal opinion); (ii) that competent adult individuals have some free will. If the reader genuinely rejects the objectivity of ethics and the existence of free will, then she will not be able to engage much with the discussions in this book!

In addition, we will be assuming that (iii) the English criminal law generally expresses popular morality, and that it does this reliably enough to secure sufficient popular support. So the law against assault, for example, is not some random regulation; it fits with widespread ethical intuitions. This also means that ethical criticisms of the law are perfectly justified.

3 The Law Commission comprises a group of practising and academic lawyers who publish detailed public reports on existing laws and recommend new ones. Many of their arguments are philosophical. We will be citing some of their Reports in our book. Sometimes Parliament accepts the recommendations (in whole or in part), sometimes it does not. See www.lawcom.gov.uk/

DOI: 10.4324/9781003351887-1

of law, with its own distinctive terminology and taxonomy, its own traditions and norms, anchored in the history and politics of a particular society.

Importantly, we have made no effort at a *comprehensive* treatment of the criminal law: we have only selected a number of issues that raise philosophical interest. Often we have simplified the legal issues and terminology in order to avoid getting bogged down; often we have omitted points of procedure that lawyers will consider important; often we have left out details from the cases. We hope for a certain amount of indulgence from the legally educated reader. In return, we are not offering "what philosophers think" or any kind of dogmatic conclusions; instead, we are offering talking points to enrich an on-going conversation.

1.1 THE CENTRAL CONCEPT: RESPONSIBILITY

To get a better idea of what the philosophical analysis of a concept involves, let's start with the most important concept. What does it mean for D to be *responsible* for X? In philosophy, this question is part of an area called the "philosophy of action."[4]

Our use of the initial "D" here follows the traditional use in criminal law discussions: D is for defendant. The idea is that D is accused of doing X, and she is *defending* herself against accusations in a court of law. Accusing D of X means tentatively holding D responsible for committing offence X. What's more, most criminal investigations begin with a victim V. So typically D will be accused of committing X against V.[5]

To understand "responsibility," we first have to distinguish forward-looking (prospective) from backwards-looking (retrospective) responsibility. If I take a job working in a shop, there will usually be a job description, listing the "rights and responsibilities" associated with the role. So I might be responsible for "looking after customers who enter the shop": dealing with their enquiries, fetching a particular product, offering advice, taking their money, etc. I am responsible for behind-the-counter service. (Following the etymology, we can say my job is to *respond* to the needs of the customer.)

Criminal law is more interested in retrospective responsibility. V has been harmed, and we want to know who did it. The criminal law is an extension of very ordinary cases of interpersonal conflict. My pen is missing. I look at my colleague and I notice that she's using my pen. "Oi," I say, "you nicked my pen!" So I am accusing her of taking my property without my consent: I am holding her responsible *for* taking my pen. She might respond in a number of different ways, depending on the facts. She might say "This isn't your pen, relax"; and she might show it to me for closer inspection. As such she is denying *causal* responsibility; she did not cause the disappearance of my pen. (And, in normal situations, by implication she cannot be *morally* responsible — or culpable — for something for which she is not causally responsible.)

4 The first of many philosophical asides: "action" is a semi-technical term in philosophy. By definition it is something done by a competent human being, freely, and for a reason or purpose, such that the reason can in principle be offered to an observer to explain the action. An action is usually more than a mere bodily movement: if I press the light switch, then my action is best described as "turning the light on" (i.e. that is my purpose) rather than "pressing the switch." In contrast, if an epileptic has a fit, her bodily movements would not constitute "actions"; and the explanation of those movements would involve reference to the brain and to biochemistry rather than reasons.

5 There is a question of whether *blame* should be the central concept of criminal law rather than *responsibility*. It might not matter, since in a lot of contexts blame and responsibility can be two sides of the same coin. However, blame is less than satisfactory as a central concept because it is ambiguous on a crucial point: it can mean either the initial, unsubstantiated accusation, or the eventual just punishment. So it's clearer if we declare that the defendant's responsibility (i.e. culpability or guilt) has to be proved *before* the state's formal blame, both logically and chronologically. That's what the presumption of innocence means.

Or she might say "Is this your pen? Sorry, it looks just like mine." Here she admits causal responsibility, but denies moral responsibility on the basis of an honest mistake. At first glance, she *seemed* to be morally responsible (criminal law uses the word "culpable"), but she provides new information which "exculpates" her (i.e. removes her guilt). Or maybe it exculpates her only *partially*, since I might then think that she has been careless in not examining the pen more closely before taking it. In this latter case, I no longer hold her responsible for the taking, but I hold her responsible for the carelessness that led to the taking.

Already things are getting complicated in this basic practice of accusation and defence. Now let's ask: when I accuse my colleague of the unconsented pen-taking, what am I *assuming*? First, I am assuming that she is *competent* (in legal speak: that she has "capacity"). That means that she has the necessary mental abilities to understand what responsibility is, and she understands how to partake in responsibility-language: what it means to hold and be held responsible, what it means to defend oneself by invoking relevant reasons, etc. All adults are presumed to be competent until they can be demonstrated otherwise (e.g. they may be insane, or have "diminished responsibility").

Second, when I accuse my colleague I am assuming that she was sufficiently free, i.e. that she had a real choice about whether to take or not to take the pen. She could have left it alone. To put it another way: she had enough *control* over the situation to determine what would happen to the pen. Third, I am assuming that she *understood* enough of the situation to realise that the pen was not hers, and that she did not have my consent to take it (and she understands enough about how property and consent works).

The second and third assumptions are sometimes called the "control" (or "freedom") criterion and the "understanding" (or "knowledge") criterion of moral responsibility, respectively. And the two criteria point toward two paths for *denying* moral responsibility. We saw earlier what my colleague said about her mistaken acquisition of my pen: in so doing she was denying the understanding criterion. It turned out that she did not understand that the pen was mine, since it looked just like hers. Alternatively, she might have denied the control criterion. Perhaps her boss summoned her quickly to a meeting, she didn't have a pen and just grabbed the first one she saw. She might say later: "I didn't have any choice." Of course, if she does say that, I might well be unimpressed with her excuse, especially if my pen is, say, an expensive heirloom; and I might have things to say about her excuse. These are the sorts of ordinary familiar conversations that lie at the heart of the criminal law, even if the criminal trial is highly formalised and structured.

There are two more points of clarification here. First, responsibility is sometimes used with the verbs holding, taking and being. So far I have been *holding* her responsible for the pen-taking. If she denies taking my pen, she denies causal responsibility, she is saying that in fact she *is not* responsible, and that I am being unfair in holding her responsible; in other words, the "holding" does not correspond to the "being." In some situations, however, I can hold someone responsible even if they are not responsible (or if I am not sure if they are responsible). This is called "strict responsibility" (or "strict liability").

Next, if D *is* in fact responsible for X (some harm), then she should *take* responsibility for X, that is, she should accept blame and fair punishment. There might be situations, however, where she is *not* in fact responsible for X but where she nevertheless takes responsibility, e.g. in order to lie to protect a friend (who is in fact responsible).[6]

6 Throughout, we have been assuming that X is *harmful*. But of course X might be something good, and then "holding responsible" involves praise and reward, and mirrors the above discussion. Obviously, the criminal law is focused on negative events, and therefore starts with the problem of ascertaining whom to blame.

The second point of clarification is about the nature of the act being evaluated. It is a *discrete* act, i.e. it occupies a relatively short space of time. It is not like the action of "attending university," which might last three or four years. My colleague sees the pen, forms the intention to take it and then takes it. And when I hold her responsible, I am holding her responsible for the taking. Everything morally (and legally) relevant is contained in those few seconds. Nothing about her biography, about her character, or about my antecedent relationship with her is relevant to my judgement. Similarly, the criminal law is normally interested only in the discrete act: did you commit the single offence on 3 January, did you commit it intentionally, and did you do so without excuses or justifications? Again, D's past (including her criminal record) is not normally relevant. D's character (whether saint or sinner) is not normally relevant.

The questions about the relevance of the past and of D's character raise two contradictory issues of justice. On the one hand, if I know about D's criminal past then I might leap too quickly to conclusions beyond the available evidence about this occasion; if I find her to be a nasty person I might act prejudicially in my response; either way this would be unjust. On the other hand, if this last instance of pen-taking is part of a longer-term pattern of uncollegial behaviour, then perhaps my annoyance at this instance is insufficient, since justice would call for a formal investigation into the pattern by the Personnel Office. As we will see, these issues of timeframe become acute in the case of domestic abuse, which we discuss in Section 8.5, and partly explain the criminal law's long-standing inability to deal with it.

1.2 THE TRIAL

For our purposes, it will be enough if our readers are broadly familiar with the television and film representations of a criminal trial in the United Kingdom or the United States. (This system is called "adversarial," and is different from the system in France and Germany, for example.) An adversarial system involves a prosecution barrister (lawyer) who presents their case against the defendant, and a defence barrister who defends the defendant. A less serious case will be processed at a Magistrates Court, without a jury; a more serious case will be processed as a trial in the Crown Court, in the presence of a jury. The jury listen to the prosecution and defence arguments and evidence, and are guided by the judge on questions of law. The jury then decides on the defendant's guilt or innocence; and if guilty, the judge will decide on the appropriate sentence.[7]

A couple of notes before we continue. In the English criminal justice system the vast majority of criminal offences are processed without trial. Consider the offence of breaking the speed limit. Here the police send the offender a letter and ask them to pay a fine by a deadline. No police investigation, no trial, no lawyers. There is also a huge number of regulatory offences governing companies and other organisations. These might involve lawyers, but will probably not involve a trial.

Second, many of those suspected of the more familiar criminal offences are informally or formally cautioned by police, or served with a fixed penalty notice, and their case is not taken further. Even when the police decide to investigate the matter with a view to preparing for a

7 The jury will be asked whether they find the defendant "guilty" or "not guilty." In our book, we will mainly use "culpable" for two reasons. First, the jury's use of the word "guilty" is *binary*, that is, it's all or nothing. In contrast, culpability is scalar: the defendant can be more or less culpable. Second, "guilt" is ambiguous between *feelings* of guilt and the *ethical status* of being guilty — obviously the two can come apart. Culpability is only about the ethical status.

trial, most defendants plead guilty, and the matter will proceed directly to sentencing without a trial. (There are generous sentence discounts for those who plead guilty.) So a trial is a rare event, and it has to be rare since trials are slow and expensive. We're going to look at the trials that take place in England and Wales, our main jurisdiction for this book.

So the police investigate an offence, and gather evidence. At a certain point, they pass their evidence and their notes to the Crown Prosecution Service (CPS), who represent the state.[8] This is one counter-intuitive aspect of the criminal law. When the offence is committed, it is committed against *the state* and not against the *victim*. Formally, the victim is no more than a witness to the offence. That means that it is the state which "defends itself" by mounting the prosecution against D. Whether the actual victim wants or doesn't want D to be prosecuted, or wants D to be punished more or less, may be irrelevant. It also means that, if D is convicted, it will be the state who punishes her. As such, criminal law is part of "public law" (the law governing the relationship between the individual and the state). In contrast, the law of tort and the law of contract (parts of "private" law) essentially involve one individual suing another individual for compensation, and the state may act as a mediator.[9]

The CPS examine the evidence and the police notes. They may drop the case if they feel there is not enough evidence. Or they may drop it if they feel that proceeding with the case is not in the public interest. If they decide to proceed with the case, they will allocate it to the Magistrates Court or Crown Court. (The two Courts can be described as "lower" courts, or as the courts "of first instance"; as opposed to appeal courts.)

The prosecution present their case against D, and their task is divided roughly into three overlapping components:

(i) The prosecution have to show that D *did it*. More specifically, that she committed the *actus reus* (the physical act) of the offence, on such-and-such a date, and against such-and-such a victim. The prosecution have to offer proof (evidence and testimony) "beyond a reasonable doubt" — note how high the standard of proof is. At this point D (or her defence lawyer) may deny the accusation, that is, she may deny causal responsibility for the act, perhaps because she has an alibi. Without sufficient proof, D has to be acquitted.

(ii) The prosecution then have to show that D performed the *actus reus* with a certain degree of culpability (moral responsibility), also known by lawyers as *mens rea* (the "guilty mind"). There is a scale of culpability, running from most culpable to least:

1. Did D *intend* to do it? Did she do it deliberately, on purpose? Was that her plan? We discuss intentional action in Chapter 2.
2. Was D *reckless*? That is, when planning to do something else, was she aware of the risk of harming V, but decided to run the risk anyway? We discuss recklessness in Chapter 3.
3. Was D *negligent*? That is, did she fail to notice/remember/check something that she should have noticed/remembered/checked, given her particular role — and this led to V being harmed? We discuss negligence in Chapter 4.

8 See the CPS website: https://www.cps.gov.uk/

9 Sometimes, as in the case of *Adomako* (which we discuss in detail in Chapter 4 on Negligence), the same defendant can be subject to a criminal process and a tort process at the same time; the criminal process may result in a prison sentence, whereas the tort process is almost always about money.

(iii) For the third component, if D offers a "defence" of her harmful action, i.e. an excuse or a justification, in the hope of reducing or even eliminating her culpability, the prosecution will have to show that the defence is not valid, on a balance of probabilities. We discuss defences in Chapter 10.

After hearing all the evidence, and listening to closing speeches from the lawyers, and the judge's summing up, the jury will deliberate, and return a verdict of guilty or not guilty. The judge will then set the sentence. If D is found guilty, then she will have the right to appeal, and from the Crown Court, this is normally to the Court of Appeal (Criminal Division). That Court then goes over the documentation from the Crown Court, first without any new presentations by lawyers, without listening to witnesses, and without meeting the defendant. At a full hearing on appeal, the lawyers will present their arguments, but witnesses are rare. The Court will allow or reject the appeal, and will give their reasons in writing.

It should be noted that most cases do not go to appeal, and therefore the argumentation of each side is not formally recorded. However, when a case does go to appeal, the judge(s) have to spell out their justifications in detail, and this is recorded and publicly accessible. This means that the majority of cases cited in a criminal law textbook are appeal cases, where the textbook can discuss the justifications. If the appeal is rejected, the defendant can appeal to the Supreme Court, although the Supreme Court will only hear this second appeal if they feel that it is in the public interest and that there is an important point of law that needs settling.[10]

We're not going to worry about further details of the process unless they are relevant to the philosophical discussions that follow; in the same way, we're not going to worry too much about differences between countries. As we said, we focus on English cases and legislation.[11] Occasionally we will make comparisons to other Anglophone "common law" countries such as the United States, Canada, Australia and Ireland where the structures, procedures and terminology are often similar. Right away we have to add that the United States actually has *50* criminal jurisdictions as well as a set of *federal* crimes, so this is complicated. One useful American document we will occasionally cite is the *Model Penal Code* (MPC), which was created by legal academics in the 1950s. It has no legal validity, but has proved influential when individual states formulate or develop their criminal laws.

Notoriously, England does not have a criminal code — a central statute with a comprehensive description of all the main crimes. A *draft* criminal code was submitted to and rejected by Parliament in 1989, and this is sometimes worth referring to. But without a central statute, where does English criminal law come from? There are some major Parliamentary statutes for certain areas of the law, e.g. the *Offences Against the Person Act* 1861 (which we discuss throughout the book), or the *Sexual Offences Act* 2003 (which we discuss mainly in Chapter 9). Most crimes nowadays have their definitions in a statute, but the detail of the criminal law comes from *cases*, or rather from appeal judgements where the judges *interpret* prior law and principles, and thereby set a precedent for future cases. At law schools, students study loads of important cases (as well as the handful of important statutes), and slowly build up the relevant chronology. So, for example, the interpretation of "recklessness" moved from a "subjective" version to an "objective" version in 1982 via the *Caldwell* case, then back to

10 Before 2009, the highest court in the United Kingdom was the House of Lords (HL), i.e. the upper chamber of Parliament. Some of its members were appointed as "Law Lords" (i.e. senior judges), and they made up the highest court. In 2009 the highest court was renamed the Supreme Court (SC).

11 Our focus is on the single jurisdiction of *England and Wales*, mainly because this is the largest of the jurisdictions in the United Kingdom. Although Scotland has a separate criminal justice system, there is only one UK Supreme Court; if a defendant appeals to the Supreme Court from a Scottish case, then the Supreme Court has to adjudicate it on the basis of Scottish Law.

the "subjective" version in 2003 via the *R v G* case. (We discuss this particular history in Section 3.2.)

English law's reliance on case law means that many areas of the law are messy, with some inconsistency and incoherence. Another disadvantage is that judges are sometimes accused of making law, when it should only be Parliament who make laws. It's true, however, that even in a country with a criminal code like Canada, there will be some contradictions in the interpretations and applications of different provisions over time. And there are advantages to the law's ability to evolve when faced with specific factual examples.

1.3 THREE OTHER PHILOSOPHICAL THEMES

There are three further philosophical themes that are so fundamental to any discussion of the criminal law that we will be returning to them again and again in this book. So it is worth introducing them here.

First, there is the problem of subjectivity, objectivity and the related notion of counterfactual speculation. When an agent acts in the world, she acts on the basis of what she believes and interprets — subjectively. But the world comprises objective facts, about which she might well be mistaken in her beliefs and memories and interpretations. This is a central tension of the human condition, and forms an on-going theme throughout ethics and the criminal law. However, there is a question about the agent's epistemic access. In Chapter 4 on negligence, we discuss the case of *Adomako*, where an anaesthetist failed to notice a dislodged oxygen tube, and the patient suffocated to death as a result. Subjectively, Adomako thought everything was fine. Objectively, there was a fact about the patient's life under direct threat from the dislodged tube. The law cannot expect the agent to notice *every* dangerous fact around her. So instead the law constructs another version of objectivity by asking: would a "reasonable person" (or in this case the reasonable anaesthetist) have noticed the dangerous fact and responded appropriately to it? If so, then that is like another objective "fact." If the reasonable person would *not* have noticed the dangerous fact, then the law cannot reproach the defendant for her failure to notice it.

The reasonable person test involves counterfactual speculation. Such counterfactual speculation goes much further in the law. For example, there is a question in tort law about the precise definition of harm. Some kinds of harm are clear enough: if someone assaults me and breaks my leg, then my leg has lost some of the natural function that it would presumably have had without the assault. As a result, I might not be able to continue my career as a professional footballer, and therefore I will lose all the future income I could reasonably have expected to receive without the assault. Such an amount can be quantified for the purposes of calculating the compensation that my assaulter owes me. In another context, say that the police have D under surveillance. She seems to be making the first moves toward committing a crime. When should the police intervene? The earlier they intervene, the less risk for the intended victim; the later they intervene, the more evidence they have of what she *would have gone on to do*. Often such speculation is straightforward, and it reveals how much we share understandings of human action and motivation. But there are other cases where it might not be clear what the agent would have done, just as it might not be clear to me what *I* would have done in some unprecedented situations.

A second major theme of the book goes by the name of "moral luck." The problem was "launched" by two articles of that name by the philosophers Thomas Nagel (1979) and Bernard Williams (1981). Normally we think of morality (and by extension, criminal law) as *immune* to luck. As we have seen, when I hold you responsible for X, I am assuming that X was entirely within your control. If you have a good excuse, then I should accept that you have less or perhaps no responsibility for X. All that seems fair. But it turns out that there are certain scenarios where some elements can affect the moral value of X despite *not* being in your control (and therefore a matter of luck), to the point where our responses might be unfair. Consider the following pairs of stories:

- D1 and D2 are assassins. They both prepare their guns and take aim at their respective intended victims V1 and V2. They both squeeze their triggers. D1's bullet kills V1. D2's bullet misses out of sheer luck (V2 moves, the wind blows, etc.) D1 and D2 are both apprehended. D1 is convicted of *murder* and gets life in prison. D2 is convicted of *attempted murder* and gets ten years in prison (i.e. it is morally less severe). And yet they both had the same murderous intention, and they both did the same thing — pulled a trigger. Neither of them could control the situation after the bullets left the guns. That seems unfair.
- D1 and D2 are reckless girl racers. They both drive at high speed along a country road at 3 am. They are both aware of the risks, and they callously ignore them. D1 hits and kills a pedestrian. D2 hits nobody. D1 and D2 are both apprehended. D1 is convicted of "causing death by dangerous driving" and gets ten years in prison. D2 is convicted of "dangerous driving," is fined, and banned from driving for a year. And yet — in terms of the control they had over their driving, while disregarding the known risks — they were both doing the same thing. That seems unfair.
- D1 and D2 are would-be accomplices (accessories). They both lend their crowbars to their friends P1 and P2, with the explicit intention of assisting the burglaries that P1 and P2 are overtly planning. P1 takes D1's crowbar to the target house, and uses it to break in. P2 forgets D2's crowbar at home, and carries out the burglary without it. P1 and P2 are arrested and charged with burglary. D1 is also arrested and charged as an accessory to burglary. Whereas D2 has done nothing wrong, and is released after interrogation. Again, both D1 and D2 have done the same thing, with the same intention, but with very different outcomes. That seems unfair.

One "solution" to the problem of moral luck would be to define the crimes entirely by their *subjective* elements, that is, the elements under the actor's control: so the two assassins would be guilty of the same intentional attempt, regardless of the outcome. Perhaps the penalty would be the mandatory life sentence for both; perhaps it would be ten years for both — but at any rate it would be the same. And yet this is not what the law does, nor is it how we would intuitively respond to the story-pairs. We will return to the story-pairs in our discussions of attempts (Chapter 6), recklessness (Chapter 3) and complicity (Chapter 7).

The third theme comprises feminist approaches to the criminal law. One of the early reviewers of the book wondered why there was no chapter explicitly on feminist philosophy or feminist jurisprudence. Both approaches are now well-established in the legal literature and philosophical literature, of course.[12] However, we have resisted the suggestion of a discrete chapter, and have opted instead to include feminist arguments and approaches throughout the book. Having a separate chapter gives the impression that feminism can somehow be

12 For further reading see Kotiswaran (2014) on feminist approaches to criminal law; on gender and the law more generally, see the textbook edited by Auchmuty (2018); Hunter, McGlynn and Rackley (2010) is thought-provoking but not limited to criminal law; the on-line *Stanford Encyclopedia of Philosophy* has an entry "Feminist philosophy of law," written by Leslie Francis: https://plato.stanford.edu/entries/feminism-law/

logically separated away from the rest of criminal law discussions (and therefore ignored), whereas we would argue that feminist criticism is essential to many discussions. For example, to complain that the traditional defence of provocation was strongly influenced by patriarchal norms is not a claim that should be made in the "feminism" chapter (if there is one) but instead in the "defences" chapter (as we have done). In addition, it is not a claim that only "feminists" should point out, it is a claim which everyone should now acknowledge as uncontroversial. Most crimes are gender-neutral, and we will be taking them as such; some crimes — domestic abuse and sexual offences are the obvious ones — involve different experiences for men and for women, and we will be acknowledging this.[13]

1.4 SIX AREAS OF LAW NOT IN THIS BOOK

Before we proceed to an outline of the book, it is worth spelling out six areas of legal scholarship with which we will not be engaging much. Some of these areas are often covered by discrete courses at law school, and have voluminous literatures, but we simply don't have the space to do any of them justice.

(i) This book is not a work of "jurisprudence" (also known as "legal theory" or "philosophy of law"). Jurisprudence is about the nature of law and law-making, of rules and rule-following, about the nature of constitutions, and about the relationship between the judiciary and the legislature. There is an overlap with political philosophy, and questions of democracy, liberalism, and equality. On occasion, we will brush up against some of these topics, but mostly we'll be starting our discussion with the familiar Western state *already* in place, with enough democratic authority, and with a broadly fair but effective criminal justice system.

(ii) We will not touch on human rights very much, where this is understood as the rights set out in various documents such as the European Convention on Human Rights and enforced by courts. Clearly most, if not all criminal offences will involve some violation of rights, but we do not believe that the *language* of rights and rights violations helps us enough to understand the nature of crime and the responsibility of the defendant. Rights become vital when we talk about fair procedures, beyond the scope of this book.

(iii) As should be evident from the discussion so far, our focus is on *domestic* rather than *international* criminal law. Ever since the Nuremburg trials in 1946, international criminal law has become complicated and dynamic, with a special role for the emerging case law from the International Criminal Court in The Hague, Netherlands. The main problem in understanding international criminal law is that most of the crimes take place in the context of some kind of military action involving large groups of soldiers.

(iv) We will not be discussing private law much. Criminal law is part of public law, governing the relationship between the individual and the state. Private law involves interactions between two individuals, often mediated by the state: tort, contract, and property laws are the paradigm areas of private law, together with large chunks of medical law, family law and employment law. Some of the crimes we discuss in this book take place in a context where other legal issues will arise in these other areas of

13 Finally, there is a debate about the degree to which the "reasonable person" standard is an irretrievably gendered concept, given the long history of its deployment in a male-dominated legal profession. In our book, we prefer to aim for a gender-neutral concept of reasonableness, while acknowledging different kinds of reasonableness in certain situations. For discussion, see Dimock (2008).

law, but we are hoping to conceptually isolate the criminal element, and the state's response, as much as possible.

(v) We will not say very much about mental health, and the exact ways that it can influence culpability. We will not discuss the defences of "insanity" (and the so-called M'Naghten Rules) or "diminished responsibility" in any great detail, nor the phenomena of psychopathy and sociopathy, nor will we look at different ways that a defendant might be "unfit to stand trial." We will not compare cognitive defects with volitional defects ("irresistible impulses"). We will not say much about the culpability of children and teenagers. All such discussion would require nuanced and detailed psychiatric explanations, which would distract too much from the philosophical issues. Ordinary competent adults are complicated enough already.

(vi) We will not be concerned in detail with criminal justice or criminology. Criminal justice is about the procedures and structures governing the police, the court system, and the prisons. Criminology is a social science that looks at patterns of criminal behaviour and incarceration, within a larger context of society. Although we have a full Chapter about punishment (Chapter 11), we are being careful to limit ourselves to philosophical issues. The full picture will obviously require some knowledge of the social reality, and we hope that our criminological and sociological readers can take away some new understandings, e.g. of the nature of culpability, that will help them in their own descriptive enquiries.

1.5 OUTLINE OF THE BOOK

Let us look at some of the typical philosophical problems that we will be discussing in each chapter. The first three chapters, Chapters 2, 3 and 4, are about the three different categories of *mens rea*: intention, recklessness and negligence. The three chapters touch on many similar themes, and could be considered one long chapter. Intentional action should be taken as the paradigm grounds for culpability. If D intentionally commits the *actus reus* of an offence, that would seem the most straightforward conceptual matter for the criminal law to deal with. But what is the difference between an intention and a desire? If I am being blackmailed, I intentionally pay the money, but I have no desire to. And there are questions about the precise object of the intention: did D assault V as an act of revenge, or merely because she was in the way? D's knowledge might also be relevant to the precise nature of the intention: if D intentionally lends P her crowbar, it makes a big difference whether D knows about P's planned burglary this weekend or not. Chapter 3 on recklessness looks at the different ways that people can recognise and appreciate risks, and how they respond to such risks, such that they end up causing unintentional harm, to themselves or others. One problem is about moral luck, and the different punishments meted out to the two equally reckless girl racers. But consider also a simple example from the medical context. There is a real question of what it means to *appreciate* a risk: do heavy smokers really understand the risk of lung cancer? Can heavy smokers really imagine what it will be like to have lung cancer? And yet most heavy smokers are competent. Chapter 4 on negligence is about a phenomenon that looks quite similar to recklessness, except that D is *not* conscious of a risk of harm — but she *should be* (especially if she occupies a role with an explicit duty of care toward the victim). Other than that structural similarity, negligence is quite strikingly different from intention and recklessness because of the absence of anything in D's head to "pin" the blame on: she has neither intended to do harm, nor has she intentionally disregarded a known risk of harm. That would seem to make D unfree at the moment of the negligent omission, and this would make blame unfair.

We then change gear a little, and Chapter 5 will look at a central metaphysical problem at the heart of all crime, regardless of the *mens rea*: what does it mean to *cause* something? In the paradigm case, I desire to cause and I intentionally cause harm, and it is then straightforward to blame me for the harm: there is a sense that I "own" the harm since I freely and knowingly brought it into the world. Ideally my causal contribution was also *necessary* for the consequence to come into being: without my contribution, it would not have happened (so another case of counterfactual speculation). But what if I make a causal contribution to something that would have happened anyway? What if I knowingly refrain from prevention, knowing that there is a good chance that harm will ensue — have I caused that harm, and is it fair to then hold me responsible for it?

Chapters 6 and 7 look at *modes of liability*, that is, different ways of committing a crime. *Inchoate offences* are those that do not produce harmful consequences but *might well have*. There are various reasons why D might attempt and fail to murder V, for example: perhaps V ducked, as in our example of moral luck above; perhaps the police intervened at the last moment; perhaps D abandoned the attempt when she learned of the police surveillance. And yet there is something paradoxical with charging D for attempting murder when she hasn't harmed anyone (indeed, the intended victim might be completely oblivious). A conspiracy involves at least two people who plan to carry out some kind of joint offence, but they fail, perhaps harmlessly, and again for various kinds of reasons. Chapter 7 looks at complicity. An "accessory" (D) assists or encourages a "principal" (P) to commit an offence. The principal is apprehended and found straightforwardly guilty; but what sort of assistance or encouragement does the accessory have to carry out in order to be culpable too? After all, if D offers P her crowbar for P's planned burglary, or if D offers encouragement to P to commit it, then surely there is a basic sense that P (if competent) makes a free, deliberate and informed choice to use the crowbar or encouragement, thereby assuming *all* the responsibility? What does it matter which tool he uses, and whose tool? And surely P cannot say "D encouraged me to do it" as some sort of excuse? One (problematic) response invokes causation: if D *persuades* P to commit a crime that P would not otherwise have committed, then D as causal origin should be held responsible.

Chapters 8 and 9 focus on two substantive areas of criminal law. Up until this point, the book has been speaking more generally — about the nature of *mens rea* (Chapters 2, 3, 4), about more metaphysical issues in causation (Chapter 5), and about modes of liability (Chapters 6 and 7) relevant to all offences. Chapter 8 is about the offences surrounding homicide and assault. Murder (intentional killing) is the most severe offence in the criminal law. However, there are interesting questions about how the requisite "intention" can be stretched to accommodate certain kinds of unintentional killing. Among the remaining kinds of unintentional killing, which are penalised as manslaughter (and on what basis), and which should be ignored as unfortunate accidents? One answer would be to say that if D is already carrying out a dangerous and unlawful act (an assault, say), then she should be held responsible for any unintended deaths resulting directly from her unlawful act. Is this fair? The Chapter concludes with a special context of assault, that of domestic abuse. Chapter 9 looks at the substantive area of law to do with sexual offences. Unlike the law surrounding murder and manslaughter, English law offers relatively tidy and comprehensive, if complex, legislation containing all the relevant offences (the *Sexual Offences Act*, 2003), and parts of this merit philosophical scrutiny, especially with regard to the nature of consent, coercion and deception.[14]

14 There are other substantive areas of criminal law that will not get their own chapter, whereas they would get their own chapter in a standard Criminal Law textbook. Property is one area; public order offences is another; information and communication offences is a third.

Chapter 10 is the longest chapter, and it discusses defences, that is, the sorts of things that D can say in her defence when accused of committing the *actus reus* with the requisite *mens rea*. Philosophers divide these roughly into justifications, such as self-defence, and excuses, such as duress and loss of control. A *justification* involves demonstrating that what appeared to be an offence is in fact not; an *excuse* involves demonstrating that a defendant who appeared to be fully responsible for committing the offence was in fact not (or not fully). Some defences might be either, depending on the facts. Obviously the various defences have to be precisely defined, since every defendant will be tempted to make use of them — and defining them turns out to be difficult. A lot depends on what the defendant believed about the threat (in the case of duress or self-defence), and about the particulars of the situation.

Finally, Chapter 11 concerns punishment. This is a topic that is not usually found in criminal law textbooks, since it is considered part of criminal justice or criminology. However, the problem of justifying punishment is a classic philosophical topic, and relies on our earlier discussions of *mens rea*. Traditionally, there are two big philosophical justifications of punishment, called "retributivist" and the "consequentialist," and they raise different questions about what a system of state punishment is supposed to do. We will also look at how parole works, and in what sense it might be considered just or unjust.

1.6 THE COVER IMAGE

Let us close this Introduction with a word about the cover image. It's a cropped version of an unsigned painting called *Judith and Holofernes*, which was found in an attic in Toulouse, France, in 2014. It has been called the "Toulouse Judith," and has been attributed to Caravaggio, but this is a matter of debate.[15] (Caravaggio had already painted the same scene,[16] but there are also versions by other painters, including Gentileschi.[17])

We wanted to avoid some of the clichés of crime and criminals — handcuffs, gavels, police uniforms, bloodied daggers, not to mention chalk body outlines on the floor. We also wanted to avoid gore, and so cropped out the cutting of Holofernes's throat, leaving us only with Judith and her servant and the raised sword. Viewers who don't know the painting will be immediately struck by Judith's provocative gaze: she's clearly up to no good. As it happens, she's committing this massive crime just "off-camera," but we don't know that yet, and need to investigate. But there are other themes relevant to this book. The servant is interesting: she's looking at Judith rather than at Holofernes. Is she warning Judith, is she worried about her? How complicit is she in the murder?

Once we know a bit more of the backstory, we also change our judgement of Judith. The Old Testament book of Judith describes how Holofernes, an Assyrian general, was preparing to invade and destroy Judith's home village of Bethulia. Together with her servant, she approaches the Assyrian camp, and informs the sentries that she wants to save herself by betraying the details of Bethulia's defences. Eventually she is led to Holofernes and left alone with him. Holofernes is interested to hear about the defences, but also interested in an evening of alcohol and sex with a pretty woman. However, she out-drinks him, and once he has passed out, takes his sword and decapitates him. As such, this is no mere murder, this is a justified political act of self-defence.

15 Reyburn S. "Is That a Real Caravaggio? It's All in the Detail" *The New York Times*, 28 February 2019: https://www.nytimes.com/2019/02/28/arts/design/caravaggio-judith-holofernes.html
16 https://en.wikipedia.org/wiki/Judith_Beheading_Holofernes_(Caravaggio)
17 https://en.wikipedia.org/wiki/Judith_Slaying_Holofernes_(Artemisia_Gentileschi,_Naples)

CHAPTER 2

INTENTIONAL ACTION

Let's start with the three-component trial structure we described in Chapter 1: the prosecution have to prove (i) that defendant D did it (the *actus reus*); (ii) that she did it with enough culpability (the *mens rea*); and (iii) that she can offer no defence (excuse or justification). We're going to assume that there is enough evidence that D did it, and we're going to look at the second component. This and the next two chapters will be about the three degrees of culpability, running along a spectrum from most morally injurious to least: intention (this chapter), recklessness (Chapter 3) and negligence (Chapter 4). Some of the main philosophical problems are located at the blurred boundaries between these three. Normally, however, if two defendants have caused the same amount of harm, with one causing it intentionally and the other causing it negligently, then the meaning of the acts and the harms will be different: intentional harm is generally more serious in that it reveals a kind of destructive, disrespectful anti-social malevolence, and therefore merits more blame and punishment. In contrast, negligence might just be the result of thoughtlessness.

Intentional action is the paradigm in discussions of moral and criminal responsibility, and the other concepts are defined in contrast to it. When I hold D responsible for the action (when I blame her), I "pin" the blame on the intention.[1] Even when D attempts and fails to commit a crime, and even if she causes no harm (and the intended victim is oblivious), she is still blameworthy because of her intention. As Ormerod and Laird (2021, p. 92) put it:

> If D has resolved to kill V and he fires a loaded gun at him with the object of doing so, he intends to kill. It is immaterial that he is aware that he is a poor shot, that V is nearly out of range and that his chances of success are small. It is sufficient that killing is his object or purpose: that he acts in order to kill.

In the "bad shot" case, if D *improbably* ends up killing V, it will be murder; if he misses, it will be attempted murder. Both crimes, murder and attempted murder, require an intention to kill, and do not depend on objective probabilities. The planned killing does not even have to be physically possible in the circumstances: perhaps D's gun was empty, but D never found out because the police arrested him before he could pull the trigger. Indeed, D's plan might involve breaking the laws of nature (as when he sticks pins in a voodoo doll), but if *D* believes it to be possible, he will still in principle be guilty of attempted murder.[2]

Confusingly, the concept of "intention" is used in three different ways in ordinary speech. First, it can be about a longer-term plan, as when I declare my intention to travel to Bognor Regis next week. Second, it can be about an immediate purpose, as when I am on the train platform and I ask the guard "Excuse me, my intention is to get to Bognor Regis now — which platform does the train leave from?" Third, once I am on the train, I can be described using an adverb, i.e. as travelling to Bognor Regis *intentionally* (as opposed to aiming somewhere

1 Murder was traditionally defined as requiring "malice aforethought." The word "malice" is better interpreted as "intention," since one can plainly commit murder without malice. "Aforethought" suggests planning, but it is plainly possible to commit murder spontaneously.

2 It is worth flagging one difference here. An intentionally *attempted* (failed) offence is a different offence from a successful offence. In contrast, being intentionally *complicit* in an offence is not a separate offence but a separate mode of culpability. If D assists P in murdering V, then D will be straightforwardly guilty of murder. But D will also be guilty of murder, as an accessory, even if he was physically nowhere near the murder scene. We discuss attempts in Chapter 6 and complicity in Chapter 7.

DOI: 10.4324/9781003351887-2

else and finding oneself on the Bognor train mistakenly). Trying to accommodate these three contexts is a long-standing problem in the philosophy of action.

One way of solving the problem might be to define intention in terms of desire. Normally, if I intend to go swimming, it is because I desire, I want, to go swimming; and if something prevents me I will try again. But this raises a couple of problems. First of all, there are situations where we do something intentionally without desiring to do it: my intention to visit the dentist for root canal surgery next week comes to mind; or the bank teller who hands the money over to the armed robber. Second, consider Antony Duff's annoyed lecturer (1990, p. 57): the lecturer has a student whom she finds persistently annoying. The student submits his assignment along with everyone else, and the lecturer marks the assignments anonymously. The annoying student ends up doing badly, and the lecturer is pleased. She desired that he do badly, but she did not act on that desire; nor did she have any intention to mark him down; instead, she acted on the intention to give each piece of work the mark it deserved.

One dominant philosophical account of intention comes from Michael Bratman (1981), and his account fits closely with the legal conception of *mens rea*. Bratman starts with the first two uses of "intention," and sees them as mental states like desires and beliefs and memories; when I act, I am — more or less successfully — carrying out the intention. The third context of intention — the adverb "intentionally" — is the tricky one for Bratman in two senses, as Bebhinn Donelly-Lazarov (2017) explains. (i) A purely spontaneous action (without any antecedent intention in the mind) can still be intentional, at least in the minimal sense that it is not unintentional (accidental, or a reflex). If someone throws a punch at me, I spontaneously but intentionally move out of the way. When you observe me dodging the punch, there is an important sense in which my intention is *in my action*, rather than — as Bratman would have it — in my mind. (ii) Consider the expression "actions speak louder than words." Maybe I have the genuine intention (the mental state) of giving up smoking, and I tell everybody about it. And I cite many of the well-known reasons to give up smoking. And yet I continue smoking, and I do so intentionally. My action would seem to invalidate my reported (mental state) intention, even if I reported it sincerely. These complications will re-emerge in legal cases too.

To further add to the complexity of the concept, we can distinguish different kinds of intentional crimes, according to different kinds of target. For this section we'll continue the focus on homicide, just because it's a conceptually clear "result" crime, and it makes sense to ask what exactly the agent intended.

In passing, most crimes are result crimes: most murder investigations begin with the discovery of a dead body. Result crimes are to be distinguished from "conduct" crimes and "circumstance" crimes. A conduct crime is defined by the agent's conduct, regardless of any result: so an agent can commit the crime of "dangerous driving" even if she does not produce any particular result, i.e. she does not hit anybody or cause any damage. A circumstance crime is defined by the existence of a particular circumstance. For example, sexual intercourse is not intrinsically wrong or illegal; but it becomes rape under two conditions: the victim "does not consent," and the perpetrator "does not reasonably believe that [the victim] consents."[3]

If D causes the death of V, the court will enquire about D's intention. If her intention was to cause the death of D, then — assuming she cannot offer any excuses or justifications — she will be charged with murder, and, if convicted, given the mandatory sentence of life in prison.[4] But even this relatively simple *legal* position conceals a more complicated *moral* position.

3 Section 1(1) of the *Sexual Offences Act* 2003.

4 Normally a judge has a range of possible sentences within which she can take account of mitigating and aggravating circumstances. Murder is the one exception in requiring a mandatory sentence of life. This mandatory sentence was introduced in 1965 as a way of compensating for the abolition of capital

These moral distinctions will not affect the mandatory sentence, but they might be relevant to the possibility of early release. We're listing these different *objects* of intention from the most specific to the most abstract:

(i) intentional targeted killing against a *particular individual*, e.g. in a spirit of personal revenge. The distinguishing point here is non-substitutability. Only the death of that individual will satisfy the perpetrator, given who that individual is or what he has done.

(ii) intentional killing against the occupant of a particular *group*, e.g. a visible minority. Here the victim is substitutable by any other member of that targeted group.

(iii) intentional killing of an occupant of a particular *role*, e.g. a security guard impeding a bank robbery. Here there is nothing personal against the individual, nor against his group identity (e.g. his race). Nor indeed is it anything against security guards in general, it merely has to do with this particular guard's perceived capacity and will to impede the robbers' plans here and now. Presumably, if the security guard could be incapacitated or removed without killing him, that would be preferable.

(iv) intentional killing of *whoever* actually happens to be affected by the fatal act. This is also known as *indiscriminate malice*. The victims are individuated only at the moment of the act, e.g. the random victims of a terrorist bomb. In one sense, this is the least morally offensive category because it is not focused on the specific individuals; in another sense, of course, it is the *most* morally offensive precisely because it is indiscriminate.

2.1 INTENTION AND MOTIVE

We mentioned in the Introduction that the law was more interested in intention than in motive. The concepts sound close in meaning. Motive is already familiar from the detective novel genre, which is obviously close to criminal law. At least half of a good detective novel is about finding out who did it and how, but often the other half is about motive.[5] The police and the detectives are trying to reconstruct the narrative around the perpetrator's actions on the fateful night in order to make this initially baffling murder intelligible. But just as the relationship between intention and desire was more complicated than first appeared, so too the relationship between intention and motive.

In many contexts "motive" will be directly and clearly linked to "intention." If you rob the bank, your intention is normally to take the money from that bank, and your motive is precisely to have more money.[6] However, the default position of the criminal law is generally to ignore motive. Here's why: if a competent D can be shown to have performed the *actus reus* with the requisite *mens rea* (e.g. intention) and without an excuse or justification, she will be found guilty of the crime, and her motivation is irrelevant. The guilt is in the commission of

---

punishment. In practice, a life sentence does not usually mean a life *in prison*. Subject to good behaviour and a risk assessment, some "lifers" can be released after they have served a minimum term, although they will remain "on licence" for the rest of their life; that is, any further criminal activity, or any suspicion of a new danger to the public, will result in them returning to prison.

5 Famously, the detective novels of Georges Simenon are often dominated by Inspector Maigret's tireless search for the perpetrator's motive, long after his discovery of his or her identity (i.e. which would conclude the legal aspect of the case).

6 In passing, there is an interesting equivocation in the word "why." When I ask why, I could be asking for an *explanation* of your action (i.e. to make it intelligible because I am perplexed), or I could be asking for a *moral justification* of your action (because I am appalled). When the famous American criminal Willie Sutton was asked why he robbed banks, he replied "because that's where the money is."

the crime, rather than in how she got there. D's motivation might be *evidence* of intention, but hardly conclusive on its own. If someone intentionally commits a crime with the best of intentions (e.g. Robin Hood), he is still guilty and the court should declare him so.

There are a number of exceptions to this general point about motives, and in such cases we can say that the motivation "colours" the intention. Looking at these exceptions will tell us more about what intention is, and how it is treated by the criminal law.

(i) *Compassion*
Some intentional killings are motivated by compassion, as when one spouse kills the other because the latter is clearly suffering from an unbearable disease and begs for death. Note the two descriptions available for D's act in such a scenario: the narrower description, according to which she intentionally kills V, so a clear murder; and the wider description, according to which (i) D assuages V's suffering (primary intention) by killing V when no other way is possible, and (ii) D responds to V's explicit request and consent by killing him. D has no intrinsic desire to kill V; quite the contrary. She does not stand to benefit in any way from V's death; again, quite the contrary. Because the law is not normally interested in motive, however, she remains vulnerable to a murder charge. In such cases, however, the Crown Prosecution Service (CPS) usually decides, after the police enquiry, that it would be against the public interest to pursue the matter to the formal charging stage.[7]

(ii) *Giving priority to one's family in a moral dilemma*
This is a variation of the first example, but involves the rejection of obligations arising from a "bigger picture." In *Steane* [1947],[8] D was an Englishman living with his family in Berlin during World War II. The German authorities threatened his family so that he would make propaganda broadcasts. After the war, he was arrested and convicted of "doing acts likely to assist the enemy with intent to assist the enemy" (i.e. treason). On appeal the conviction was quashed, however, because his intention had been to save his family, and in his particular circumstances, he reasonably calculated that making the broadcasts (his subsidiary intention) was the only way to do this. The Court of Criminal Appeal stated:

> if on the totality of the evidence there is room for more than one view as to D's intent, the jury should be directed that it is for the prosecution to prove the intent to the jury's satisfaction. They would not be entitled to presume a criminal intent if circumstances were consistent with an innocent intent such as a desire to save his wife and children.[9]

7 Instead of intentional killing, one spouse might be sufficiently motivated by compassion to intentionally assist the other's suicide. Assisting a suicide is illegal according to the *Suicide Act* 1961. This is a curious crime, because suicide itself is not illegal. Clearly the prohibition against assistance is designed to protect many vulnerable people who seek suicide under the influence of temporary despair. However, in formal recognition of the possibility of compassionate suicidal assistance, and following the high-profile case of Debbie Purdy in 2009, the CPS published a set of prosecution guidelines See: www.cps.gov.uk/legal-guidance/suicide-policy-prosecutors-respect-cases-encouraging-or-assisting-suicide

8 When a name (or initial) is italicised like this, it refers to the name of the defendant in a legal case. We will use the convention of square brackets around the date for legal cases, and round brackets around the date for bibliographical references. The end of the book lists all the cases discussed, and provides their full legal references. Many cases take the form of *R v Smith*, which stands for *Regina (Rex) v Smith*. For simplicity, we will always omit the *R*.

9 The problem with this reasoning is that it suggests that Steane was not responsible for any contributing to German propaganda, and yet he well knew he was so contributing. An alternative way of acquitting Steane would have been to recognise a defence of duress to his intentional treason, but Steane's defence

(iii) *Sentencing*

If a mother steals expensive medicines from a pharmacy in order to treat her sick child, then she may still be convicted of theft, but her sentence will probably be more lenient because of her motive. Most crimes have a *range* of recommended sentences, allowing the judge discretion based on the particulars, including motivation. She is still guilty of intentionally and knowingly breaking the law, but she deserves less punishment because (i) there is less selfish malice in her for society to respond to (a "retributivist" justification) and/or (ii) she does not need to be deterred from re-offending (a "consequentialist" justification).[10] Again, this example is important for our discussion of the relevant description of the action: within the mother's perspective she was not *simply* "stealing medicines," she was "stealing medicines *in order to* treat her child" (i.e. as a single action). For her, the action-package which she contemplated and then carried out contained a direct reference to the future beneficiary, and it was presumably a last and desperate resort.[11]

(v) *Sexual gratification*

The motivation of sexual gratification is part of the definition of the offence of voyeurism. According to Section 67 of the *Sexual Offences Act* 2003, "A person commits an offence if (a) for the purpose of obtaining sexual gratification, he observes another person doing a private act, and (b) he knows that the other person does not consent to being observed for his sexual gratification." What is interesting about this offence is that it does not require direct physical or mental harm caused to V; most cases of voyeurism are on a victim who is oblivious. Part of the purpose of the prohibition is to deter future acts of voyeurism; but part is to establish the thought that the victim, even when oblivious, suffers what might be called a "metaphysical" harm. One way to unpack metaphysical harm would be to say: once the victim discovers the facts of the voyeur's observations, she will suffer at the thought that she had been observed last Thursday evening. But some victims might never find out, and we would still say that they had been harmed. Compare: if someone steals money from my bank account, and I never find out, I am still being harmed.[12]

(vi) *Weaponry*

A single empty house is burgled by two different burglars on two consecutive nights, and they perform the same physical actions and run off with goods of the same value. It would appear that they have committed the same offence. But D1 carried a loaded gun to the burglary and D2 did not. The gun will aggravate D1's offence, and make D1 deserve a greater penalty, even if D1 never uses the weapon — as defined by Section 10 of the *Theft Act* 1968. The point is: he *might have* used the weapon. And

team did not propose this, perhaps because the threats against Steane's family were not concrete and imminent enough. See Chapter 10 on defences. Ormerod and Laird (2021 p. 97–8) stress that Steane's "honourable" motive was also relevant. If Steane had assisted the enemy to feed his alcoholism, the court would not have been so impressed, and yet the point about different levels of intention would still hold. Note Rubin (2003), who claims that new evidence undermines Steane's credibility and his professed loyalty to Britain during the war.

10 We will be examining the justification of punishment in Chapter 11.

11 We will not have much to say about the complexities surrounding sentencing. But see the UK Sentencing Council for more details: www.sentencingcouncil.org.uk/outlines/

12 The same can be said about another offence, the possession of indecent images of children (criminalised by Section 45 of the *Sexual Offences Act* 2003). Any harm to the child occurred back when the photograph was taken; when D1 later possesses and enjoys the image, or passes it on to D2, it might seem the child cannot be harmed *any further*. Hence the need for something like metaphysical harm to capture the intuitive wrongness of it. We will discuss sexual offences further in Chapter 9.

the presence of the weapon expresses a greater degree of ruthlessness in the burglar's preparations for and execution of the burglary.

(vii) *Terrorism*
Terrorism offences are exceptional in many ways precisely because of the sheer scale of the potential harm, and the huge potential for public anxiety. So a terrorist motivation will tend strongly to aggravate ordinary crimes, as well as lowering various thresholds designed to protect suspects: thresholds for searching premises, thresholds for attempt and conspiracy and complicity, thresholds for possession of potential bomb ingredients. The underlying thought is that ordinary crimes are discrete in their scope, and therefore merit a discrete response; whereas terrorism is aimed at an entire society. In addition, while most people can avoid most crimes most of the time, nobody can avoid a terrorist attack, which can strike anywhere at any time. For both these reasons, the state is justified in responding with much greater pre-emptive caution and investigation, even at the risk of impeding the lawful activities, civil liberties and privacy of citizens. Terrorism will comprise a regular exception to many of the principles in this book.

(viii) *Oppressive attitudes*
We already saw how the possession of a weapon can aggravate a burglary. Racism can also aggravate the seriousness of the crime. Assume D1 assaults V1 and D2 assaults V2. The two sets of physical injuries are identical, and the two victims suffered equal pain. If D1 is motivated by racism and D2 by personal *animus*, the legal and moral significance of the two actions will differ. D1 will have *done* something qualitatively more serious, and will therefore receive a harsher punishment; in addition, V1's experience will be worse, including as it does the denigrating message underlying the attack.

One problem with aggravation from hostile attitudes is that it is governed in a fairly ad hoc way in different parts of the law, and in each case with different criteria.

- In the *Crime and Disorder Act* 1998 Sections 28 and 29, assault can be aggravated by racial prejudice. ("Race" is interpreted fairly widely.)
- The *Equality Act* 2010 lists the following "protected characteristics": age, disability, gender assignment, marriage or civil partnership, race, religion or belief, sex, sexual orientation.
- Section 66 of the *Sentencing Act* 2020 imposes a duty upon courts, when considering the seriousness of any offence, to treat the following as an aggravating factor: (a) racial hostility, (b) religious hostility, (c) hostility related to disability, (d) hostility related to sexual orientation or (e) hostility related to transgender identity.
- Section 269 of the *Criminal Justice Act* 2003 determines the minimum term in relation to mandatory life sentences. The main minimum is 15 years, with extra years depending on, among other things: the type of weapon used, the number of victims, and motivation by sexual gratification, sadism or racism/religious hatred or homophobia. (The details are in Schedule 21 of the *Act*.)
- In the Law Commission's (2021) *Report no. 402. Hate Crime Laws: Final Report*, they proposed a number of measures to make the situation more coherent and consistent.[13]

13 Interestingly, the Commission described their consultations on the matter, and concluded that they did not support the inclusion of *sex or gender* as a protected characteristic, mainly because they felt the risks (to women and girls) would outweigh the likely benefits of doing do. See Section 5.378 *ff.* However, the

2.2 CHARACTER, BIOGRAPHY AND IDENTITY

So apart from the above exceptions, D's motive will normally be irrelevant to criminal responsibility. In this section we're going to explore a similar point about D's character, biography and identity: normally they, too, are irrelevant to criminal responsibility, and for the same good reasons. Whether D is a saint or sinner, whether she had a good or bad childhood, whether she has few or many past convictions, whatever her origin, class, race or gender, she will only be judged on whether she committed the *actus reus*, with a minimum *mens rea*, and without a sufficient defence. That all seems right. But notice two important assumptions behind this approach: first, that all the relevant details about culpability are contained roughly in the moment of performance. (We say "roughly" to include the moments just before the performance, i.e. when she may have been forming her intention and carrying out preparations.) This is sometimes called the "time-slice" assumption. Second, as discussed in the Introduction, that the defendant was sufficiently *free to refrain* from performing the *actus reus*: in not refraining, she chose to perform it, she owned the action.

But when we look more closely at character, we might have cause to doubt these two assumptions. One's character comprises a set of dispositions to behave in certain ways in certain conditions. Some morally positive character traits are called virtues, some morally negative ones are called vices. Consider the vice of irascibility. An irascible person is reliably disposed to get too angry, too quickly, and to lash out too harmfully, in a situation where such an angry response is not appropriate. Part of becoming a well-balanced adult is to overcome natural childish irascibility, and learn a certain degree of control over one's emotions, as well as learning to "read" a situation to understand the correct emotional response.

There is a paradox here, however. On the one hand, we are inclined to *blame* a person for their irascibility: we are reminding them that they have not conformed to acceptable behavioural standards of competent adults. Again, though, blaming someone only makes sense when we assume that they were free to refrain from the offensive behaviour. But the problem of irascibility is precisely that the anger seems to overwhelm the agent, and she is *not* free to control it, either on the given occasion, or over the longer term. One's character is not the sort of thing that one can choose to alter from one moment to the next. At the same time, however, the irascible agent is not *unfree* in the way that an epileptic would be; in most contexts of her life, the irascible agent is perfectly competent, and can be held fully responsible by her friends, by strangers, and by the criminal law. If the irascible agent tries to say "I'm sorry, I don't know what happened, I just lost it," we are inclined to respond by saying "Get a grip."

Here we anticipate a discussion we're going to have in Chapter 10 on defences. The *Coroners and Justice Act* 2009 Section 54 recognises a defence called "Loss of Control" (traditionally known as "provocation"). The thought is that in some cases of intentional killing, the defendant might claim that she was so angry that she lost control of herself and was therefore not fully responsible for her actions. If she is successful in this defence, she will probably still go to prison — but for manslaughter, not for murder, and therefore for a shorter length of time. There might be *two* kinds of intention at stake here. In narrow terms, there was clearly an intention to kill: D has to grab the gun, aim it at the right part of the victim's body, etc., and all that will require a certain amount of control. In broader terms, she could sincerely say that she acted only once the "red mist" had descended. Once she has cooled off, she can sincerely regret the killing, and declare that she had no intention to kill anybody.

Commission did recommend that the offence of "stirring up hatred against entire groups" (Chapter 10) be extended to cover sex and gender, as a response to violent "involuntary celibate" ("incel") ideology. See the Law Commission website: www.lawcom.gov.uk

But here's the important part: the "loss of control" defence is *not* designed to excuse the irascible defendant. Instead, it is designed for a person of *normal* character who is pushed to extreme action by an extreme situation in her life. The loss of control has to be attributable to the victim's words or conduct which "constituted circumstances of an extremely grave character, and caused D to have a justifiable sense of being seriously wronged" (to quote from the *C&JA* 2009). The words "grave" and "justifiable" refer to *objective* norms of conduct; the irascible person, on the other hand, cannot claim that her response was justifiable, and cannot claim that the victim's words were grave just because she thought they were.

Inevitably, however, there are blurred boundaries here. It's all very well saying that a well-balanced adult should have control over their emotions except in objectively definable extreme situations, but the category of "competent adult" can include plenty of people with very different characters, and different degrees of control, and there will be an on-going tension in whether the criminal law deals with them fairly.[14]

A person's character is of course deeply shaped by their childhood upbringing. At before, we would normally say that the defendant's biography is not relevant to their culpability during the time-slice within which the defendant acted. There is a long-standing debate among criminologists about the longer-term causal effects of early childhood family and social deprivation on the subsequent lives of the competent adults that such children become. There is certainly a strong argument for using the criminological data to ground reforms in the state's social policy. However, we will agree with the general assumption by the criminal law that the defendant's background cannot be claimed as an excuse.[15]

One aspect of the defendant's biography will be her criminal record. Here there is a livelier controversy about its relevance. At first glance, one would consider it as irrelevant as motive, character and biography. The defendant should be judged on her action within the time-slice alone. However, one can already see that exceptions can be made for a first-time offender, who, despite her competence, could be plausibly described as lacking sufficient understanding of what she was doing, and therefore as not being fully responsible. She might "know" that shoplifting is wrong and illegal, but she acts under peer pressure and has not yet "felt" the sting of the wrongness or its illegality: it might suffice for a police officer to give her an informal or formal caution and she will "get the message." Similarly, if a first-time offender gets to court and is found guilty, then a lenient punishment could be justified. Beyond such a concession, however, the court should keep the criminal record secret from

14 Irascibility is a specific kind of vice involving the loss of control over one's emotions, usually in response to a misinterpreted situation or personal frustration. But we have to stress the wide variety of vices that work in various different ways. Cowardice is very different from irascibility, for example. In addition, there are important character traits of callousness, brutality, sadism etc., and these would seem to aggravate offences in a way that would merit a harsher penal response.

15 Sometimes the debate is expressed in terms of a competent adult's "rotten social background" (RSB), and whether the *causal* influence of the RSB is sufficient to qualify that adult for a partial excuse for her criminal activity. This is linked to the arguments of social activists, backed up by social scientific data, that it is better to see crime as a socio-economic issue rather than a personal responsibility issue: the best response to crime, these activists claim, is economic support for deprived communities rather than mass incarceration. In terms of individual culpability, an RSB might offer some degree of excuse. The idea is that the adult spent her childhood with abusive parents, or in conditions of deprivation or neglect, and as a result she failed to fully develop the basic pro-social attitudes required for responsible interactions with others. As a result she was less inhibited when seeking to promote her self-interest through criminal activity, and she will fail to learn any moral lessons from state punishment. The default position of the criminal law is to say that an RSB provides no excuse: part of being a competent adult involves overcoming one's earlier deprivation and its causal influences, and *choosing* to obey or not obey the law. (We return to this question in Chapter 10 on defences and Chapter 11 on punishment.) For an article broadly sympathetic to the social activism account, see Delgado (1985). For a philosophical argument that rejects any attempt to excuse the defendant on the basis of her background, see Chau (2018).

the jury; because if the defendant has a *long* record, then this might well prejudice an otherwise undecided jury that she "must have" done it. On the other hand, there is a question of whether the defendant with a long criminal record is no longer sufficiently deterred by the threatened sanctions, and therefore merits a harsher sentence (i.e. within the range allowed by the sentencing guidelines for a particular offence type). This is controversial because in theory, she has *already* been punished for the earlier offences, and on each occasion has re-entered society with a newly clean slate. We will return to this question in Chapter 11, on punishment.

The time-slice approach of the criminal law is problematic for certain kinds of action. Many discrete actions have longer temporal scopes: for example, "I intend to take part in a training course next year." Some crimes would seem intuitively to require an extended temporal definition, and the wrongness might therefore get lost under a time-slice approach that ignores history. Consider stalking: this is defined by a pattern of behaviour, such that any individual time-slice action within that pattern might not be very serious. Being followed or observed on *one* occasion is very different from being followed or observed on *many* occasions. And the intention will be quite different if it actualises around a single occasion or is sustained across many occasions. To deal with stalking (and harassment), Parliament passed the *Protection from Harassment Act* 1997 and other statutes. Consider domestic abuse, which we will be discussing in Section 8.5. Although one instance of domestic violence might be dealt with as discrete assault, it would under-describe the meaning of the violence: first, the time-slice would miss the context of the violence within an intimate relationship and (usually) within the home (so that it is no longer mere violence, but also involves deep betrayal); second, it would miss the context of the violence within the pattern of sustained intimidation and control. Once again, the exact nature of the defendant's intention will depend on all these distinctions.

Parliament responded by defining "coercive control" within the *Serious Crime Act* 2015, Section 76, as follows:

> (1) A person (A) commits an offence if— (a) A repeatedly or continuously engages in behaviour towards another person (B) that is controlling or coercive, (b) at the time of the behaviour, A and B are personally connected, (c) the behaviour has a serious effect on B, and (d) A knows or ought to know that the behaviour will have a serious effect on B.

Before this legislation, the defendant could be charged at most with individual acts of intentional assault on particular occasions, and such a charge sheet would not capture the intuitive wrongness of the *systematic* and *sustained* domination and humiliation of the victim. (Indeed, the patterned behaviour might not involve much physical violence as such.) The offence of "coercive control," on the other hand, essentially spans a lengthy time-frame, and allows a different kind of intention across that time-frame, an intention with increasing cumulative malice, greater than the "sum" of malice in any individual acts. On each occasion, there will be a local intention to assault or humiliate the victim, but this is interpreted as expressing the over-arching intention within the context of the on-going relationship.

Using time-slices to capture the wrong of domestic violence also leads to the following paradox about *habit*. Tadros (2007, p. 216) comments:

> It may well be the case that the more systemic violence becomes, the less reflective the perpetrator becomes about it. The first instance of violence may well be done with a high degree of reflection. But as violence becomes habitual, it may well be that the perpetrator thinks less and less about it, just in the way that we commonly think less and less about non-violent habitual action. But surely that should not lead us to conclude that the defendant becomes less and less culpable for his violent acts. On the contrary; that the violence is habitual ought to incline us in the opposite direction.

So the perpetrator's understanding of the situation has shifted over time, to a point where he no longer feels anything of the intuitive aversion to violence against the victim that he presumably felt when he first moved in with her. (To put it another way, he now feels himself more "entitled" to hit her, and therefore he requires less intentional "energy" to overcome any residual aversion or sympathy.) This is not just a point about the victim's subjective *understanding*, however, which may be undermined by internalised oppressive norms and distorted by the relentless humiliation; it is also a point about the objective *meaning* of the action and the intention, beyond anything that perpetrator or victim might say about the matter. Part of the objective meaning comes from the systematic and sustained campaign of coercion and control; another part, not spelt out in the legislation, is the cohabitational and intimate *context* of such coercion.

2.3 OBLIQUE INTENTION

Our earlier discussion of motive and intention brings us to the classic problem of "oblique intention." This is part of a wider issue known as the problem of "double effect." I intend to drink a lot of wine tonight, I'm looking forward to it. But I know that I will be badly hungover tomorrow, a predictable side-effect of my actions. Of course, I don't *intend* to get hungover. But imagine that tomorrow's a workday, I come into work late, and once there I perform poorly. Can I tell my employer: "I didn't intend to be hungover"? Surely not. After all, it was not as if the hangover was a freak accident, like many illnesses would be. I am clearly responsible for my hangover, I could have easily avoided getting hungover, and therefore I am a legitimate target of blame and perhaps disciplinary action from my employer.

This is directly relevant to the law of murder. In the paradigm situation, D's killing of V has to be *intended* for it to be classified as murder — otherwise it would be the less serious crime of manslaughter. But Glanville Williams (1987, p. 423) imagines the following. D plants a bomb on a cargo plane, with the aim of claiming the insurance money from the destruction of the cargo. That is his primary intention. Of course, the pilot is *virtually certain* to die in the mid-air explosion, and D knows this. The plane takes off with the cargo, it explodes and the pilot dies; D is apprehended. Intuitively we would want him to be charged with murder, but D will deny that he *intended* to kill the pilot; indeed he could even say that he had sincerely hoped that the pilot had survived. Does that mean we have to rest content with a manslaughter charge? That we would describe D as having done no more than recklessly take a risk that the pilot would die? That would seem to under-describe the cynical ruthlessness of D's project.

For many years English law endorsed the notion of an "oblique intention" to capture this scenario: the bomb-planter would be described as obliquely *intending* to kill the pilot, and therefore he could be convicted of murder. The intention is to be "stretched," as it were, to include the pilot's death. However, oblique intention requires a double-threshold about virtual certainty:

- The objective threshold: the facts have to be such that, given D's action, there was an objective virtual certainty that V would die;
- The subjective threshold: D has to be subjectively aware of that objective virtual certainty.

If either the subjective or objective threshold is missing, then an oblique intention to kill cannot be imputed onto D. This structure was established in the case of *Nedrick* [1986].[16] D had a grudge against V1. In the middle of the night, D visited V1's house, poured paraffin oil

16 The structure was confirmed in *Woollin* [1998], and this case name is often used as a shorthand.

through the letterbox, and set the house on fire. V1 survived, but V1's child V2 died in the fire. So the question was whether D intentionally or recklessly killed V2. D claimed he had no intention to kill anybody, but only to frighten V1 and greatly inconvenience her; he did not even know that V2 was in the house. Unlike the bomb on the plane, setting the house on fire can, in most cases, plausibly be described as creating a possibility but *not* a virtual certainty of death. (This will depend on the facts, of course — some fires are much more violent than others.) Here is the relevant passage from the Court of Appeal's judgement:[17]

> Did he foresee the consequence? If he did not appreciate that death or serious harm was likely to result from his act, he cannot have intended to bring it about. If he did, but thought that the risk to which he was exposing the person killed was only slight, then it may be easy for the jury to conclude that he did not intend to bring about that result. On the other hand, if the jury are satisfied that at the material time the defendant recognised that death or serious harm, will be virtually certain (barring some unforeseen intervention) to result from his voluntary act, then that is a fact from which they may find it easy to infer that he intended to kill or do serious bodily harm, even though he may not have had any desire to achieve that result.[18]
>
> *(p. 1028C-F)*

In *Nedrick*, D was deemed to *lack* the oblique intention to kill. However, he was certainly reckless about the risk of someone dying in a house fire, and he freely ran that risk. For that reason he was still guilty of manslaughter for the death of V1. *Nedrick* represents the current "scope" of intention in the law of murder in England today. It expresses well the fuzzy boundary between intention and recklessness, and we will be revisiting this in the next chapter. In addition, Chapter 8 examines the difference between murder and manslaughter more systematically, and describes two other ways of "stretching" intention: the "GBH rule," and the principle of "transferred malice."

Nedrick and the whole idea of oblique intentions have been criticised, and we will mention three criticisms. Antony Duff (1989, p. 61) deploys the "failure test" to distinguish genuinely intended effects from virtually certain side-effects. If D has an intention to X, then she aims to bring about X, she makes X her project; and she will consider herself to have failed if X does not come about (and so she may try again). If the bomb in the plane fails to go off, D has failed in his project. But if the bomb goes off but the pilot miraculously survives, then D will be indifferent, and perhaps glad, of the pilot's fate. Therefore, concludes Duff, it cannot be said that the bomb-planter intended the pilot to die, and we have to find another way to charge him with murder.

17 The facts of *Nedrick* are very similar to the facts of an earlier case, *Hyam* [1975]. And yet Hyam was charged with murder. Lord Hailsham held that intention could also exist where D

> knew there was a serious risk that death or serious bodily harm will ensure from his acts and he commits those acts deliberately and without lawful excuse with the intention to expose a potential victim to that risk as the result of those acts. It does not matter in such circumstances whether the defendant desires those consequences or not.
>
> *(p. 79)*

Two different thresholds should be noted, however. In *Hyam*, the House of Lords believed that it was "highly probable" that setting a house on fire would kill someone, and that D must have known it was highly probable, but proceeded anyway. Therefore she obliquely intended the deaths. This threshold changed to "virtually certain" by the time of *Nedrick* [1986], barely a decade later. It is rare for the House of Lords to overrule itself so explicitly, in such a short time period. The *Hyam* case is discussed at length by the philosopher Antony Duff (1989).

18 In *Woollin* [1998] the House of Lords suggested that the word "infer" in the last sentence of this quotation should be replaced by "find": that is, the jury cannot simply presume that the intention must be there, they have to find evidence that D actually intended his action.

Incidentally, this "failure test" also justifies taking intentional action as more culpable than reckless action even when they both produce the same quantum of harm. Someone who intentionally harms has thereby associated herself explicitly with the harmful consequence, and thereby reveals a bad character that is likely to lead to further intentional harm; she therefore deserves more punishment than someone who unintentionally harms.

Second, Goff (1987) accepted that the bomb-planter should be charged with murder, but not by imputing an intention that is not there. Instead, the definition of murder should be expanded to include not only the paradigm case of an intention to kill, but also a secondary type of case describing the bomb-planter's *attitude* to the foreseen death of the pilot. Callous indifference would be one way of describing it. Goff himself prefers the term "wicked recklessness," borrowed from Scots law. Wicked recklessness is to be distinguished from ordinary recklessness, where the emphasis is simply on the conscious disregard of risks. Goff (p. 54) cites Sherriff Gordon: "Wicked recklessness is recklessness so gross that it indicates a state of mind which is as wicked and depraved as the state of mind of a deliberate killer."

Third, to accommodate the bomb-planter, the Law Commission suggested creating two degrees of murder, such that "second-degree murder" would include "unlawful killings intended to cause injury or fear or risk of injury where the killer was aware that his or her conduct involved a serious risk of causing death."[19] A *Nedrick*-style set of facts could then be examined, first to see whether there was an intention to cause fear, second to see whether the risk of causing death was "serious" enough, and third to deduce whether the killer was sufficiently "aware" of the risk. (We say a bit more about this proposal in Section 8.1.)

2.4 CONDITIONAL INTENTION

In this final section, we will consider one more twist on the basic paradigm of intentional action. In the paradigm case, I have the intention to X and then I carry out the intention by performing X intentionally. But what if my antecedent intention is conditional? That is, I have the intention to X but only *if and when* condition C obtains. As we shall see, this problem is relevant to conspiracy, self-defence and attempts, which we will return to in later chapters. It also occupied a central place in the recent Supreme Court case of *Jogee* [2016], which altered complicity law in England and Wales (discussed in Chapter 7).

A classic case here is *Easom* [1971]. Easom was suspected of pickpocketing and theft in cinemas, so the police mounted a sting operation. A policewoman sat in front of the suspect with her handbag on the seat beside her, attached by a thread to her finger. Easom noticed the handbag, opened it, and looked inside it to see if there was anything worth stealing, at which point he was arrested by the policewoman and charged with attempted theft. In fact, the handbag was empty; but it was plausible that if there *had* been something valuable in the handbag (the condition) Easom *would have* intentionally attempted to steal it.[20] Notoriously, the Court of Appeal allowed his appeal. They argued that Easom's conditional intention was not enough for culpability because it could not be an intention or an attempt to steal *a particular object* — he didn't know what was in the handbag. At the moment of arrest, he had been merely curious, and of course he only confessed to such curiosity. To punish Easom for a conditional intention was tantamount to punishing him for his mere thoughts.

19 Law Commission Report no. 304 *Murder, Manslaughter and Infanticide* (2006), Section 2.70 *ff.*

20 In anticipation of our discussion in Chapter 6 on inchoate offences, the perpetrator is considered to have launched an attempt — and is therefore liable to arrest and prosecution — once she has carried out a "more than merely preparatory" step.

Intuitively, something has gone wrong, and it raises the question of how to re-define the situation to catch Easom. Ideally the policewoman would have placed something valuable and steal-able in the handbag so that she could then apprehend him *in flagrante*. Could we say, for example, that Easom was attempting to steal the "the contents" of the handbag — in a similar way that malice toward "some person" can be transferred?[21] The problem with that analogy is that transferred malice still involves a victim, whereas Easom did not actually end up harming anyone on this occasion — but the redescription of the intention is on the right lines. John Campbell (1982) describes Easom as harbouring not a conditional *intention* but a conditional *execution*. The condition is "external" to the intention. Easom approaches the handbag already with the *un*conditional present intention to steal something, based on his knowledge that handbags typically contain valuable objects: he plans to examine the interior of the handbag, and then decide whether to execute the intention or not. So in opening the handbag, Easom had indeed revealed his settled intention to steal, and had launched the attempt. If the handbag had been empty, Easom would have simply taken his settled intention elsewhere, to another purse or coat pocket in the cinema.

Campbell contrasts such an "external" condition to a situation where the condition is "internal" to the intention. In such a case a person is genuinely of two minds, and waits upon the condition before forming her intention. So Abigail says to Bertram "I want to go out tonight," and she checks the cinema listings to see if anything good is showing. She does not presently intend to go *to the cinema*, but if she discovers something good in the cinema listings, she will then form the intention to go there.

As John Child (2017) points out, however, there is still something problematic in trying to distinguish the conditional from the unconditional:

> Where criminal offences such as attempt and conspiracy require a defendant (D) to intend future conduct, D's intention will always be conditional. D's intention may be explicitly conditional (e.g. D intends to rob the shop, but only if unable to pay her rent), or implicitly conditional (e.g. D intends to rob the shop, but if asked, would not do so if she found it surrounded by police).
>
> *(p. 311)*

All of our future planning is governed by conditions, most of which are too obvious to spell out. I intend to rob the shop only if I am not feeling sick, only if my mother doesn't need my help for something urgent, only if a piano does not fall on me! Improvisation is essential to human endeavour. In contrast, says Child, when I move to execute an intention here and now, then I can only do so *un*conditionally: I have already deliberated about whether the conditions are right, whether to take the risks, whether I need to know more, etc., and my conclusion is that *I will act now* — there are no *further* conditions in play, explicit or implicit. Of course, I may not succeed in carrying out my intentions, for any number of reasons, foreseeable and unforeseeable; but that does not alter the unconditionality of the intention under which I acted.

21 We discuss the principle of "transferred malice" in Section 8.1. If D shoots at V1, with the intention to kill V1, but V1 ducks and V2 is killed instead, then D will be convicted of the murder of V2, even if she did not intend to shoot V2. Her "malice" (intention) is transferred to V2.

CHAPTER 3

RECKLESSNESS

In any book about criminal law, it's tempting to focus on intentional acts. It's "cleaner" if D intentionally does something bad, and therefore obviously deserves punishment, as if she was "asking for it." It supports a cleaner understanding of the world as divided between bad'uns and the rest of us. The rest of us are in control of our lives, obey the law, and keep out of trouble. In contrast, recklessness is messy because it's so often about "the rest of us," law-abiding people with good intentions, people just looking for a bit of fun, taking a short cut, relying on their memory, people who say, "I'm sure it will be all right." Recklessness is also messy because of the massive role of cruel gratuitous luck. Already with intention we saw that luck was involved, but luck pervades recklessness scenarios at so many levels that it seems deeply unfair to blame and punish the unlucky offenders who were just as reckless as their lucky neighbours.

Recklessness is all about risk, and we all take risks all the time. Every time we get in a car we take a risk, even if we obey all the traffic laws. But even if we avoid driving, we still have to cross the road sometimes, and that's risky. Every time we bank online we take a risk, but it's too convenient to avoid. Every time we go to a crowded shopping centre during a pandemic, we take a risk. Every time we let our child walk to school alone, we take a risk. In theory we can distinguish reasonable from unreasonable risks and lead a safer life; in theory we can learn from experience and become more cautious with age; in theory we can predict and quantify the risks, and prepare for them through insurance and back-up plans. But it would be impossible to lead any sort of interesting life if we tried to avoid all risks. And when the risk "actualises," and we or someone else suffers, then a lot of reassuring notions of past reasonableness become idle.

There are three dimensions of risk: the probability, the severity and the context. An air crash is very improbable (in terms of inductive generalisations from past statistics) but very severe; does that mean that some people's fear of flying is irrational? Rain in Ireland is really probable but rarely severe — unless we took our risk in the context of planning a picnic, which is now ruined. Recall our example from the last chapter (Section 2.3) of the person planting a bomb on a cargo plane, intending only to destroy the cargo and to claim the insurance money; she claims that she did not intend to kill anyone. And yet she knows that there is a very high probability (a "virtual certainty") that the pilot will die (a severe consequence) in the mid-air explosion. Technically she is being no more than reckless, but the risk is so probable and so severe that we can impute on her an "oblique" intention to kill the pilot, and convict her of murder. This is one aspect of the "fuzziness" of the boundary between intention and recklessness on the ladder of *mens rea*.[1]

3.1 THE *MODEL PENAL CODE* DEFINITION

There is a distinction at the heart of recklessness: between a "subjective" and an "objective" version. Fascinatingly, in general, English law adopted a subjective approach until 1982, then the objective approach took over until 2003, after which the courts went back to the subjective

1 A note about organisation: in this chapter we're looking at recklessness and risk more generally. In Section 8.2. we will describe the different kinds of recklessness and negligence that results in manslaughter.

DOI: 10.4324/9781003351887-3

approach, where it is today. We will discuss the English developments in the next section. For the moment, a clearer place to start is the unambiguously subjective definition of recklessness from the American *Model Penal Code* (MPC) Section 2.02(2)(c):

> A person acts recklessly with respect to a material element of an offense when he consciously disregards a substantial and unjustifiable risk that the material element exists or will result from his conduct. The risk must be of such a nature and degree that, considering the nature and purpose of the actor's conduct and the circumstances known to him, its disregard involves a gross deviation from the standard of conduct that a law-abiding person would observe in the actor's situation.[2]

Let's take an example to focus our intuitions here. For a bit of fun, D (a competent adult) gathers some old cardboard and paper into a plastic wheelie bin in an alley, and sets it alight. The fire grows larger and faster than she anticipated, and sets the neighbouring wooden house on fire, causing extensive damage. D did not intend to set the house on fire. But she was conscious of the risk of the fire spreading, and disregarded that risk. That would seem to make her responsible for the criminal damage. (As we will see, several of the central English cases concern reckless arson, so this schematic example is apt, and it links in with our discussion of *Nedrick* in the last chapter.) Now let's look at the MPC definition:

(i) The risk has to be *unjustifiable*. A surgeon will take lots of risks, and if some of them actualise the patient might well die sooner as a result. However such risks will typically be justified by (i) the expert risk/benefit comparison of the options (including the option to do nothing) and (ii) the competent patient's informed consent.[3] In contrast, if D's only "nature and purpose" is to have some fun, this is not going to justify any big risks to other people and property.

(ii) D has to be *conscious* of the risk. If D is a competent adult, she can be presumed to understand enough about what fire can do to property and to people. Clearly, she understood the risk to the wheelie bin. But there is a question of whether she was conscious of the risk *to the house*. The facts of the case will be relevant here: how physically close was the bin to the house? How obvious was it that the house was made of wood? The focus on consciousness is what makes the MPC recklessness subjective (also known as "advertent"). But consciousness remains ambiguous:
   1. If, the day before, a reporter were to ask D whether fire poses a general risk to wooden houses, of course she would not deny it; but as she sets fire to the wheelie bin contents, can she sufficiently imagine *this* fire spreading so rapidly to *that* house — perhaps she has no direct experience of how quickly fires can grow.
   2. We might distinguish between "cognitive" and "affective" consciousness here: she knows the risk in the abstract, but does not *feel* it sufficiently to be worried about it?
   3. Or perhaps she sees herself as sufficiently cautious, e.g. she is ready to pull the wheelie bin away from the house if the fire grows too big, without thinking that it might become too hot to approach.

2 The MPC was drawn up in the 1950s by a group of American academics, and regularly revised since. It has no legal force, but has influenced many criminal law statutes of individual American states, and is a useful focal point for academic discussions and appeal judgements.

3 To be more specific, the legal justifiability of the surgeon's risk-taking would depend on whether the surgeon can show that a significant number of other doctors with similar expertise (not necessarily a majority) would have also taken the same risk. If she can show that, then she can defend herself against an accusation of negligence. This is called the "Bolam test" and comes from the case of *Bolam* [1957].

4. Or perhaps her excitement grows as the fire does, and she simply does not think about the risk to the house until it is too late?
5. None of these considerations are *excuses*, of course; but they might complicate the MPC requirement of "consciousness."

(iii) She has to consciously *disregard* the risk. This is important because disregarding is an intentional act of turning one's attention away. Even if there is no intention to harm, there is still an intention to risk harm, which means she is still in some sort of control, and therefore it will be fair to hold her responsible. By intentionally disregarding the known risk, she effectively consented to the possibility of the risk actualising, and therefore to the possibility of being caught and held responsible for the harm she caused.

(iv) Notice that the risk is that "the material element *exists* or will *result* from his conduct." This links up with the difference between circumstance crimes and result crimes. In our example, she is disregarding the possible result of the house catching fire. But one can also take a risk about a circumstance e.g. in buying this attractive television from my friend, I am disregarding the risk that it might be stolen, and that I could therefore be charged with "handling stolen goods."[4]

(v) What would a *law-abiding* person do in the actor's situation? In English law this is phrased in terms of what a "reasonable person" would do. This idea of the reasonable person standard does a lot of work in criminal law, precisely because it is impossible to specify in advance the many ways that one can be reckless. We take the defendant, and we compare her behaviour to what a "reasonable person" would do and not do, would notice or not notice, would remember or not remember. There are shared norms for all these things, and the assumption is that all competent adults are capable of reliably perceiving and abiding by these norms. We return to this question of "reasonableness" below.

(vi) What is a *situation*, exactly? Obviously the main situation in our example is that of contemplating the flammable contents of the wheelie bin in front of me, next to a wooden house. But there is a certain ambiguity about "situation." Is D's *age* part of her "situation"? We called her a competent adult, but an 18-year-old will be less experienced, more impulsive, with a greater need to impress peers with dangerous behaviour etc. Again, this is not enough to give D an *excuse*, but it does undermine some of the fairness of the comparison with the law-abiding or reasonable person: for maybe it takes less effort for a 30-year-old adult to avoid certain risks.

Now recall one of our "moral luck" story-pairs from the Introduction: the two *equally* reckless drivers, one of whom is lucky and gets home without incident, while the other kills a pedestrian. The point of moral luck is that it seems unfair to penalise the two actors differently

4 There's an interesting epistemological point about how much suspicion (that the TV is stolen) is required to inculpate the buyer. Section 22 (1) of the *Theft Act* 1968 states that "a person handles stolen goods if… knowing or believing them to be stolen he dishonestly receives the goods." But "knowing or believing" sounds like a high threshold. Here's a more precise definition from Boreham J in *Hall* [1985] at p. 260:

> Belief… is something short of knowledge. It may be said to be the state of mind of a person who says to himself, "I cannot say I know for certain that these goods are stolen, but there can be no other reasonable conclusion in the light of all the circumstances, in the light of all that I have heard and seen."

Strictly speaking, then, I might well actually not *believe* that the television is stolen: but the objective circumstances present that reasonable conclusion to me, and so the stolen-ness of the television is *believable* in the absence of any alternative reasonable explanation.

when they were doing the same thing and they had the same limited control of the situation. Let's adapt the story-pair to two reckless arsonists, Amal and Bettina, who set fire to their respective wheelie bins next to wooden houses. The contents of Amal's bin burns itself out without incident; the contents of Bettina's bin cause a fire that sets the neighbouring house on fire. They are both apprehended, but penalised to different degrees, depending on the amount of criminal damage they caused.[5]

Moral luck and recklessness

Harry Frankurt (2008) argues that because they performed the same voluntary reckless acts with the same culpability, they should get the same punishment. The punishment can be high (appropriate to the risk) or low (appropriate to their culpability), but it should be the same. How would one defend the current criminal law, with its different sentences for Amal and Bettina? There are two strategies available, based on the descriptions of the relevant actions:

- *The prospective view.* This starts by agreeing with Frankfurt that Amal and Bettina performed the *same* action, but that the action is not limited to the voluntary. The narrow action description reads: "They recklessly chose to set fire to the wheelie bin contents." But a wider description reads: "recklessly chose to set fire to the wheelie bin contents *and to accept* the direct, probable and foreseeable consequences." In being conscious of the risks, they both implicitly accepted the possibility of the fire spreading, even if they did not desire, endorse or intend it. So insofar as the *potential* fire-spread is already part of the chosen action, then the *actual* fires-spread is as well. And therefore it is not unfair to punish them differently.
- *The retrospective view.* This starts by disagreeing with Frankfurt: surely Amal and Bettina performed *different actions.* Amal performed the action of "setting the bin contents on fire" and Bettina performed the action of "setting the bin contents and the house on fire." Against Frankfurt, it is implausible to separate the house fire from the bin contents fire when we enquire about what Bettina did. Only a highly improbable freak accident would be logically separate from Bettina's bin fire in the way Frankfurt describes. The house fire was quite probable, and quite foreseeable.

There is a third, very different strategy for responding to Frankfurt. Imagine if Bettina's fire not only destroyed the wooden house, but also killed someone in that house, as in the case of *Nedrick*? According to Frankfurt, this is just bad luck. But we can test our intuitions here by imagining how the dead person's family would respond to Bettina. Would they accept that it was just bad luck, as if the house had been struck by lightning? Or would they be angry at Bettina precisely because of her reckless disregard for the risks? Certainly, the family can accept that Bettina did not intend the death, it wasn't murder. But Bettina still chose to take a really stupid risk, resulting in a completely foreseeable and avoidable death; and the fact that Bettina was willing to take that risk for the sake of mere fun reveals a callousness about the interests of others that must surely be blameworthy in itself (as per our discussion of character in the last chapter). As such, the punishment has to reflect the seriousness of the harm caused.

What of Frankfurt's argument that Bettina could not control the path of the fire (or the presence of the person in the neighbouring house)? True, she couldn't. But insofar as setting

5 English law has a threshold of £5000. Damage worth less than that is treated very differently from damage worth more than that. See the CPS site on criminal damage: https://www.cps.gov.uk/legal-guidance/criminal-damage

the bin contents on fire was a necessary cause of the particular house fire (and the death), then she *could* have moved the wheelie bin away from the house, and she *could* have refrained from starting the fire! Whenever we are tempted to claim that Bettina was not in control of the consequences, we have to remind ourselves of the control she had before the fire.

Importantly, Frankfurt's argument relies on the comparison between Bettina and Amal. But this is not the appropriate comparison to make, for within the context of Bettina's own fire-setting, it doesn't matter what Amal was doing. She was a different agent, responsible for her own choices, and answerable separately to the criminal law. The right comparison is between the actual reckless Bettina, and her counter-factual cautious, reasonable self (maybe the voice of her conscience) that she intentionally ignored.

3.2 A BRIEF HISTORY OF ENGLISH RECKLESSNESS

Now that we better understand the *subjective* definition of recklessness from the MPC, we can look at the back-and-forth of English definitions. Normally we would not be too concerned with legal history for this book, but this particular story raises interesting philosophical questions. The traditional common law definition of recklessness had been subjective for years, and this was formally recognised by the case of *Cunningham* [1957]. Cunningham broke open a coin-operated gas meter in order to steal the money inside. The gas leaked out of the meter into a neighbouring house, poisoning the occupant (though not fatally).[6] He was clearly guilty of criminal damage and theft. But the question was whether he was also guilty of "maliciously administering a noxious thing," contrary to the *Offences Against the Persons Act* 1861 Section 23. The Court of Appeal quashed his conviction, saying that "maliciously" should be read as intentionally causing harm or being reckless as to the possibility of causing foreseeable harm, and that this question should have been left to the jury to decide on the basis of the facts.

While Cunningham could be presumed to know that the gas was *flammable*, he might genuinely have believed that it was not particularly *poisonous*. Or he might genuinely have believed that not much gas would escape, and that it would dissipate without entering the neighbour's house in sufficient quantity to poison her. In other words, the jury might have agreed with Cunningham that the risk of poisoning was not reasonably foreseeable, and so he had not intentionally disregarded that risk as he prised the meter open.

Some of the problems with Cunningham-style subjectivity became apparent in 1977, with the amusing case of *Parker* [1977]. Parker was trying to make a telephone call in a public booth, and could not get a dial tone, at which point he angrily slammed the plastic receiver against the phone body, shattering the receiver. He was charged with reckless criminal damage, under Section 1 of the *Criminal Damage Act* 1971. Parker claimed that as a competent adult he was of course *generally* aware of the likely fragility of this kind of plastic object, but *at the moment* of smashing the receiver his mind was so full of anger that it pushed the awareness aside. In other words, his knowledge of the risk was, at the moment, latent rather than occurrent, and so he argued that he could not be reckless according to the Cunningham precedent.

Nevertheless the court upheld his conviction precisely because the knowledge of the fragility of plastic was there, "at the back of his mind." The court added that Parker *would have been able* to bring the latent knowledge up to consciousness if he had stopped to think, or if

6 Not just *any* occupant, but in fact his future mother-in-law — not the best way to begin their family relationship!

he had been asked by a third party. And with this argument we are entering an "objective" definition of recklessness.[7]

Caldwell

The Cunningham conception remained in place until 1982. In that year the House of Lords ruled in the case of *Caldwell* that awareness of risk was no longer to be required for recklessness. Caldwell held a grudge against a hotel owner, his former employer. One evening Caldwell set fire to the hotel with the intention of causing criminal damage. As it happened, the fire spread quickly, and the hotel was successfully evacuated: nobody was hurt, but for a time there was a real risk of injury to some of the hotel occupants. Caldwell was charged under Section 1(2) of the *Criminal Damage Act* 1971, which reads:

> A person who without lawful excuse destroys or damages any property, whether belonging to himself or another —
>
> (a) intending to destroy or damage any property or being reckless as to whether any property would be destroyed or damaged; and
> (b) intending by the destruction or damage to endanger the life of another or being reckless as to whether the life of another would be thereby endangered;
>
> shall be guilty of an offence.

Caldwell intentionally set fire to the hotel, and so was straightforwardly guilty of criminal damage — that he could not contest. The question was whether he was also guilty of recklessly "endangering" the lives of the hotel guests and workers. It was clear enough that he did not intend to kill anyone or to endanger anyone, his intention was *only* to damage the property and thereby harm the interests of the owner. He claimed that it had not occurred to him that the fire would spread so quickly to the point of endangerment.

Once again we see the role of luck in the spread of the fire. Given the *same* physical actions by Caldwell (pouring the petrol, lighting the match), we can imagine four different consequences of increasing seriousness: (i) the fire went out or was put out quickly and so did not represent any real danger to the guests (but still caused damage, of course); (ii) the fire spread far and fast enough to pose a real danger to the guests, even if they managed to get out without injury (what actually happened); (iii) the fire spread far and fast enough to seriously injure one of the guests; (iv) the fire spread far and fast enough to kill one of the guests.[8] The clear possibility of options (iii) and (iv) perhaps persuaded a majority of the House of Lords to uphold Caldwell's conviction for reckless endangerment, even though the House accepted that the endangerment had genuinely not occurred to Caldwell at the time he was lighting the fire. Whether or not Caldwell was conscious of the risk was no longer the question; instead, the question was whether the risk would have been "obvious" to any reasonable person in Caldwell's situation. This is objective recklessness.[9]

7 Sudden anger like Parker's is also relevant to the defence of loss of control, although the latter is only applicable in murder cases. See Section 10.5.

8 So depending on luck, Caldwell might have been guilty of four different crimes: (i) criminal damage; (ii) criminal damage and reckless endangerment; (iii) criminal damage and recklessness leading to grievous bodily harm; (iv) criminal damage and recklessness leading to death (manslaughter). We discuss the last case in Section 8.2.

9 There is another complication in that Caldwell was drunk at the time of setting the fire, and claimed plausibly that this would have reduced any awareness of the risk of endangerment even more. Drunkenness

So the trend set by *Parker* [1977] was confirmed by *Caldwell* [1982]. The decision was immediately controversial. In philosophical terms, it seems to go directly against a deep principle of morality called the "ought implies can" principle. If we impose a moral duty on an agent to do X, we tell her she ought to do X, then we imply that she can do X, and therefore has the choice of whether to do X or not. And this should apply to the criminal law as well. Now the House of Lords will say that Caldwell *could have* contemplated the risks if he had put his mind to them. But in order for Caldwell to put his mind to the risks, it first needs to *occur* to him that there might be a risk worth turning his mind to. And he could not control what occurred to him and what did not. In saying that it might occur to a reasonable person, the House of Lords seem to be saying that Caldwell was not a reasonable person — but how can we blame Caldwell for not doing what *someone else* would have done, if he was not able to do so at the crucial moment? Objective recklessness therefore seems to amount to negligence, and we will see the same arguments against *Caldwell* when we discuss negligence in the next chapter.

A different justification for objective recklessness would make reference to its *deterrent* function. The thought runs as follows: even if it was unfair to charge Caldwell with reckless endangerment, at least the publicity of the *Caldwell* case means that other people contemplating arson would themselves be more careful about the risks of endangering people in the property they wanted to burn down, and this will lead to less bad consequences. The classic problem with any such "consequentialist" justifications is that it ignores the individual's particular desert, and effectively uses them to achieve an (otherwise laudable) social aim. The "retributivist" would say that our response to Caldwell should depend entirely on Caldwell's culpability, which should depend on his choices, regardless of whether or not society is better off with a conviction. (We discuss consequentialism and retributivism in Chapter 11 on punishment.)

One year after *Caldwell*, this fundamental problem was brought into focus in the case of *Elliott v C* [1983]. C, a 14-year-old girl with learning difficulties,[10] broke into someone's shed late at night, and set fire to some white spirits with the intention of keeping herself warm, whereupon the shed caught fire and burned down. The court accepted that she had not fully understood the risk of the fire spreading, and yet in accordance with the new *Caldwell* precedent, the court had to sentence her for reckless criminal damage because of a risk that would have been obvious to a reasonable person. And the court also accepted that her ignorance or lack of imagination was directly connected to her youth, inexperience and learning difficulties, and in that sense she was unable to act reasonably in this context. Needless to say, her conviction struck many as deeply unfair.

Reasonableness

Who is the "reasonable person," then? Let's pause in our discussion of the English history of recklessness to examine this idea, since it will be relevant in several future chapters. Reasonableness comprises a set of norms: norms of behaviour, norms of perceptiveness,

has a special place in the criminal law, as we will discuss in a later section of this chapter. Suffice to say here that the criminal law usually *ignores* drunkenness and thereby rejects any claimed diminished awareness of risk; Caldwell was treated as if he had been sober.

10 We declared in the Introduction that we would not get into discussions of mental health because of their complexity. Suffice to emphasise here that C was competent enough in most contexts of human activity, but in the facts of this case, her learning difficulties were obviously relevant to her lack of sufficient imaginative appreciation of the risks.

norms of deliberation and to a certain extent norms of appropriate feelings. The idea is that every competent adult has been brought up to learn these norms, and to be capable of acting on them. Most of the norms of reasonableness have to do with protecting and promoting one's self-interest. Some of them will involve the longer term and a more enlightened conception of self-interest. Some of the norms are moral in the basic sense of pro-social.

It is tempting to be sceptical about the existence and normative force of such norms, especially when one thinks about the huge differences in various norms across various social groups, even in a single Western society. Nevertheless, in a basic sense there *has to be* enough homogeneity and broad acceptance of such norms for any society to hold itself together over time, let alone for any legal system to command broad obedience. While there will be plenty of disputes in borderline cases, such disputes do not undermine the broad agreement of paradigm cases, such as those taught in primary school. Think of a simple norm such as queueing. The child learns what queueing is and when it is required; and with that it learns that butting into the queue is unreasonable (as well as rude).[11]

Norms of reasonableness also govern interpersonal understanding, and this includes jury members trying to understand the defendant's behaviour on the night in question. To take a simple example: if I am visiting you in your home, and suddenly you get up and open the fridge, I can understand what you are doing. I understand what a fridge is, what is typically contained in a fridge, I understand what food is and what hunger is. Even if I am not hungry right now, I understand that you might be (and that you feel that distinct kind of discomfort), that you are looking for food to deal with your hunger, and that you are looking in an appropriate place. Part of my understanding of your actions and your feelings involves an act of imagination: what would *I* do in your situation? And here the relevant situation involves at least the following: (i) the physical location of me in front of a fridge; (ii) the feeling of hunger; (iii) the nature of human foods, what they look like, how to consume them; (iv) the fact that it is *my* fridge, and that I am entitled to open it, removes things and consume them (norms of property ownership). But I also might *fail* to understand your eating the food from the fridge, because another element of your situation is that you are due to play football in front of your house in about ten minutes: and so I ask you, again on the basis of the norms of reasonableness that I presume we share, whether it would be wise to spend a lot of time eating something complicated right now, and wise to fill your belly before intense physical activity. You might have a satisfactory answer to my question, and our conversation might continue; but then again you might not, and I might be struck by a stubborn opacity in your engagement with this small part of the world (i.e. the opacity of your perception, deliberation, feeling and action processes). There is room in the "system" for a certain amount of opacity and misunderstanding, for weakness of will, for incomplete information, as well as for half-explanations (and apology). But I might also *warn* you not to eat too much before the game, just as I might *blame* you when you get the cramps during the game, and such a warning/blame expresses the idea of "I would not have done that in your situation."

Part of the problem of reasonableness and interpersonal understanding has to do with a *situation*. Consider C again. The court blamed her for not noticing risks that would have been obvious to a reasonable person in her situation. They clearly had in mind the situation of being cold in a shed at night. But in the same way that C found herself in the shed,

11 There is a debate in feminist legal philosophy about whether the concept of a "reasonable person" is actually gender-neutral in practice. See Dimock (2008).

found herself in a state of being cold, why can we not say that she found herself "in" a state of being young and inexperienced, "in" a state of having learning difficulties. In this case, the relevant comparison would not be with a "reasonable person" but rather with a reasonable person of the same age and with the same learning difficulties; and the relevant question would be about what *that* reasonable person would and would not have noticed as "obvious." Hart (1968, p. 154), in a discussion of negligence, thinks that any definition invoking the reasonable person should be explicitly accommodating to the defendant's actual limits: "Could the accused, given his mental and physical capacities, have taken those precautions?"[12]

After extensive academic and public discussion, the House of Lords eventually overturned *Caldwell* in 2003 in the case of *R v G*, thereby bringing subjectivity back to the definition of recklessness. *R v G* was another case of children (this time aged 11 and 13), and another case of arson. They were burning things for fun behind a shop, and the fire spread to the shop and some neighbouring buildings, causing £1 million worth of damage. Although the boys, like C, were old enough for criminal responsibility, it was clear that they did not appreciate the risk of the fire spreading, a risk that would have been obvious to a reasonable *adult*. Henceforth,

> A person acts recklessly [...] with respect to:
>
> (i) a circumstance when he is aware of a risk that it exists or will exist;
> (ii) a result when he is aware of a risk that it will occur, and it is, in the circumstances known to him, unreasonable to take the risk.
>
> (at 41)

So here we have D's *actual* awareness of the risk, regardless of what a reasonable person would or would not have been aware of; and we have the circumstances as *actually* known to D, regardless of what a reasonable person would have known. However, note that there is still one (small) objective element: D must still *deliberate* reasonably, given the risks of which she is aware and the circumstances known to her.

Dangerous driving

It is always tempting to take driving as a paradigmatic avenue of recklessness; everyone (drivers and pedestrians) understands the risks posed by cars, and all drivers understand the temptation to drive quickly. In England, driving is governed by an explicit statute, the *Road Traffic Act* (RTA) 1988. At first this included an offence called "reckless driving," but the act was amended in 1991 to create a new offence. Section 2A(1) states that D will be guilty of the offence of "dangerous driving" if:

(a) the way he drives falls far[13] below what would be expected of a competent and careful driver, and
(b) it would be obvious to a competent and careful driver that driving in that way would be dangerous.

12 Some legislation allows some of the defendant's properties to enter the "situation" in the reasonable person comparison. Thus the *Coroners and Justice Act* 1989 Section 54 defines the new defence of "loss of control" in terms of what can be reasonably expected of "a person of D's sex and age." See Section 10.5.

13 For completeness, there is a second, less serious offence called "careless driving" (Section 3ZA), which is the same as "dangerous driving," except that the driving is merely "below" rather than "far below" what would be expected.

This is an objective standard of recklessness. So despite much of English law adopting an (almost) subjective standard with *R v G* in 2003, dangerous driving remains an exception. The offence is defined by two objective facts: first a fact about substandard driving, and second a fact about whether its dangerousness is "obvious."[14] There is no reference to the driver consciously disregarding any risks while driving. The prosecution can therefore take e.g. CCTV evidence to establish the two objective facts without consulting the defendant at all. (The defendant will still have the opportunity to offer an excuse or a justification for why she was driving so dangerously, but the onus will then be on her to prove this.)

In addition to this definition of "dangerous driving" (DD), there are two separate offences, "causing death by DD" (Section 1) and "causing serious injury by DD" (Section 1A). So while DD is a *conduct* crime, "causing death by DD" is a *result* crime. Once again we recall our discussion of moral luck in the Introduction, and the story-pair about the two dangerous drivers. One of them makes it home without incident, and the other hits and kills a pedestrian. They are both apprehended, the first is charged with DD and may get a fine and some points knocked off her licence, and the second with "causing death by DD" and faces a prison sentence. As we saw, Harry Frankfurt would call this unfair because the two dangerous drivers were *doing* the same thing, with the same state of mind, and with the same limits to their control of the situation; therefore they should get the same punishment regardless of the luck of a pedestrian crossing their path. In our "retrospective" view, we responded by saying that in fact the two drivers were *doing* different things, and this is precisely what is reflected in the two offence descriptions of the RTA 1988: the second driver has "caused a death" — and it was entirely within her control whether she got into the car and whether she drove dangerously.

The *RTA* 1988 contains one more offence that is worth mentioning:

> 3ZB.[15] A person is guilty of an offence under this section if he causes the death of another person by driving a motor vehicle on a road and, at the time when he is driving, the circumstances are such that he is committing an offence under —
>
> (a) Section 87(1) of this *Act* (driving otherwise than in accordance with a licence),
> (b) Section 143 of this *Act* (using a motor vehicle while uninsured).

In our discussion of Caldwell and C, we already had some doubts about the fairness of holding them responsible despite the risks genuinely not occurring to them. But 3ZB goes one stage further to a kind of strict liability. For it says that whoever drives unlicenced or uninsured and causes a death will be held responsible, *even if* she is a very competent driver and even if she drives very carefully. In *Williams* [2010], D was driving a car, and V stepped out in front of it, such that D could not avoid killing him. As it happens, D had neither a driving licence not car insurance, so he was already breaking the law. Controversially, the Court of Appeal claimed that D's illegal driving "caused" the death; once D had made the decision to break the law, then he could be held responsible for all the direct harmful consequences of that driving. However, as Ormerod and Laird point out (2021, p. 67), it was not the lack of a licence and insurance that "caused" anything, it was D's driving, and there was no suggestion that the

14 The "reasonable person" has been expanded to include an explicit reference to the appropriate degree of driving skill and the appropriate caution while driving. This is a little odd, since it is the state who determines whether a driver is "competent" enough to pass its driving test. Anybody driving without a licence would already be guilty of a separate offence under Section 87(1) the *RTA* 1988.

15 This strange numbering tells us that the offence was added to the Act at a later date: in this case, it was added by the *Road Safety Act* 2006 (and was amended in both 2015 and 2019).

driving itself was negligent. The UK Supreme Court effectively overruled *Williams* in *Hughes* [2013], and now 3ZB is applied only rarely.

3.3 PRACTICAL INDIFFERENCE

There are two awkward cases for the subjective account of recklessness to accommodate. The first is exemplified by *Parker* (who smashed the telephone receiver in anger), who seemed genuinely unaware of the fragility of the receiver because he was in such a state of anger. The second is of someone who has *so little regard* for the legitimate interests of others that she genuinely does not consider the risk of harmful consequences arising from her intentional actions. On a subjective account of recklessness, both people would have to be acquitted, and this seems wrong. One solution is that of *Parker*: that Parker *was* conscious of the risk, but at the back of his mind. But that solution, already questionable, won't work for the second awkward case.

Antony Duff (1990 p. 163) introduces a special category of person who is "practically indifferent" to the legitimate interests of others. For example, a bridegroom is found drinking in a pub on the day and time when he should be in the church for the wedding ceremony. The bridegroom claims, let's assume quite genuinely, that he completely forgot about the wedding ceremony, and under any subjective conception of recklessness, we would be forced to acquit him of blame. And yet, argues Duff, he does not have the correct attitude to the ceremony or to the bride or to the bride's family — the wedding ceremony details are precisely the sorts of things that he as bridegroom *must not forget*, if we are to continue taking him and his professed intentions (to marry the bride) seriously. Importantly, this is worse than ordinary recklessness: for we are not saying that the bridegroom is guilty of a particular failure of awareness and willpower on this occasion; we are saying that this occasion's failure reveals a deep and systematic practical indifference to the life of someone he professes to hold dear.[16]

Victor Tadros (2007) offers a similar account. Again we have the problem of a person who is genuinely indifferent to the harmful consequences of the risks he is planning to take, and would therefore have to be acquitted on a charge of subjective recklessness. Tadros takes one step into the past, and asks whether the defendant, genuinely unaware of the risks in the present, at least made a reasonable effort to *investigate* the risks.

> A defendant may form a belief that there is no risk because he is too careless or lazy to investigate the risks … In doing so the defendant clearly shows that he has insufficient regard for the interests of those who might suffer from the risk materialising. (Tadros 2007, p. 255)

Now certain people will not be inclined to investigate the risk because of certain character defects: (i) they are too ignorant or unimaginative or clumsy or insensitive (i.e. unilateral defects), but this is compatible with them *normally* having sufficient regard for the interests of others. In contrast, Tadros wants to target those who fail to investigate the risks because (ii) they are cruel or selfish or greedy or jealous or more generally just callous (what might be called *other-oriented* character defects). Glanville Williams (1987) took a similar line, and

16 The Law Commission, in its *Consultation Paper* no. 177 (2005) argued for a category of "reckless indifference," as opposed to "simple recklessness," and this seems to map onto the phenomenon described by Duff. In the special case of *killing* by reckless indifference, they propose that this occupy a new category of "second degree murder." Such a "construction" is similar to the way that the cargo plane bomber's gross recklessness was "constructed" into an "oblique intention" to kill, thereby making the bomber eligible for a murder charge.

argued for an account of recklessness that could be called "conditionally subjective": the court would first ask (i) whether D was aware of the risk, and if not, (ii) whether she had the capacity to *make herself aware* of the risk, and if so, (iii) whether she chose, out of a general indifference, not to exercise that capacity.

We can flesh out the distinction in two ways, says Tadros. First, we can imagine the agent trying to use an adjective from either batch of traits as a defensive explanation. (i) It *might* work for someone to say, "I'm really sorry for accidentally spilling my drink on you, I'm just so clumsy," although that is already pretty weak. (ii) It definitely won't work for someone to say, "I'm sorry for accidentally spilling my drink on you, I'm just selfish."

Second, we can imagine a third party *reminding* the defendant, during her reckless behaviour, of the risks to others that her behaviour currently runs. The clumsy or unimaginative person will be horrified to learn of the risks, and will cease their activity immediately in order to investigate; in contrast, the cruel or selfish or callously indifferent person will not be troubled in continuing with the risky activity.

Duff's and Tadros's concerns are well placed, but it is not clear whether any attempt to gather such agents into the net of subjective recklessness would end up being too complicated to guide juries in their deliberations. It is already difficult enough to determine what the defendant intended and what the defendant was aware of; asking them to speculate about character traits and about hypothetical scenarios might lead to too much inconsistency and confusion.

3.4 INTOXICATION

This brief final section will consider the problem of voluntary intoxication. When Caldwell set fire to the hotel he was intoxicated. This almost certainly contributed to his inadvertence to the risk he was creating for the hotel guests. Voluntary intoxication[17] is a problem for criminal law because it is so common, and so often associated with crime, especially with criminal damage and arson — Herring (2020, p. 73) states that 88% of criminal damage cases are fuelled by alcohol and drugs. Again, insofar as our conception of recklessness is subjective, then the very drunk individual might genuinely be unaware of the risks associated with her conduct, and this will be exacerbated by the probable lack of memory the next day.

The criminal law responds with two classic fudges. Let's say the drinker starts drinking at 6 pm. By 11 pm, she is very drunk, staggers out of the pub, and starts smashing shop windows. The first fudge is to ignore the drink, and declare that the drinker *was* aware at some level (or perhaps at the back of her mind, like Parker) of the likely criminal damage as she started throwing cobblestones, precisely because she would have been aware of the risks if she had been sober. The second fudge involves expanding the timeframe by describing the criminal action as effectively beginning *at 6 pm*, when the drinker starts drinking, aware (at 6 pm) of the risk that she will later become drunk and violent, and yet consciously disregarding this risk by freely choosing to drink on. This controversial methodology is sometimes called a "tracing" account, because it attempts to "trace" responsibility in the present (when the agent appears unaware) back in time to a previous competent and voluntary decision that had the required freedom and awareness.

17 We will only be speaking about voluntary intoxication in this section: involuntary intoxication, e.g. having one's drink spiked, usually absolves the drunk or drugged person from liability.

The tracing strategy is somewhat plausible in other contexts, as with the epileptic who starts to drive in full knowledge of the risk of having a fit at the wheel (the American case of *Decina* [1956]). When the fit strikes, she becomes incompetent, and therefore not responsible for any damage caused. But if it can be shown that she knew of a high risk of a fit, but chose to drive anyway — and without any overriding justification for driving — then she can be treated as having chosen to risk causing the damage. In the case of alcohol, the tracing strategy might work for cases of habitual heavy drinking with a habitual disposition to alcohol-fuelled violence, but would be less plausible for ordinary social drinkers.

CHAPTER 4

NEGLIGENCE

This is the third of three *mens rea* chapters, descending the "ladder" of culpability. Intentional action was the most culpable, and most criminal theorists take it as the paradigm of wrong action. Recklessness is a bit less culpable since one does not intend to do wrong: one intentionally disregards a known and unjustified risk of causing harm. The third rung down is negligence. We have already discussed something similar to negligence, "objective" recklessness, as characterised by *Caldwell* (1982) and by the *Road Traffic Act* 1988 definition of "dangerous driving."

Negligence is perhaps the most mysterious of the three rungs, and in one sense is radically different — for there is no intention or choice in the agent's mind. Indeed, there might not be anything at all in the agent's mind: that's precisely the philosophical problem. With intentional harm and recklessness, we can "pin" the blame on the intention, i.e. we can hold the unexcused agent responsible for the intention, and this is fair because she had the freedom to refrain from acting on that intention. As such the intentional or reckless agent can be said to own her action; it originated from inside her. With negligence, we can't pin the blame on anything: all we can do is describe what happened, as if from the outside. The agent herself might not even realise that she has been negligent, and once this is pointed out to her, she might have no clue what went wrong, or why.

So what exactly is negligence? As in the previous chapter, we might as well start with the *Model Penal Code* (MPC) 2.02.

> (d) A person acts negligently with respect to a material element of an offense when he should be aware of a substantial and unjustifiable risk that the material element exists or will result from his conduct. The risk must be of such a nature and degree that the actor's failure to perceive it, considering the nature and purpose of his conduct and the circumstances known to him, involves a gross deviation from the standard of care that a reasonable person would observe in the actor's situation.

This wording maps directly onto the *MPC* definition of recklessness: the same "substantial and unjustifiable risk" and the same "gross deviation from the standard of care." The key difference is that the reckless agent is *aware* of the risk and disregards it, while the negligent agent is *not* aware — *but should have been.* This "should have" is crucial, and it is what distinguishes negligence from what might be called honest ignorance. After all, there are plenty of substantial risks that we are not aware of, but we are not expected to be either.

The *MPC* definition is a bit misleading for two reasons. First of all, the wording makes it look merely like a "thinner" form of recklessness, whereas the gap between them is much bigger because of the negligent actor's lack of any intention. Second, because the third word is "acts" and there is a reference to a "standard of care," this might look like the agent's *conduct* is the essence of negligence. But the essence of the above definition is also the "should be aware" and the "failure to perceive" — in other words, criminal negligence is more about the agent's beliefs (including perceptual beliefs), or lack of them.[1]

1 In contrast, negligence in *tort* law focuses mainly on action or inaction. Tort law is mainly about one individual (the complainant) suing another individual (the defendant) for financial compensation for the harm she has suffered. To add to the confusion, English tends to call *criminal* negligence "gross negligence," to distinguish it from the ordinary negligence of tort law. Certainly, in a context such as medicine, ordinary

DOI: 10.4324/9781003351887-4

Negligence might well involve a "failure to perceive" a risk, but it is much broader: it includes the failure to remember, to check, to anticipate, to consult somebody, or to think something through, when the agent should have remembered, checked, anticipated, consulted, or thought it through. Importantly, it includes a situation where the agent mistakenly *thinks* that she knows the situation, or that she has things under control, or that she has remembered everything — and therefore believes that she does not need to check or to consult. There is a fuzzy border with recklessness here; for a reckless arsonist might be aware of the general risk associated with fire, but negligently unaware of the *specific* risk of her small fire spreading to the neighbouring building; or she might know about the existence of the risk but not *appreciate* it, as in the heavy smoker.

Finally, we have the same reliance on the "reasonable person" as we had with recklessness (see the previous chapter), and the same problems arising from such reliance. With negligence, there is often a new twist on this standard; since the defendant is often negligent in her performance of a *role*, then we have to define her negligent failure partly in terms of what a reasonable *occupant of that role* would have done.

To make this more concrete, we're going to look closely at a famous example of negligence, from the context of medicine. The big advantage of the medical role is that it is relatively easy to define (i) the "standard of care" that a reasonable doctor "would observe in the actor's situation," (ii) the best interests of the patient who is supposed to benefit from the doctor's work and (iii) the over-arching purpose of medicine. With these structures in place it is easier to judge the doctor's performance accordingly. Doctors have a long and systematic training in medical schools and most go on to a post-graduate specialised training and practice, where they acquire the skills and knowledge to deal with all the foreseeable contingencies of their specialism. The medical profession then monitors their progress and performance throughout the training and their professional work, with the real power to investigate mistakes and discipline their members.

We can summarise this by speaking of the doctor's *duty of care*. Now all of us have a basic duty of care whenever we interact with strangers. Some of us have a more precise duty of care when we occupy a role toward, e.g. a client, or a student, or to one's child. But because the medical patient is so much more vulnerable, and because the doctor is in a position of doing so much more damage, then the duty of care has to be codified much more precisely than that of other roles. And the doctor, insofar as she voluntarily pursued her medical career through each stage, has implicitly committed herself to this duty of care to all her patients. In addition, if the doctor, *qua* specialist, has been allocated a particular patient on a day and time for a particular medical procedure, then the doctor has a particular duty of care to that particular patient.

One last point before looking at the central case. There is a long-standing principle in English law that one is *not* liable for omissions. This is most evident in so-called Bad Samaritan cases: if I am walking by a shallow pond in a park and I see a toddler drowning, such that I could easily rescue her without significant cost to me, I am not under any explicit legal obligation to do so. (This is to be contrasted with the European mainland, where there normally *is* such an obligation to rescue.)[2] The underlying idea here is that an omission is not an action, and therefore I cannot be held responsible for it. The main exception to this non-liability is

(tort) negligence is common enough, whereas gross negligence is rare. But despite its rareness, it is philosophically interesting enough to justify a whole chapter. We will have something brief to say about tort law later in this chapter.

2 See Dressler (1999). The exception for this is where an individual *assumes* a duty of care over a stranger by taking the first steps of looking after her. In the case of *Rufell* [2003], V was visiting D, and while there, V injected heroin, and then became unwell. The following morning, V was still unwell, and D pulled

precisely when I have an explicit duty of care. With that preamble in mind, let us look at the case.

4.1 ADOMAKO

Adomako [1993] is the classic case of gross negligence manslaughter in English criminal law. In this chapter, we are focusing on negligence more generally. One can be negligent about many different acts. In Section 8.2 we will return to the case as part of a discussion of manslaughter more specifically.

Adomako was a mid-career anaesthetist working in the NHS, assisting during a routine operation. Being an anaesthetist is a role with a very precise definition of the qualifications necessary (certified knowledge, skills and experience) and of the tasks that make up the job, before, during and after the operation. During the operation itself, he must put the patient under, monitor him, and then revive him, all the while being ready for certain typical problems, and ready to respond in accordance with the appropriate protocols, using his knowledge and skill. In the context of the NHS, we can say that taxpayers pay anaesthetists a lot of money for this.

On the fateful day, the patient was in for a routine eye operation — so no life-threatening risks were anticipated. The patient was also relatively young, and in good health. Adomako put the patient under, set up the monitors, and everything was running smoothly. The patient was supplied with oxygen through a tube and a mask. Suddenly the tube fell out ("dislodged"), but Adomako did not notice. The patient slowly suffocated, and a bit more than ten minutes later he was dead.[3]

It is important to stress that it is not unusual for oxygen tubes to dislodge, and in normal cases the anaesthetist will notice it and replace it "within 15 seconds" (to quote the appeal judgement) without harm to the patient. It was Adomako's job to watch the tube (among the other things he was supposed to watch), and Adomako knew it was his job. Nobody else in the operating theatre was supposed to check, and nobody noticed it. Why did Adomako not notice the dislodged tube? The judgement does not say. And for the purposes of determining negligence, it doesn't matter: the prosecution needs to establish that he did not notice (and fix) what he was supposed to notice (and fix), with catastrophic results. But even if we ask Adomako why he did not notice the tube, what could he possibly say? He certainly didn't have any good excuse. It was probably something banal: maybe he was distracted by a messy divorce he was going through, maybe he was rehearsing his upcoming promotion application, or maybe he was reminiscing about a fun night out the previous weekend. Who knows? None of this would come close to a satisfactory explanation because if it was a distraction, he should

him outside, where V died of hypothermia and opiate intoxication. D was convicted of gross negligence manslaughter. We return to this in Section 5.1.

3 For context, Adomako was actually subject to *two* parallel legal processes. According to the first, he committed the tort of negligence, and was therefore vulnerable to being sued by the patient's family in a civil court. Negligence torts are the most common kind of negligence, especially in medicine. In anticipation of negligent mistakes, doctors are legally required to take out personal malpractice insurance. Usually the insurance company lawyers will work out a settlement with lawyers representing the patient, and this will dictate the compensation payable to the victim (or victim's family) without the issue proceeding to court.

The second, parallel legal process for Adomako was the *crime* of "gross" negligence, which is a criminal matter. Here the punishment might be a fine, but it might also be prison. In the real *Adomako* case, he accepted the settlement of the civil case, but appealed against the criminal case. His appeal was dismissed, and he was given a suspended sentence. The full text of the appellate criminal judgement is available here: https://www.bailii.org/uk/cases/UKHL/1994/6.html

never have allowed himself to be distracted — and again, he knew that full well. Indeed, Adomako was justified in believing that he could resist any distractions precisely because he had resisted them successfully enough over the past years on the job. He was not a junior doctor, and this was a routine operation.

The tragedy is compounded by the simplicity of the omission, and the ease for a layperson to understand what happened. This is the main thing that led to the charge of *gross* negligence rather than *ordinary* negligence. This was hardly an esoteric failure where Adomako might appeal to his colleagues to defend him under the "Bolam Test."[4] Anybody can understand the idea that the patient needs oxygen, that the dislodged tube would prevent the flow, and that the anaesthetist would be responsible for watching the tube. This mind-boggling stupidity makes it very difficult to sympathise with Adomako, except perhaps for two aspects. First, as soon as he suspected that something was wrong, he admits: "After things went wrong I think I did panic a bit," and such panic would only have made things worse. But then again, anaesthetists are not supposed to panic. Second, we can be struck by the awful bad luck of the particular contingencies "lining up" with an agent who would not notice them on this occasion — it was surely not an accident "waiting to happen," given Adomako's successful record to date. If the ventilator had been physically closer to him, he would have easily noticed the dislodgement; if the ventilator had been further away, he might have been concerned enough to move it closer. And it's bad luck that none of the operating room staff noticed the tube either. If the operation had taken place a week earlier or a week later, Adomako might have been more alert and attentive. If the ventilator had failed in any other way, it would have set off an alarm that Adomako would have noticed and dealt with appropriately. None of this comes close to an excuse, of course, but it does raise the problem of moral luck in a striking way.

4.2 JUSTIFYING NEGLIGENCE LIABILITY

Now that we have that case to focus on, we can look at the central philosophical problem of negligence. On the one hand, we are inclined to blame Adomako for his omission in the strongest terms. He so obviously failed, and his patient died. End of story. But on the other hand, we can ask whether it would be fair to blame him, given how many times *in our own lives* we have been distracted, and failed to notice something important. So there is a strong sense of "there but for the grace of God go I ..."

Moreover, blaming him means holding him responsible; and as we saw, it is only fair to hold someone responsible for something if they understood what they were doing and had the freedom to refrain from doing it. True, there was no external obstacle preventing Adomako from checking the tube. But before he checked the tube, it would have to *occur* to him to check it. If it did not occur to him, then he was not actually free to act on the thought that the tube might be worth checking. And if he was not free, then it is not fair to blame him.

This is one interpretation, which we will call "narrow." (We will return to the "broad" interpretation, below.) This is the position taken by "negligence sceptics," like Alexander and Ferzan (2009) and Hurd (2014). The question for such sceptics is whether to re-classify negligence as a non-culpable accident and acquit the defendant from *criminal* charges (while allowing the *tort* process to compensate the victim's family in the usual way). If we retain the strong intuition (along with English law) that Adomako is *to blame*, and was *at fault*, then how are we to

4 This is the standard test for negligence for English doctors. The test comes from the *Bolam* [1957] tort case. If the doctor can show that her acts or omissions "reached the standard of a responsible body of medical opinion" (not necessarily a majority), then she will not be deemed negligent.

respond to the negligence sceptics? Let us consider three strategies from the academic discussions, and apply them to *Adomako*.

(i) *The harmful character trait.* The first strategy draws its inspiration from David Hume, and we already saw it in Antony Duff's discussion of "practical indifference" in the last chapter. The negligent agent was guided by a harmful character trait, such as a callous lack of interest in other people's legitimate interests, or an arrogant sense of infallibility, or indifference to rules, or a general moral insensitivity — or some combination of all three. Seana Shiffrin (2017, p. 204) describes a person who composes a text message while driving, and suggests not only arrogance, but also a lack of self-knowledge and indeed a lack of interest in pursuing self-knowledge:

> [she] may overestimate her abilities or underestimate her vulnerabilities and flaws. An inflated sense of self may propel the conviction in action that, on this occasion, her aim is sufficiently true to render safety precautions merely advisory for her or a practical sense that her focus while driving is expansive enough to permit texting.

The presence of any of these character traits means two things. Although the negligent actor has no intention on which to "pin" our blame, the character trait is a second-best target. Moreover, we can assume that the agent has indirect long-term control over his character (self-improvement through habituation), and she can be legitimately blamed for not having intentionally taken steps to eliminate this character trait in the past. As such, the blame for present negligence is "traced" back to regular intentional omissions in the past.[5]

This might work for *some* cases of negligence, but it does not seem to work for Adomako. First of all, there is no evidence of any arrogance or callousness from the Appellate Court judgment. Second, Adomako had several years of successful enough professional practice behind him. Whatever his failings in the past, he had never faced serious disciplinary action before, and so never had any evident reason to self-improve. Third, part of what it means to have a character trait is that we retain the freedom to act *out of* character if and when the situation requires it. In order to perform their jobs (sufficiently well to avoid disciplinary action), doctors have to learn to suppress many natural character traits as it is. Finally, what can we say to the victim or the victim's family by way of explanation? Telling them that the doctor was "arrogant" or "callous" does not help them much to understand what happened.

(ii) *Tracing back to a previous choice.* The second traditional avenue for blaming the negligent action on the agent uses the same kind of "tracing" strategy, but focuses on a clear choice in the past. So in the New York State case of *Decina* (1956), the agent was aware of his epilepsy, but chose to drive. While driving he suffered a fit, lost control and caused damage. Clearly he should have been driving with due care and attention, and insofar as the fit prevented this, then he could be described as negligent. However, the blame could be traced back to his previous choice to ignore the known risk of a fit, and that's what we can blame him for.[6]

Here the first question is whether to describe *Decina* as a case of recklessness rather than negligence. In normal reckless driving cases, I am aware of the risk of an external event: a pedestrian walking into my path. Decina was also aware of the risk of an external event: the

5 "Habituation" is a term from Aristotle's theory of virtue. A virtue like kindness is a disposition to perceive the right way, to deliberate the right way, to feel the right way, and to act the right way, all in response to an appropriate object. The non-kind person cannot decide from one moment to the next to *be* kind (she cannot control these four aspects of virtue), but she can "fake it till she makes it." She can *pretend* to be kind, while watching others who are already kind. In theory, with enough of the right kind of sustained effort and attention, she may well acquire the genuine virtue over time. The thought then is, if she does not have the virtue *now*, it is because she intentionally chose not to habituate herself into acquiring it earlier.

6 For a discussion of this point in a different context, see Padfield (1989).

epileptic fit. Although such an event was internal to Decina's *body*, it was external to his choice-making *self*.

Be that as it may, it is not clear whether we can use the *Decina* tracing strategy for Adomako, again because of Adomako's longer-term record as a successful enough doctor. He could reasonably conclude that he could do his job well, which meant noticing the things he was supposed to notice and checking the things he was supposed to check. If someone had asked him just before the operation whether he would ever fail to notice something as obvious as a dislodged tube, he would probably have laughed at the question.[7]

(iii) *Exercising capacity*. The third traditional strategy comes from H.L.A. Hart (1968).[8] Recall the "narrow" interpretation, above: that at the moment that the tube dislodged, Adomako was not free to check the tube since the idea of checking had not occurred to him, and so he had no idea to act on. Hart would say: Adomako could still *have checked the damn tube*! He could still turn his eyes toward the tube, at which point he would certainly have noticed its dislodgement and would have certainly intervened to re-attach it (almost without thinking). Again, it's not as if there was anything preventing him from checking it. Moreover, it is false to say that checking the tube did not occur to Adomako *at all* — it was part of his duty of care, part of his training, part of his job, and part of the normative structures within which he moved in every operating room. He *knew* that he should check the tube, he had the "capacity" to check it, but he did not "exercise" the capacity, as Hart puts it. That it was not a conscious choice, that Adomako did not stand before the two ideas of "to check" or "not to check," does not matter. There is still enough to pin the blame on.

To put it another way, Adomako had chosen to become a doctor (and had continually "re-chosen" to remain a doctor), and with that to assume the required duty of care to the future patients who would be allocated to him. He had also chosen to become an anaesthetist (and had continually re-chosen to remain one), and thereby to assume, when on duty, the specific responsibilities attached to the role. The etymology of the word "responsibility" is important here. Adomako chose to take responsibility for the patients allocated to him, and this involved the readiness to *respond* as appropriate to the needs of the patient, including the readiness to respond as appropriate to any mechanical defects in "his" operation-room equipment.

The "narrow" interpretation suggested his lack of freedom to check the tube. The "broad" interpretation would suggest a different lack of freedom. Given his continuing over-arching re-commitment to the job and the associated duty of care, he did not have the freedom to *let himself become un-free* to notice the tube.[9] Again we are in a murky world of choice. Philosophers of action, like criminal law theorists, are too quick to assume that a choice must be intentional and explicit, between at least two options of which the chooser is conscious — and otherwise it is not a choice, but some kind of caused event taking place through the person's brain and body. (And this caused nature of the action might therefore make it unfair to blame the person, the negligence sceptics will say.)

7 For a recent critique of "tracing" strategies, see Greenberg (2021).

8 Hart discusses two examples: (i) a roofer, placing tiles on a roof, and negligently throwing building material down onto the street below without checking (Hart, 1968, p. 147); (ii) a signalman, negligently ignoring his signalling duties in order to play a game of cards (p. 150). The latter involves role-related negligence (like Adomako's), but the first is a more general negligence that would apply to anyone who finds themselves on a roof. And while the roofer probably just wasn't thinking, at least he was focused on his job; the signalman's negligence seems much worse because he was engaged in something wholly irrelevant to what he was being paid to do.

9 We thank David Prendergast for this way of putting it.

But there are degrees of choice: Adomako's semi-conscious unexercised capacity, his "letting himself become un-free," is obviously less than the paradigm, but it is more than a caused event. Although we cannot blame him as much as if he had intentionally dislodged or recklessly ignored the tube, we can still blame him, and the force of that blame is magnified by the ridiculous ease with which the problem could have been corrected, and by the severity and irreversibility of the consequences. Indeed, precisely because of these consequences, it would seem that the "should" underlying the normative structures defining his role (as in "he should not fail to check") is actually too soft: when it comes to the tube, it would be better to say that the anaesthetist *must not* fail to notice its dislodgement.

Hart's "broad" interpretation of the failure is still not a full explanation — we can still ask *why* Adomako did not notice the tube. And we might be inclined to accuse Hart's analysis of merely re-describing the problem. *Of course*, Adomako should have noticed the tube, and Adomako is the first to admit this. *Of course*, Adomako could have and should have exercised his capacity. But Adomako — and we — remain utterly baffled as to how he failed.

We can combine Hart's approach with the tracing strategy. There must have been earlier moments — without harmful consequences — when Adomako would have noticed that he was losing his grip. And at that point he had a conscious choice of whether to "get a grip" via a new effortful policy of double-checking and heightened vigilance, perhaps to the point of drawing up a printed checklist that he would go through methodically before and during each operation. Part of the doctor's duties include a duty of *self*-care: they should watch their own physical and mental health for symptoms, and seek help if the symptoms risk undermining their job performance. If necessary they can recuse themselves from an operation if they are not feeling up to it. Evidently Adomako did feel up to it on this occasion. But he should have been aware of the risk of unreliable introspection from any harmless slip-ups in the recent past. We might call this a case of "prior" negligence.[10]

Apologising for negligence

In order to test some of the intuitions raised by the Hartian account, we can consider a slightly different context beyond the law. Imagine that Adomako is morally serious, and feels terrible about what happened. He wants to apologise to the victim's family. Can Adomako personally apologise to the family of his victim?[11] Our first answer would be: of course, he can and should apologise to the victim. However, there is a subsequent question of what exactly he is apologising *for*. Yes, he can apologise for *what happened*; but we're not sure he can apologise for *what he did*. We can call this a "shallow" as opposed to a "deep" apology. This maps onto the problem of trying to pin the blame onto the negligent agent. Not only is Adomako baffled by what happened, but his bafflement will turn to frustration because he cannot apologise deeply for it. However sincere his expression of bafflement as a follow-up to the words of apology, it will inevitably sound lame to its intended audience.

10 Stark (2016, Chapter 8) thinks that Hart's account is on the right lines, but does not go far enough. His chapter provides a detailed and nuanced account of how Hart's account might be developed to accommodate what he calls the Standard Account of negligence in common law jurisdictions.

11 We're not talking about apology as part of, e.g. an organised restorative justice or reconciliation programme, nor are we talking about apologies that legally admit culpability. Instead, we are asking about unforced "personal" apologies, that take place after all the legal business has concluded. There is a question of whether the victim's family would *care* about the apology. They might be satisfied with the tort settlement, together with the knowledge that Adomako had been struck off; since they know the facts of the case, they might say "what more could he possibly say to us?" This section is a compressed discussion of Cowley (2024).

Effectively the shallow apology would amount to no more than Adomako's acceptance of the legal description of his negligence, together with an expression of his genuine sorrow; which is all well and good, but would not amount to the moral achievement that Adomako seeks. A deep apology would only be possible for an act that was *owned* by the agent rather than one that happened "through him." Normally I can only own an act when it involves my choice to carry out an intention. If I intentionally ignore a known risk and recklessly harm someone, I can apologise deeply for that choice and therefore for its consequences. A deep apology will be driven by a genuine remorse, where remorse conceptually presupposes that I made the wrong choice; whereas a shallow apology will only be driven by a sorrow separate from my agency. In summary, we can say that the reckless agent's remorseful apology is more satisfying (for both apologiser and apologisee) because it comes from the "inside," whereas the negligent agent's sorrowful apology is more frustrating because it comes from the "outside" (i.e. her accepting the external description of the events).

Note, however, there is again the problem of the fuzzy boundary between recklessness and negligence. Although the negligent Adomako might be baffled by what happened, a reckless agent might be equally baffled. She might say to herself "I knew the risks! Why did I disregard them? What was I thinking?"

4.3 TWO OTHER NEGLIGENCE CASES

In order to get a sense of the sheer variety of negligence, we're going to look at two other cases, both medical (or quasi-medical). In 2011, trainee doctor Hadiza Bawa-Garba was struck off the medical register for the grossly negligent care of her 6-year-old patient, leading to his death. In 2016, the Court of Appeal (Criminal Division) rejected her appeal. However, in 2018 the Court of Appeal (Civil Division) ruled in her favour in relation to the decision of the General Medical Council to strike her off the medical register. They accepted her argument that her negligence had been caused by the lack of sufficient resources and staff at Leicester Royal Infirmary's children's assessment unit. Quite simply, she had been given too much to do, she was exhausted trying to do her job, and so serious misjudgements and corner-cutting were inevitable sooner or later. It's fine in principle to tell doctors that they should recuse themselves from an operation if they are feeling unwell, but they cannot do that too often. Maybe Bawa-Garba felt that her career and performance could not afford the closer scrutiny that a further recusal would attract from NHS Personnel. The negligence itself took place in 2011, at the beginning of a long period of Conservative government austerity, and therefore one can assume that the pressure on junior doctors can only have got worse with each passing year. While it's true that the medical school and career system selects extraordinarily strong and able individuals — if we are to judge by the small percentage of original applicants who get into medical school and have the stamina and commitment for long years of training — there will be mental and physical limits even on these individuals, and at some point the politicians have to trust the hospital clinical directors' requests concerning the number of staff they need, and how much such staff can be asked to do while maintaining a minimally safe quality of care.

The *Bawa-Garba* case is interesting, since it challenges the *individualist* presumption underlying most of the criminal law and the philosophy of action. According to this presumption, the only proper focus of the law is the individual, her choices at a given moment and the causal consequences of those choices. And negligence presents a problem precisely for that focus. The *Bawa-Garba* judgement in relation to her status as a doctor explicitly acknowledges the institutional framework within which the doctor had been acting, and raises the question of the reasonableness of the expectations placed on the coal-face participants of such a framework, rather than taking such expectations as given. Clearly there is a sense where it is too easy to "blame the system" for individual failings, and so working arrangements need to be continually monitored and adjusted with a view to fairness. In *Bawa-Garba v General Medical Council* [2018], her conviction was quashed.

The second case is not medical but ancillary to medicine: optometry. *Rose* [2017] is an example of what we might call "second-order" negligence. D was conducting a routine examination of an 8-year-old boy's eyes, with a view to offering him appropriate glasses. During that examination, she should have examined — but did not — the "optic discs" at the back of the eye; if she had done so she would have (and should have) noticed a certain swelling. This characteristic swelling is a possible symptom of the build-up of fluid in the brain, and optometrists are explicitly trained to notice that symptom and to refer the patients immediately for a proper ophthalmological and neurological investigation. Five months after the negligent omission, the boy died precisely from the build-up of the fluid, and D was convicted of gross negligence manslaughter. One year later, the Court of Appeal quashed the conviction, however.

What is interesting about this case, compared to Adomako, is that the negligence is at one remove from the death. Adomako could have and should have noticed the dislodgement of the oxygen tube, and the dislodgement led directly and foreseeably to the patient's death. Rose's failure to notice the swollen discs did not lead directly to the patient's death, since she was not qualified to diagnose the cause of death — the pressure on the brain. But she should have checked the discs, and in this respect she was found to be *negligent* but not *grossly negligent* by the Court of Appeal, and so her conviction for criminal manslaughter was quashed. (She remained subject to professional disciplinary proceedings and to a compensation settlement process.) If she had actually examined the optic disc and *not* noticed the swelling (or not considered it worthy of referral), *then* she would have been grossly negligent; but because she did not examine the discs in the first place, she was not in a position *to miss the symptom*, and so could not be grossly negligent. And yet her omission causally led to his death.

4.4 NEGLIGENCE ARISING FROM INDIFFERENCE

Negligence is easiest to grasp in the context of roles like doctor or parent where the duty of care is relatively clear. But it also concerns less formal relationships, where there are many ways of being negligent (even if we might use a less legalistic word such as "careless" or "thoughtless"). We might just blame someone for not doing what they agreed to do, what they promised to do, what they normally do — or what simply should have been done. We're going to group all these into two larger classes. On the one hand the negligence might involve a failure to notice something, to check something, to imagine something, or remember something —and we will take all of these as types of cognitive failure (varieties of *blindness*). This is what Adomako and the MPC were all about. On the other hand, I might notice or remember things perfectly well, I might be sensitive to risks and to people suffering, but I just don't care — in a context where the immediate but impotent response would be: "But you should care!" Again we come back to *indifference*, an attitudinal failure. Importantly, the attitudinal failure might cause harm directly, or it might lead to a cognitive failure; and a cognitive failure might lead, over time, to an attitudinal failure.[12]

12 We are not including here the case of *wilful* blindness, turning a blind eye in response to evidence of wrongdoing, precisely in order to avoid the responsibility of having to do something about it.

Intuitively, indifference sounds worse than blindness. In many contexts, if I say "I just didn't notice," that might sound somewhat innocent; if I say "I just didn't care," much less so. Indifference (or indifference as inferred from negligent blindness) is also interesting because it could end up playing three different roles in criminal cases. First, it could be irrelevant, insofar as the legal enquiry will content itself with the presence of a clear intention. Second, it could *aggravate* when e.g. an attitudinal failure will be deemed to have contributed to the unusual brutality of the crime. Third, it could potentially *mitigate* by offering the basis for a partial excuse, or by reducing culpability from apparent recklessness to negligence.

Kenneth Simons (2002, pp. 220–221) shows the influence of indifference across a number of examples, and we're going to briefly discuss two of them:

> *The Remorseless Negligent Driver.* Suppose that a distracted driver, engrossed in conversation with a passenger, accidentally strikes and kills a pedestrian. The driver reacts to the tragedy with utter indifference.

This seems a straightforward case. The driver was distracted and therefore negligent and therefore killed the pedestrian, and that should be the end of a complete legal story. Anything *after* the killing is irrelevant to his culpability at the moment of the killing. There is a question, however, whether the post-collision indifference is not evidence of a pre-collision indifference that exacerbated the negligent driving by dulling the driver's appreciation of the risks? Maybe — but it would not affect the legal interpretation of what happened as a negligent killing. There is a second question about whether the post-collision indifference could be perceived as a kind of *insult* to the victim and her family, and whether this could be grounds for a harsher sentence; whereas genuine remorse would comprise some degree of mitigation.

The above negligent driver can then be compared to the following reckless driver:

> *The Indifferent Reckless Driver.* A speeding driver endangers numerous pedestrians and reveals that he does not care whether or not he causes injuries. (Suppose the driver runs several lights. At each, he is aware that he has barely missed hitting a pedestrian. He never applies his brakes. His passenger urges him to slow down, but he maintains his speed at the final light, where his car strikes and injures a pedestrian.) (p. 222)

In one sense this driver is reckless since he is aware of barely missing the pedestrian. But his indifference almost makes him negligent. This case falls within the fuzzy border territory between recklessness and negligence. The driver is aware (and so is not cognitively deficient, as the MPC would require) but he doesn't care — and yet we want to say that he *should* care; he should have been shocked enough by the first near miss to slow down and drive more carefully. And so Simons's point is that the indifference would aggravate the eventual offence of injuring the pedestrian.

There is another interesting aspect of this example, and that is the timespan. As we have seen before, the criminal law prefers time-slices, and might interpret the example as a series of discrete offences: running each red light was a separate offence; and then injuring the pedestrian was another, much more serious offence. If the law only examined the collision, it might not see the underlying indifference. It is only when the light-running and the collision are taken as a *single* action through time, including the ignoring of the near-misses, that we can understand the full relevance of the indifference to the seriousness of the final collision.

4.5 NEGLIGENCE, TORT LAW AND MORAL LUCK

In our discussion of *Adomako*, we made reference to two parallel legal processes: the criminal process and the tort process. It is worth saying something brief about the latter here, and especially about the role of moral luck. For the concept of negligence (especially when it reaches the news) is much more common in tort than in criminal law.

Tort law (as part of "private" law) is about the relationship between two individuals, be they individual human beings, or "legal" individuals like corporations. Under a typical tort of negligence, one individual, the defendant, has breached her duty of care, and this breach has harmed another individual (the "claimant" or in other jurisdictions "Plaintiff"). The harm can be formally quantified in money terms, and the claimant seeks compensation, ideally to return her to the *status quo ante* (i.e. the situation before the harm).[13]

One important difference between criminal and tort negligence is the focus of blame. In criminal law, as we have seen, it tends to be on the negligent agent's mistaken or absent *awareness* of relevant facts or risks; in this way the blame is "personalised," as Findlay Stark puts it (2016, p. 180). In tort law, the focus is on the harm demonstrably caused by the negligent agent's substandard *conduct* (i.e. compared to the hypothetical conduct of the reasonable role-occupant), and the agent's beliefs or awareness are usually legally irrelevant.

Now let's consider moral luck, and look again at the story-pair in the Introduction about the two reckless girl racers, one of whom hits and kills a pedestrian. In Chapter 3 we discussed how the criminal law might justify different punishments for the two drivers even if they were allegedly doing the same thing. Now let's take the two drivers as equally negligent rather than equally reckless, and ask about what tort law would say. We will follow the argument of Goldberg and Zipursky (2006 — henceforth G&Z), in their discussion of the example of the drivers named Fate and Fortune by Jeremy Waldron (1997). The former hits and seriously injures a motorcyclist, who sues Fate for a million dollars. The latter hits nobody. G&Z start by acknowledging that the tort situation is *even more unfair* than the criminal situation. At least in the criminal situation, the "lucky" driver still pays some penalty (the fine), whereas in the tort situation, if there is no injured party (or if the injured party does not sue), then there is no tort and therefore nothing to pay. What's more, moral luck will also govern whether one victim is more fragile than another and therefore suffers more harm; and whether one victim has a greater income — and therefore loses a greater future income — than another.

In our discussion of the criminal law response, one strategy was to reject the comparison between the two drivers, and focus entirely on the one who caused the death. G&Z adopt a similar strategy here, but they go further. The essence of tort law is to be non-comparative. The two-driver examples rely on comparison to make their central point about luck and unfairness: in both cases, the two agents were doing the same thing, and therefore they both deserve to pay the same compensation.

In comparison, the single question for tort law is: who wrongfully injured whom? As such, there is no essential reference to any other cases for comparison. In the Fate and Fortune case, all that matters is what *Fate* did to the motorcyclist; what Fortune did or did not do is irrelevant. After all, there will always be people who are luckier and people who are unluckier than I. Tort law involves basic corrective justice, in the spirit of "if I break it, I pay for it." There will certainly be debates over the quantification of the harm. But ultimately a harm has come into the world, and the court is faced with the problem of who should pay for it: the

13 The quantification of the harm is a highly complex science. Theft and damage to property is fairly easy to quantify. But injuries resulting in the loss of a limb or an eye will result in a conventional valuation. In addition there will be quantifiable distress. Finally and controversially it might include compensation for the loss of predicted future income: so the promising footballer will get much more compensation than the nurse, despite having identical career-ending injuries. See the case of Sean Highdale, a promising young footballer who was seriously injured in a car crash in 2008, and secured compensation of a "seven-figure sum": https://www.dailymail.co.uk/sport/football/article-2330817/Sean-Highdale-picks-seven-figure-compensation-wrecked-career.html

complainant, the defendant or some combination of both. If the defendant has been negligent and the claimant has not, then it is surely fairer that the defendant pay. (If the complainant is guilty of some "contributory" negligence, then the compensation can be reduced.)

We mentioned that one part of the luck had to do with whether the victim was more or less fragile when hit by the car, and this may affect the amount of compensation owed. Again, comparison is irrelevant, one has to "take one's victim as one finds them." An extension of this idea goes by the odd name of the "thin skull" rule. The basic idea is that some people, as a matter of luck, are born with thinner skulls than other people, but the thinness is not visible or common; indeed, the owner of the thin skill might not even be aware of it. So a thin-skulled person gets into a bar-room brawl, during which his opponent knocks him over; on the way down he hits his head on a chair, and he dies from the resulting brain haemorrhage. (The assumption is that a normal-skulled person would not have died in the circumstances.) The opponent's clear intention was only to injure the victim's face and knock him down, within the broadly accepted "rules" of clean fighting in such a context. Normally we can believe the opponent when he claims that he had no idea of the victim's particular vulnerability. But a person is dead, and both the criminal and the tort law have to respond to the "facts on the ground," without reference to what happened in other bar-room brawls, or what might have happened in this one. We will return to thin skulls and the case of *Blaue* [1975] in the next chapter, Section 5.2.

4.6 STRICT LIABILITY

For completeness, we want to spend this final section on the phenomenon of "strict liability." If we recall the ladder of culpability that has structured this and the previous two chapters, we can descend from the highest liability of intentional action (including the tolerance of known harmful side-effects), then to recklessness, then to negligence, and below all this will be strict liability. Examining strict liability is also useful because it "book-ends" negligence: just as there was a fuzzy border between recklessness and negligence, so too there is a fuzzy border between negligence and strict liability.

We're also looking at strict liability because, perhaps surprisingly, the vast majority of crimes are in fact crimes of strict liability — we're thinking of the thousands of *regulatory* crimes that govern mainly business activity (and some individual activity), most of which we are not aware of.

Negligence (in criminal law) involves a situation where the agent should have been aware but was not, and as a result caused harm (or broke the rule). As we saw, the "should have been aware" is crucial. Strict liability asks whether the agent caused harm (or broke the rule) *full stop*. It does not matter whether the agent was aware or not, whether she should have or could have been aware, whether she had or had not been cautious — there is no enquiry into that at all. At first glance, this is controversial: even if the agent had done everything that could be reasonably expected from her in her situation to guard against causing the harm (or breaking the rule), then if she causes the harm (or breaks the rule), she will be still held liable. Strict liability is therefore essentially unfair.[14]

The big advantage of strict liability is that it is efficient. As long as there is sufficient evidence of the agent causing the harm or breaking the rule, then penalties can be applied

14 Recall the "negligence sceptic," who claimed that negligence was essentially unfair, since it was not possible for the agent to refrain from committing the harm, given what she knew and didn't know at the moment of commission. Such sceptics would argue that negligence effectively amounts to strict liability.

directly — no need for an enquiry, no need for a trial, no need even to interrogate the defendant. Allowing efficiency to trump fairness can be justified because the crimes in question are not very stigmatic, and the efficiency is widely accepted by the public: the strict liability regulations against pollution, for example, are hardly very controversial, and every chemical company now accepts them as a cost of doing business (and usually purchases insurance to cover the fines).[15] After all, however unfair strict liability might be at the moment of discovering the harm, every company had the prior choice of whether to engage in *that* business, given the regulations governing it and the risks of breaking them.

The most familiar example of strict liability for ordinary citizens is speeding. I am caught on a speed camera. A few days later I get a letter in the mail, ordering me to pay a fine. I'm annoyed, because I was in a hurry for an important meeting, and my speeding did not come close to harming anyone. But the criminal justice system doesn't care: there is no enquiry into whether it was an honest mistake, whether I was endangering others or not, or how skilful a driver I am. They have the evidence that I broke the speed limit, and they tell me: cough up and don't do it again. Most people accept this system, since it is not *too* unfair: after all, it is easy to obey the speed limit, and it is widely understood that slower cars cause fewer accidents and harm fewer people (and consume less petrol).

When we said there was no enquiry into possible good reasons for speeding, that's not quite true, but there is an interesting change in procedure. Let's say I was speeding in order to bring a sick family member to hospital, and three days later I get the letter asking me to pay the fine. I can appeal the ruling after I receive the letter; and I may succeed and have the fine cancelled. However, notice the reversal of the burden of proof. Normally it is the prosecution's job to prove intention or at least recklessness, by showing that I was aware of and consciously disregarded the risks without good reason: I am innocent until proven guilty. With strict liability, once there is evidence of my guilt, then I am guilty until I can prove that I was innocent (or at least justified in breaking the law).

We will close with four other examples of strict liability in criminal law, at least strict liability in relation to some element of the offence.

(i) *Causing death by driving: unlicensed or uninsured drivers* (Section 3ZB of the *Road Traffic Act* 1988). We mentioned this in Section 3.2. The thought was that however skilful a driver you are, and however carefully you are driving, the mere fact of lacking a licence or insurance will make you strictly liable for any death you end up causing, even if you are not blameworthy at all.

(ii) *Crimes of possession.* If I am caught with burglary tools or counterfeit-making equipment or class A drugs, then I can be charged regardless of whether or not I was doing or even planning to do anything with them. Here the unfairness of the individual charge is balanced against the deterrent effect of the known public penalty for mere possession, which is designed to dissuade burglary and counterfeiting and drug use *at an early stage* in the planning, and to dissuade colleagues from "minding" the tools for their more criminally inclined friends. In addition to the unfairness, there is also an underlying controversial claim about human character here: if someone already has

15 Other familiar cases of strict liability include a food manufacturer's liability for the quality of the food, a car manufacturer's liability for the safety of the car, a business's liability for the health and safety of its employees, an employer's "vicarious" liability for the crimes committed by their employees while on duty, and the owner of a dangerous animal for the safety of her neighbours. If I own a tiger, and I take every reasonable precaution to keep it behind bars, and yet it manages to get out and harm someone, then even if my behaviour is not blameworthy in any way, I will be held strictly liable.

a class A drug in her possession, then she has revealed that she is the type of person who will be tempted to use it and/or distribute it onward.

(iii) *Terrorism*. Another category of prohibited possession concerns equipment or supplies that are "capable" of being used for terrorist purposes; of course, the problem is that virtually anything is capable of being so used. Here the Draconian and vague policy is justified by the broad and indiscriminate destructiveness of terrorist attacks, and so the criminal justice system is permitted to intervene on the back of much less conclusive evidence than for ordinary crimes. If someone purchases 200 litres of fertiliser, without an obvious application to farming, then she will almost certainly attract suspicion and perhaps even arrest, if enough circumstantial evidence is already available.

(iv) *Rape of a child under 13*. This circumstance crime is defined by Section 5 of the *Sexual Offences Act* 2003. To commit the crime, it is enough for D to intentionally penetrate V when V is aged under 13. It is legally impossible for a child under 13 to consent to penetration, whatever she says. But more emphatically, D cannot claim that he had good reason to believe that V was 13 — even if she looked older, even if she told him she was older, even if she had plausible false identification. There will not be any enquiry into this at all. If this is unfair, then it is justified by the enormous likelihood of life-long harm to be suffered by V. (We discuss Sexual Offences further in Chapter 9.)

CHAPTER 5

CAUSATION

Now that we have a better idea of the concepts of intention, recklessness and negligence, we can look at something more fundamental that unites all three. Causation is a *huge* and very technical philosophical topic. It is also a *huge* and very technical topic in legal theory (in several different areas of law, but especially in tort). In this chapter we will try to avoid getting bogged down in the technicalities of either discipline, in order to focus on a small number of interesting philosophical problems relevant to both. This will help our understanding of the issues in several other chapters in this book.[1]

Let's return to the basic structure of the criminal investigation of a result crime, as adumbrated in the Introduction. A dead body has been discovered. The ambulance arrives on the scene, and already the paramedic is speculating about the *cause* of death. Was it a natural physiological failure, such as a heart attack? Was it a natural external event such as a falling branch? In asking these questions, the paramedic will rely on a basic understanding of how the human body works, the typical ways it can malfunction, its typical vulnerabilities in its encounters with the world, as well as a broad familiarity with the way the world works. These are all *causal patterns*, and the paramedic's expertise is merely a slight extension of our general understanding of the social and natural world, and of our place in both, which all competent adults can be assumed to have. Such a general understanding is necessary for us to act in the world, to learn from our mistakes, to plan for the future, to help and ask for help — and, as we saw, to commit intentional and reckless crimes.[2]

The paramedic continues her thoughts and her rough investigations. Was the death the result of human agency? Did the dead person cause it herself (accidentally or deliberately)? Or did another person cause this (accidentally or deliberately)? The body will be taken to a mortuary where a pathologist will look for more detailed evidence pointing to various natural or human causes, and in the latter case, the method of killing. If a homicide is suspected, the police will examine the scene for evidence about who might have caused the death, how — and why. Once they identify the dead person, they will examine the last days and hours of her life for further evidence of an underlying causal history. They will interrogate witnesses at the scene, as well as friends and family of the deceased, to see who might have a motive, which might generate a reason for someone to act. (We discuss the relation between causes and reasons, below.)

Most such investigations, by the pathologist, by the crime scene investigators, by the police detectives and by the prosecution lawyers, might presuppose a fairly simple account of causation. If and when the case reaches the courtroom, the first question will be: did the

1 The locus classicus for the technical philosophical discussion is John Mackie's *The Cement of the Universe* (1974), as well as the substantial literature following that. The locus classicus for the technical legal-theoretical discussion is HLA Hart and A Honoré's *Causation and the Law* (1959), as well as the substantial literature following that. See also Michael Moore's *Causation and Responsibility* (2009).

2 The central metaphysical problem of agency is about how a human being can act freely in a causally saturated world. The scientific picture of one event necessarily causing another event, in accordance with strict laws, simply has no place for human freedom. No matter what the human being might *think* about her freedom, she can never deny the possible influence of biochemical causes in her brain, of genetic causes in her upbringing, of socio-psychological causes in her social interactions. For the purposes of this chapter, and indeed most of this book, we will *assume* that competent adult human beings can make genuinely free choices to causally intervene in the world, and that they can therefore be appropriately held responsible for the consequences of their voluntary causal interventions (where "holding responsible" presupposes that the agent was sufficiently free to have refrained).

DOI: 10.4324/9781003351887-5

defendant do it (i.e. cause it) — or not? For such simple cases, most of this chapter's discussions will not be necessary. But there are a number of problematic types of cases where we can ask: what is causation, exactly? What does it mean to find evidence of a particular cause? How might causation be linked to responsibility?

5.1 CONCEPTUAL DISTINCTIONS

Let's introduce some of the distinctions and some of the technical terms. We'll leave the dead body to one side for the moment, and look instead at a very simple example of a human causing a change in the world: I strike a match and it bursts into flame.

Sufficient and necessary cause

Clearly my striking it is a *sufficient* cause for the match to burn, otherwise it would not have ignited. Was my striking it *necessary* for it to burn? Yes and no. We can imagine other things that would have set the match on fire, such as it being held over a naked candle flame. If there had been a naked candle flame and if the match had been just above, the match would have burst into flame without my striking it. So my striking it was not necessary. But *given* that there was no lit candle nearby, or any other known ignitors, then we can say that in this situation, here and now, my striking the match is indeed a necessary cause. Without the striking, the match would not have ignited (and I reliably know that, and other people can reliably assume that I know that).[3]

Lawyers call the necessary cause the "but-for" cause, as a shorthand for the following statement: *but for* my striking the match, the match would not have burst into flame. Section 2.03(1) of the *Model Penal Code* runs as follows: "(1) Conduct is the cause of a result when: (a) it is an antecedent but for which the result in question would not have occurred."[4] And such necessary causal responsibility would seem to ground moral and criminal responsibility, absent any exculpating or mitigating circumstances. The important implication of this is that if an agent *is* the necessary cause in a given situation — and they know they are the necessary cause — then they control whether the consequence will occur (and they know they have this control, and others can reliably assume that they knowingly have this control). And they can therefore be fairly blamed for the consequence.[5]

3 Note that timing can be important, even if the longer-term outcome is the same. In the case of *Dyson* [1908], V was suffering from meningitis, which made him weak. D struck V on the head, and V died. The meningitis, in making V weak, clearly contributed to the death; but expert opinion confirmed that V would not have died *at the time he did* but for the blows, thus making it murder. Even if the patient had been close to death because of the meningitis, and even if D's causal contribution had been small (but more than negligible), the death would have been *hastened* and this would be enough for murder.

4 Another popular phrase for a necessary cause is "*sine qua non*" — "without which not." So the striking of the match is the *sine qua non* cause of its bursting into flame.

5 Recall our discussion from the Introduction about the different meanings of "responsibility." When we look at natural events, we can trace *causal* responsibility, and this just means causal efficacity. So the lack of oxygen was responsible for the patient's death — this is a reference to the causal chain, without human involvement. But we can also say that "Jones was responsible for the death of Smith," and this can mean (i) Jones was *causally* responsible for the death (she killed him); but it might also mean that she was *morally* responsible for the death (she did a wrong action, and is therefore blameworthy). Normally the second presupposes the first.

Causes and conditions

But my striking it is not sufficient on its own. Imagine a large airtight glass box, maybe about a meter wide, with sealed rubber gloves allowing me to hold objects inside the box. If the air has been sucked out from the box, and I strike the match against the abrasive side of the matchbox, it will not ignite. This is because environmental oxygen is a necessary *condition* for combustion, part of the normal background against which the successful match-striking would be understood as "the" cause. But now imagine that I am striking the match again and again in the vacuum box, nothing is happening, but then my friend suddenly opens a tap and releases air into the box, and the match bursts into flame. In such a case we might say that the oxygen was the (necessary) cause of the ignition; or we can also say that my friend's opening of the tap was the (necessary) cause.

That means that the air and the striking are both necessary conditions for the ignition. But by convention, we say that the thing that *changes* will be the cause, and the other stable elements of the situation will be conditions. But we could go further in listing the conditions. The abrasive surface is necessary. A certain speed of striking will be necessary (too slow will fail to generate the spark). A certain dryness of the match will be necessary (too wet and the match will not ignite). A certain chemical composition of the matchhead will be necessary.

We can also list two huge — indeed, infinitely huge — sets of necessary conditions that would not normally occur to anyone trying to describe the scene, but which *might* be relevant in certain special cases. (i) There are an infinite number of things which *must not happen* in order for my striking to cause the ignition: e.g. I must not have a heart attack; a massive asteroid must not land on the building. (ii) An infinite number of necessary events had to take place *in the past* in order for me to get here, now, with this box of matches in my hand. For a start, my mother had to meet my father and cause me to exist, all those years ago. But of course it would be very odd to say that my parents *caused* (via a "chain of causation") my match to burst into flame!

So for most result crimes, it is enough if the defendant was the but-for cause of the immediate criminal consequence. When we find the dead body and the pathologist concludes that the person has been shot, then we are simply looking for the person who shot her (and the accompanying question about *mens rea*) — on the assumption that the shooting was necessary for the death, i.e. that she would otherwise have survived.[6]

Causes and reasons

There is also a philosophical debate about the difference between causes and reasons. Generally we will be assuming that causes are part of the description of natural events (the falling branch

6 Sometimes there is a set of conditions, all of which were necessary, and we choose one of them to accord with our moral intuitions about responsibility. In *Pittwood* [1902], D operated a railway level-crossing, and one night he negligently failed to close the crossing, with the result that a cart entered the crossing, was hit by a train, and as a result of the collision, a passenger on the train died. One can say that the cart's arrival caused the passenger's death, and this event was independent of D's actions. And yet surely D's negligence caused the collision, which caused the death. Why? Child et al (2022, p. 94) put it this way:

> While causation frequently depends on physical, mechanical relationships between actions and outcomes … causation is also often, but not always a function of moral and policy evaluations about D's responsibility for the event. When we state that Pittwood's dereliction "caused" an accident, we are articulating a view that he was responsible for that accident through his behaviour.

caused the skull fracture); and causes are also part of the description of voluntary human bodily movements (e.g. the stabbing caused the loss of blood). Reasons are what *motivate* free human agents to do things; but reasons do not *cause* people to do things, for that would imply a lack of freedom. Someone with strong reasons to do X can still refrain from doing X.[7]

That's the basic distinction, but there will be more complicated hybrid scenarios. Some event (the presence of a similar-looking umbrella) might cause the human agent to falsely believe that P ("Jones stole my umbrella"), and this then generates a reason for action Y (I freely take Jones's umbrella).

Causal over-determination

Let's return to the match-striking example, and our inclination to say that, once all other necessary conditions are in place, the match-striking was the but-for cause of the flame. But there remains a problem. Imagine a slightly different example. I am striking the match as part of an effort to set fire to a wooden house owned by my enemy. I have poured petrol over the base of the exterior wall, and I strike the match. The side of the house explodes into flame. That sounds like a but-for cause, as a component of the crime of arson. At the same time, on the other side of the house, another arsonist is at work with another can of petrol and another set of matches. (The house owner has many enemies.) The other side of the house explodes into flame. The house quickly burns to the ground.

Now we are left with a paradox. It *seemed* that I was the necessary cause of the fire; and yet if I had not lit my side of the house, then the house would have burned down anyway by the other arsonist. So my actions were not actually necessary for the fire. And the other arsonist could say exactly the same thing: *her* actions were not necessary because the house would have burned down anyway as a result of my action. Conclusion: neither of us is the but-for cause. And that's a problem, since it seems to let both of us off the hook. Sometimes this problem is phrased as follows: the but-for account is "under-inclusive"; it is unable to include examples which we intuitively think it should.

Hart and Honoré (1959) solve this problem with an ingenious but complicated solution that we're only going to sketch here. The idea is that there is a set of conditions — including the wooden house, the petrol, the oxygen, and my striking of the match — that constitute a *set* of conditions which is sufficient to cause the fire. And the match-striking is a "necessary element" within that "sufficient set" (an "NE" in that "SS," hence the "NESS" test). So far so good. But on that fateful day, mine was not the *only* set sufficient to cause the fire. There was another set — the wooden house, the petrol, the oxygen, and *the other arsonist's match-striking* — which was also sufficient to cause the fire. And *her* match-striking is a necessary element to that set.

There may be other sufficient sets too (e.g. a third arsonist). But that's not a problem. All that matters is that my match-striking is necessary in one set, and the other arsonist's match-striking is necessary in another set, at roughly the same time, and so we can *both* be held liable for causing the fire. (For most crimes, there will only be one set, of course, and so the NESS account collapses into the but-for account as normal).

7 Recall our discussion of reasons in Chapter 2. At any moment in time I stand before an infinite number of possible actions that I can realistically contemplate as within my causal power. But I only have reasons to perform some of those actions. I can survey my reasons to see which action the reasons incline me toward most strongly. When I eventually perform the action, I do so for certain reasons: the motivating reasons. After the action is performed, the police investigation will seek the agent's motivating reasons to *explain* the action, i.e. to answer the question: "Why did she do it?"

Actions and omissions, events and absences

We've encountered the distinction between acts and omissions in previous chapters. We saw that it was slightly counter-intuitive to say that an agent's omission can cause something; it might seem even more counter-intuitive to say that an *absence* can cause something. But recall *Adomako* from our discussion in the last chapter, on negligence. What exactly caused the death of the patient? It depends on the "resolution" at which you're describing. At the highest resolution, at the molecular level, we can say that certain normal biochemical processes (e.g. glycolysis) use oxygen, and these processes broke down when the normal supply of oxygen was removed for long enough (irreversible cell damage begins after about five minutes, cell death after about ten) — so surely we *can* say that the sudden absence of oxygen, as a disruption of a hitherto stable pattern, caused the death of the cells; we can blame the death on the lack.[8] If we scale down to a lower resolution, we can then say that the dislodgement of the tube prevented the oxygen from flowing to the patient's lungs, to his blood, to his brain, and so caused the brain death. Again, it might seem strange to say that the dislodgement (another negative concept) causes anything. But if the oxygen flowing through the tube is the normal state (the normal function of the ventilator), then the dislodgement interrupts this.

And at the lowest resolution, we have Adomako's failure to notice (and fix) what he should have noticed (and fixed). As discussed in the last chapter, the "background state" here was not only the properly functioning respirator and tube, but also a properly "functioning" anaesthetist, carrying out the duties that he committed and re-committed to carrying out. And so it is the omission that is the exceptional event, the disruption, thus supplying the causal impetus. Antony Duff (2007, p. 107) has argued that instead of asking whether an omission is a cause, it would be better to focus on the concept of *control*: if an agent can knowingly control (or at least strongly influence) a result, whether by act or omission, then she should be understood as causally responsible for that result. Hence Adomako's causal responsibility for the patient's death.[9]

Limiting the chain of causation

Lawyers sometimes speak of a chain of causation, as when event A causes B, which causes C, which causes D, and all the causes are but-for. This is a bit of a simplification, since it would be more accurate to speak of a "fan" of causation: A causes B, C and D, yes, but *each* of those consequences themselves go on to cause further consequences. To speak of a "chain" therefore implies a chosen focus on *certain* consequences relevant to our legal enquiry. Either way, there is an obvious problem here. All the consequences are necessary causes of subsequent consequences — does that mean that I am causally responsible for all of them? And if not, then for which of them? (And again, remember that in the same way that I cause the fan of chains of

8 Tadros (2007 p. 172) offers the example of the lack of rainfall. At a certain time of the year, in a given geographic area, the rainfall is regular and reliable: that's why we planted the crops. When the rain doesn't come, that exception to the pattern is the obvious thing to blame in our diagnosis of the crops' failure.

9 If an agent's omissions can cause harm, this raises a question of whether the state should institute legislation to punish "Bad Samaritans." France, along with many countries on the European mainland, has such legislation. The United Kingdom and Anglophone jurisdictions tend not to. The basic idea is that (i) I come across a stranger in trouble, (ii) I have no antecedent duty of care to that stranger, (iii) I can see that I could help her at no great risk or cost to myself, and yet (iv) I do not help her, nor do I inform the authorities about her plight. I am therefore a Bad Samaritan, my omission has *causally facilitated* their suffering, and in France I can be prosecuted for this facilitation. For a defence of the Anglophone approach, see Dressler (1999).

causation stretching forward from my choice, so too there are multiple chains of causation leading to my choice, including the event of my parents meeting.)

This is sometimes called the problem of "over-inclusiveness," and there is no easy answer. We might try to speak of "direct" consequences, but that doesn't help much when we consider the many indirect consequences that both intentional and reckless agents can be held responsible for. Another way would be to speak about the consequences that were reasonably foreseeable by the agent as she acted, but this is problematic too. Ultimately, lawyers have to rely on the case law, informed by ordinary intuitions of appropriate remoteness.[10]

Enabling and facilitating

This distinction concerns complicity, and so we will return to it in Chapter 7 on that subject. However, the distinction is important for our understanding of causation. Complicity is about a human "principal" causing harm, with the assistance of a human "accessory" (also known as an accomplice). By definition, the accessory typically does not cause harm or do wrong; but she (intentionally) causally contributes to the principal's harm-causing or wrong-doing. There are two kinds of contribution, enabling and facilitating. This distinction does not really exist explicitly in criminal law — one is either an accessory or one is not — but it can have an impact on sentencing. (We're drawing on Mellema 2016.)

When the accessory *enables* the principal's harm-causing, that means the accessory intentionally provides some assistance that is a necessary condition — and the accessory knows it is a necessary condition — for the principal to cause the planned harm: let's say the accessory intentionally provides the gun which the (otherwise unarmed) principal then uses to shoot the victim, as planned. Here we have the same point about control: if the accessory withholds her gun, then the principal (lacking ready access to other guns) would not be able to shoot the victim. (He might harm the victim in other ways, but the accessory would not then be complicit.) Because of this control, the enabler bears greater moral responsibility.

In contrast, when the accessory *facilitates* a harm, that means that her assistance makes it more likely that the harm will happen, but she cannot prevent the harm merely by withholding the assistance. The assistance makes a causal contribution, but not a necessary one. Let's say I knowingly drive the principal to the scene of the planned shooting, but I know that if I refused the lift, the principal would take a bus to the same place, with the same purpose. I still bear some moral responsibility, but perhaps less since I could not prevent it.[11]

10 There is a famous American tort case called *Palsgraf v. Long Island Road Co.* [1928]. Mrs Palsgraf was waiting on a train platform. Nearby, a man was boarding a crowded train with enough difficulty that he had to be helped by two railroad employees on the platform. In the process, the man dropped a package that he was carrying, it happened to contain fireworks, one of which was set off by the drop, the firework flew through the air and hit a large weighing scale on the platform, knocking it over onto Mrs Palsgraf and injuring her. If we assume that the railway employees had been negligent in their assistance, did that negligent assistance *cause* Mrs Palsgraf's injuries? It certainly seems that the injuries would not have taken place but for the negligent assistance. But the New York Court of Appeals ruled that the injury was (i) too remote, and (ii) too freakish and therefore not reasonably foreseeable by the railroad employees.

11 Sometimes a decision has to be made about whether to describe a multi-actor scenario as complicity or not. In *Pagett* [1983], D takes V hostage as human shield, and emerges from a flat surrounded by police. D fires at police, and the police fire back in self-defence: V dies from a police bullet. This *might* have been taken as D "encouraging" the police to kill V, a kind of complicity. Instead, D was found guilty of manslaughter because he *caused* V's death, albeit indirectly. D intentionally placed V in a position where V would foreseeably suffer and possibly die from the police officer's justified conduct.

The novus actus

Another important legal principle is that a chain of causation can be "broken" by an extraordinary natural event or by another human choice, a *novus actus interveniens* (intervening new act). The natural event has to be extraordinary in the sense of being not reasonably foreseeable. So if I assault Jones and leave him unconscious on the seaside beach at low tide, and the tide comes in and drowns him, then I will be charged with assault and manslaughter, because I can be expected to know about how tides work on beaches. What did I *do*? I assaulted him, and then disregarded the known risk that he would drown. Technically it was the water that killed him, but the water behaves in regular ways which all seaside inhabitants learn about at an early age. (This is based on the Australian case of *Hallett* [1969].) On the other hand, if an earthquake strikes, releasing a boulder which rolls down onto the beach, killing Jones, then I will not be liable for the death.

If, while Jones is unconscious on the beach, and the beach is deserted, but later an opportunistic thief stops to search Jones's pocket and steal his wallet, then I will not be liable for the theft, *even if* the thief would not have been willing or able to take the wallet *but for* my leaving Jones unconscious at that time and place. Here we can say that my assault was a "factual" necessary causal condition for the theft, but not a "legal" causal condition, because the thief has interrupted the chain of causation with her own free, deliberate and informed act, and thereby assumes full responsibility for the theft. The question is whether the thief's actions would be reasonably foreseeable and the stipulation was that the beach was deserted.[12]

In *Roberts* [1971], Roberts picked up a woman at a party, V, and offered to drive her home. While driving, he started groping her, and in a panic V jumped from the moving vehicle, sustaining serious injuries. While there was no doubt about Roberts's liability for the assault in the car, did he cause V's injuries outside the car? Again, any reliance on but-for causation answers the question too quickly: clearly, but for the assault, V would not have sustained those injuries. One interpretation of the events would be to say that V *chose* — as a *novus actus* — to jump from the moving vehicle, and she therefore assumed full responsibility for her injuries, with Roberts's groping a separate and discrete act now confined to legal history. In contrast, the court focused on V's panic, and judged her jump to be only partly voluntary, closer to a reflex than to a reasoned choice. Even if Roberts could not reasonably foresee V's *actions*, he could reasonably foresee V's *fear*, and therefore he was deemed liable for the consequences of the fear which he had caused.[13]

5.2 BLAUE

Following on from the discussion of the *novus actus*, above, the same issues came to the fore in the philosophically fascinating case of *Blaue* [1975]. Before we begin, recall the discussion of "thin skulls" from the last chapter (on negligence), and the general principle that the defendant has to "take the victim as he finds them."

12 Insofar as another agent's actions *are* foreseeable, then those other actions are "built into" the original assault as risky consequences. If there are shifty-looking people nearby, and the beach is notorious for regular robberies, then I will have recklessly left the unconscious Jones in a state of specific vulnerability to robbery as well as to drowning.

13 But see *Williams & Davis* [1992]. Here three Ds picked up V, a hitch-hiker. Once V was in the car, the Ds started threatening him with intent to rob him. V leapt out of the car, and was killed. On appeal, the manslaughter conviction was quashed, because there was not enough evidence that the Ds' threats were severe or credible enough to make V's reaction proportionate — as a result, V's act was taken as a *novus actus*.

Blaue forced his way into V's house, and attempted to rape her. V defended herself and tried to get away. In his frustration, Blaue grabbed a kitchen knife and stabbed V several times, and then ran off. V managed to stagger outside, and a neighbour called an ambulance. By the time V reached the hospital, she had lost a lot of blood, but she was competent enough to refuse a blood transfusion because she was a Jehovah's Witness (JW) — and as a result she died. (A JW will refuse a blood transfusion since she believes that it will spiritually pollute her.)[14]

The question here was: did Blaue *cause* V's death? It is clear that Blaue is guilty of attempted rape, and guilty of assault occasioning bodily harm: he could hardly deny any of that. It is also clear that ultimately, V died from a loss of blood through the very stab wounds intentionally inflicted by Blaue. If V had bled to death in her house, there would be no doubt about the causation, or about Blaue's responsibility for her murder.

However, such were the circumstances of the case that V had a clear opportunity to save her own life by accepting the blood transfusion. Medically, blood transfusions are straightforward and safe; there really was no significant medical risk involved. Of course, within her JW religious understanding of the situation, saving her *biological* life would undermine her *spiritual* life in heaven; and further biological life (at most a few decades) could never compete with an eternity in heaven. Given her religious beliefs, she could therefore not take seriously the physician's warning about certain biological death, because for her, biological death would be no more than a transition.[15]

Regardless of the reasons for her decision or her understanding of the medical options, however, Blaue argued that what mattered was that V had competently chosen one course of action over another, a *novus actus*, and therefore she bore full responsibility for that choice. She found herself in hospital with a medical problem, the doctor offered a solution, and she refused; by that point, the origins of the problem were no longer legally relevant, argued Blaue. As a competent adult, she was of course free to refuse any medical treatment, but Blaue should not have to "pay" for *her* choice.[16]

Against this, the prosecution argued successfully that V did *not* have a choice regarding the blood transfusion. As a devout JW, she felt she had to reject the blood, given her fear of spiritual pollution. (Whatever we may think of the rationality of her beliefs, we have to accept that *given* her beliefs, her fear is intelligible.) This was not a whimsical or merely psychological aversion, e.g. like needle-phobia; this was an essential principle of a religion to which she had been deeply committed for a good stretch of time. As such she had been placed, by Blaue, in a coercive situation that did not allow a *novus actus*, and therefore the chain of causation could be reliably traced back to Blaue's free action of stabbing her. The judgement reads:

> It has long been the policy of the law that those who use violence on other people must take their victims as they find them. This in our judgement means the whole man, not just the

14 Note the background principle of medical law that any competent adult patient can refuse any medical treatment, even life-saving treatment, for any reason (even for no reason).

15 There is a question about the strength of her conviction. It's one thing to have a religious belief, but this may be shallow and conventional; but when it comes to such a serious matter as determining who caused a death, the law should not believe the patient's claims simply because she declares them. In the *Blaue* case, the depth of V's beliefs was clear by her simple willingness to die rather than accept the transfusion.

16 Compare this to the facts of *Wallace* [2020]. D, angry at her boyfriend V's decision to leave her, poured acid on his face as he slept. V suffered not only disfigurement, but paralysis and untreatable pain. He returned to his native Belgium, where he eventually requested, and was granted, lawful euthanasia. D was acquitted of both GBH-rule murder and UDAM-manslaughter because either (i) D's decision was free, deliberate and informed, or (ii) the Belgian doctor's lawful decision to administer euthanasia was free, deliberate and informed. Either way, the acid-throwing was relegated to causal history. See the discussion in Section 8.3.

physical man. It does not lie in the mouth of the assailant to say that his victim's religious beliefs which inhibited him from accepting certain kinds of treatment were unreasonable.

However, could it not be argued that she *chose* to join the religion (in the past), and therefore she was responsible for accepting the risk that she would later find herself in a situation of being compelled to refuse the transfusion necessary to save her biological life? This would be a variant of the "tracing" strategy described in Chapter 4 on negligence. However, this account is not true to the phenomenology of religious belief. Many people do not choose to join as if they were joining a social club or interest group; they feel *called* to join. Alternatively, they have grown up in that religion, have never known a time when they were not part of it, and so never *chose* to join it. At any rate, regardless of how or when she became a JW, she had "grown into" it, to a point where she identified with it, and where her religious beliefs entirely shaped her outlook on the world and on herself, and with that the compulsion that she experienced.[17]

In the end, Blaue was charged with murder, but this was reduced to manslaughter on the grounds of diminished responsibility, since it was discovered that he had been suffering from mental health issues that would have affected his ability to control himself and to understand the original conflict situation with V in her house. But the manslaughter conviction still expressed Blaue's direct causal role in V's death.[18]

5.3 DRUG-DEALER CASES

There is a long line of problematic criminal causation cases concerning the relationship between a drug dealer and an addict. The basic scenario usually runs thus: the dealer offers the drugs, the addict takes the drugs, self-administers, and dies of an overdose. The question then is whether the dealer caused the addict's death, and should therefore be guilty of manslaughter. On the face of it, the addict is competent at the moment she buys (she is not yet under the influence), and she is sufficiently informed about the risks; so this would suggest a free, deliberate and informed *novus actus*, relegating the dealer's supply to causal history. And that's how the courts usually decide.[19] On the other hand, the addict is addicted, presumably sees herself as "needing" the fix, and so not entirely free. At the same time, at the moment of supplying the drugs, the dealer knows that V is an addict, knows what she plans to do with the drugs he supplies her, and knows the risk of an overdose. All of this would seem to increase the dealer's reckless responsibility for her death, however competent she might have seemed.

17 There might be a problem with the status of the religion in question. Jehovah's Witnesses are Christians, and therefore a part of the mainstream religion in the United Kingdom. What if Blaue's victim had justified her refusal of the transfusion on the grounds of membership of an obscure Satanic cult? If she was still deemed competent, then it would have been a straightforward refusal of treatment, but with regard to Blaue's previous stabbing, it would probably have been deemed a *novus actus*. (Conceivably, her Satanic beliefs might have been taken as sufficient evidence of incompetence for the doctors to override her expressed wishes and transfuse her by force, in her best interests.)

18 For completion, it is worth mentioning a variation to *Blaue*. Imagine that Blaue2 stabs V2, she gets to hospital, is offered a transfusion, and she accepts eagerly. But the doctor is Adomako, and because of his gross negligence, V2 dies in a situation where the routine transfusion would almost certainly have saved her life. This would be taken by the courts as a *novus actus*, and Blaue2 would not be charged with murder.

19 For example, *Kennedy (no. 2)* [2005]. Interestingly, the Court of Appeal in this case considered D to be acting in concert with V, and therefore bore joint responsibility for V's death. However, the House of Lords overturned this, and reinstated V's *novus actus*. *Kennedy* is importantly different from cases where D injects the drug into V with her consent, e.g. *Cato* [1976]: there D did not intend to cause V's death, but was convicted of "unlawful and dangerous act manslaughter" (see our discussion in Section 8.2). In addition, the Court allowed that D's action might not be the but-for cause, but if it accelerated a death that was going to happen soon, then this was enough to inculpate.

Needless to say, the addict's partial freedom is very different from the JW's partial freedom in *Blaue*. We can say that the addict's actions are partly determined by the biochemistry of addiction, whereas the JW's actions are partly determined by her deep religious beliefs.

Consider the following variation. V is so weak that D has to hold the syringe while V presses the plunger. This would not be D injecting V; this would not be D recklessly handing the drug to V to inject, knowing the risk. Instead, it would best be described as a *joint action*: the two were freely and knowingly engaged as joint principals in a reckless criminal venture with the foreseeable and likely result of serious harm or death. The dealer, as the only survivor of the joint action, could still be pursued it. If we can accept that scenario as a joint action, there is a real question about whether we couldn't accept *all* drug-dealer scenarios as joint actions, precisely because of V's questionable autonomy.

The drug-dealer problem brings us back to questions about necessary conditions in causation. Recall our discussion of the fire: the oxygen is a necessary condition for the fire in the sense that if there is no oxygen, there will be no fire. Analogously, is the drug dealer's sale of the drug a necessary condition of the addict's death? The answer is ambiguous. On a "global" scale, if *this* dealer had refused to sell to *this* addict on *this* occasion, then the addict would almost certainly have found a different dealer to buy the same amount of the same drug, and may well have overdosed. What's more, if the addict dies from an overdose, it is not as if she died from this one, latest injection alone; she dies from months or even years of cumulative abuse, via a habit fed by many dealers (i.e. we are not discussing a first-time user). So that would mean that this dealer is far from a necessary condition. However, on a "local" scale, *given* that this addict bought this drug from this dealer, then this dealer's sale was necessary as the final step (the "last straw") for *this* death to occur at the time and place and in the manner that it did. Yes, the addict might have gone elsewhere, but she did not, and we simply can never be absolutely sure if she would have gone elsewhere; whereas we can be sure she went to this dealer, and died. But, is the dealer's status as a necessary condition at the "local" scale enough to make him liable for manslaughter? In *Kennedy*, the House of Lords ruled that the victim's injection was a sufficiently competent *novus actus*. (The dealer would still be guilty of supply and possession-related offences, of course.) This fits with a long-standing pattern of judges being reluctant to call adult behaviour incompetent, except as a result of confident and specific expert medical testimony about the defendant's psychiatric status.

Importantly, however, the Lords in *Kennedy* did not mention the issue of V's addiction. Were V's request for the drugs and his subsequent self-injection truly autonomous? It depends. At the moment of the request and of the self-injection, he was not under the direct influence of *this* drug, and so he can be presumed to be acting autonomously. But given the *indirect* influence of the drug on V over time, was V really in a position to refuse the drug? Again, D knew very well that V was addicted, and D could predict with almost virtual certainty what V was planning to do with the drug once D handed them over.[20] The trial

20 In this respect, there is a question of whether *Kennedy* is or is not compatible with the more recent case of *Rebelo* [2021]. D was offering a weight-loss drug (DNP) over the internet, and V made regular purchases until eventually she died from it. V had a complex history of mental health, so there was the same question of whether her continued use was sufficiently autonomous. D accepted a conviction for "placing an unsafe food on the market," but stated:

> Ms Parry was an autonomous woman who decided to make a foolish decision in the exercise of her free will and killed herself, as she was entitled to do. The appellant's act of placing DNP on the market was too remote. Putting DNP on to the market did not cause her death and he bore no responsibility for Ms Parry ingesting it. It was not possible for him to have foreseen the possibility that she would take a handful of the capsules.
>
> (at 14)

judge considered D to be engaged in a joint venture with V, and that would have kept D responsible for the outcome; alternatively, it would be plausible to describe D as having a duty of care toward V, which he breached by allowing V to inject an overdose, and for failing to summon medical assistance as soon as D realised that something was wrong? That would bring D within the ambit of gross negligence manslaughter (on which see Section 8.2, and the discussion of *Broughton* [2020]).

5.4 BLAND

In this final section, we discuss a famous medical case, *Bland* [1993], which raises interesting questions about causation and intention. It also represents a case where legal concepts were twisted in such a way to allow the result that nearly everyone intuitively sought, but not without raising deep further questions that have still not been satisfactorily answered.

Tony Bland was 19 when he was crushed in the 1989 Hillsborough stadium disaster, as a result of which he fell into a coma, or permanent vegetative state (PVS). Importantly, he was able to breathe unaided, and all his internal organs were working fine. He therefore needed only artificial nutrition and hydration (ANH) and hygienic nursing care, together known as "basic care." By 1993, the coma had lasted four years, and seemed likely to continue for many more years, perhaps decades. Bland's family therefore asked the doctors to remove the ANH, thereby allowing Bland to die. The doctors were unsure whether this would be legal, and so consulted the court.

At the heart of the *Bland* case is the distinction between basic care and medical treatment. Bland was receiving basic care, administered by nurses rather than doctors, and by definition this was a minimum that could never be withdrawn from a patient. "Medical treatment," in contrast, has the status of an extraordinary intervention, and as essentially "unnatural";[21] if such treatment could heal or cure or fix the patient, fine. But if it is considered futile, then it is morally and legally permissible to withhold or withdraw it. So, for example, aggressive life-saving treatment is routinely withheld when a very sick patient is judged to have irreversibly passed into the dying phase.

However, Bland was not dying, and did not need "medical treatment," he just needed basic care (including the ANH). So in a remarkable bit of conceptual engineering, the House of Lords assembled a series of striking claims:

- The ANH was to be re-defined as "medical treatment," on the grounds that the naso-gastric tube had to be inserted by a trained healthcare professional. (Once inserted, however, it would not need any special training to maintain it, or to replace the nutrient bags.)
- Since the ANH was "medical treatment," it could be potentially withdrawn if it was "futile." But the ANH was not futile, it was doing exactly what it was supposed to do, it was feeding and hydrating Bland. In addition, ANH is hardly a medical treatment

The Court of Appeal declared that V was not sufficiently autonomous, that D knew this, and that D was aware of the risk of harm in supplying the drug. For this reason he was convicted of gross negligence manslaughter. For discussion see Laird (2021). The question then is whether the 2021 Court of Appeal would have considered V's autonomy in *Kennedy* to have been similarly compromised.

21 The word "unnatural" is very difficult to use coherently, as can be seen by those who condemn homosexuality as "unnatural," whatever that means. In addition, *most* of medicine is "unnatural" insofar as it fights things like "natural" infections, "natural" cancers, and the "natural" deterioration associated with ageing.

since it *essentially* contains the same sorts of things that Bland had been consuming for all of his conscious life.

- The ANH was declared futile because it was not helping Bland to recover his conscious life. It was merely prolonging his unconscious state, and being permanently unconscious was against Bland's best interests.
- So *given* that it was judged to be against Bland's best interests to remain in the permanent unconscious state, then it would be better if he died.
- It would be impermissible to *kill* Bland by a lethal injection. But removing the ANH would not amount to "killing," but to "letting him die" — despite the fact that removing the ANH was *more* than virtually certain to cause the dehydration and death of Bland (recall the discussion of "virtual certainty" in the chapter on intention). That does sound very much like intentionally causing Bland to die.

In addition, (i) removing the ANH would mean a slow death from dehydration, lasting as long as a week, and (ii) allowing a patient to die from preventable dehydration carries a symbolic resonance with the worst kinds of negligence under a duty of care. (If a parent were to withhold food and water from their child, that would be clear and heartless murder.) (iii) Although the *Bland* decision was not formally an execution, there was a clear decision to allow Bland to die an easily preventable death. In those states of the United States that allow capital punishment, the condemned person is allowed a full diet of food and water, and the execution is meant to be "humane," i.e. as swift and painless as possible.

Despite these terrible legal and philosophical missteps, the *Bland* decision remains law, and has become standard practice in coma cases. It is remarkable that a better legal or philosophical argument could not be constructed to support an outcome with which a lot of people would essentially sympathise. Importantly, the request for removal of the ANH still has to be initiated by the family; the doctors would not make that decision on their own, and probably not against the family's will.

CHAPTER 6

INCHOATE OFFENCES

An inchoate crime is a crime that is launched but somehow fails. And right away we can ask: at what point does a launched crime become culpable, and justify punishment? As with recklessness, there is also the question of harmlessness: if the launch fails and nobody is harmed (the intended victim is oblivious), then how do we justify criminalising it and punishing it? And if we want to punish the failed launch on the basis of her intention, then we have the problem of moral luck and the different punishments.

There is an important difference between harmless recklessness/negligence and a harmless inchoate offence. The dangerous driver who makes it home without incident has already committed an offence precisely because she *might have* caused harm (and because, encouraged by her luck, she might drive dangerously again in the future, without the same luck). This counterfactual harm is contained within the meaning of the harmless reckless action. When we evaluate the harmless reckless action, we consider not only what happened but at the same time the "shadow" of the harm that might have happened, alongside the reality.

Inchoate actions are also about endangerment. But in contrast to recklessness, an inchoate action is guided by the agent's or agents' intention, along a certain trajectory, with a certain momentum, toward the future. While the harmless reckless action draws part of its meaning (at the moment of performance) from the counterfactual present, the harmless inchoate action draws part of its meaning (at the moment of failure or abandonment) from the future, from the "shadow" of the harm that was planned and intended.

This chapter will discuss the two main inchoate offences, attempt and conspiracy.[1] We will also say something about a third, less common offence: incitement. Before we start, two brief comments. If the agent succeeds, she will be judged by the nature of the completed offence; whereas the inchoate action by definition fails or is abandoned. In theory, a successful murderer could be charged with *both* murder and attempted murder, since she needed to attempt it in order to succeed. But in practice the successful offence legally overrides the attempt. Second, it might be tempting to describe an inchoate offence as "incomplete." But as we discuss below, there is an ambiguity here: the agent can complete an attempt (she has done all she can) and *then* fail, if, e.g. the laws of nature do not cooperate. So we will distinguish between complete and incomplete attempts (all of them failures). Some writers use the word "non-consummate" to describe inchoate offences, and sometimes they include recklessness and negligence under this label, and sometimes they include possession (which we discuss under the label of "strict liability" in Section 4.6).

6.1 ATTEMPTS

Let's start by imagining two timelines: that of the agent (who becomes a defendant), and that of the criminal justice system. The agent plans, prepares, and intentionally carries out the (result) offence through to its (she hopes) successful conclusion, all the time moving forward (with the occasional glance backwards to see e.g. whether she has covered her traces). The criminal justice system lurches into gear typically upon discovery of the result of a crime (e.g. a dead body). The first question is: "What or who caused this?," and it then essentially

1 The classic work on attempts is Duff (1993). See also the later monograph by Yaffe (2010).

DOI: 10.4324/9781003351887-6

works backwards in time to reconstruct the events. This means that the vast majority of failed or abandoned attempts are never discovered, of course. It's only when (i) the police receive a tip-off, and can begin surveillance with a view to preventing the attempt, or (ii) there is enough evidence of a failed attempt (more or less close to success) for the police to launch a retrospective reconstruction; (iii) sometimes the prosecution might have the choice about how to describe D's actions: if D is beating V severely, but the police intervene and V survives, this might be a case of "grievous bodily harm" or it might be "attempted murder."

An attempt is a different offence than the substantive offence at which it aimed.[2] Recall the two assassins in our discussion of moral luck in the Introduction. Under one description, they have "done" the same thing: merely "pulled a trigger" with the same intention; and yet the law treats them very differently, and this seems unfair. To justify the law's differential approach, we can say that in fact they did *not* do the same thing. Indeed, *neither* of them were merely "pulling a trigger." D1 stands in the courtroom, accused of "murdering V1," exactly as she intended, and given the huge severity of the result, any further discussion of whether she pulled a trigger or not is a technicality. D2 is accused of "attempting to murder V2," and that is much more than trigger-pulling, for her murderous intention was *in* the trigger-pulling. With the unsuccessful V2, it might be harder to prove her intention beyond a reasonable doubt, since there is no body with her bullet in it. But we might find her bullet in the wall next to where V2 had been standing.

But we would go further: murder is radically different from attempted murder because of the different transformations of the agent in each case. A successful murder turns the agent into a *murderer.* This is something that she will be for the rest of her life, regardless of how much she is punished, whether she is ever released early from her life sentence, and whether she has since devoted her life to good works. There is no such thing as an ex-murderer. In contrast, someone who tries and fails to murder might take up two attitudes toward the failure: she might be frustrated, and start plotting a new attempt; or she might be jolted by the terrifying recognition of how close she came, and thank God that she failed. (See Cowley (2015) for further discussion of this idea of transformation.)[3]

As we know, crimes can be divided into result, conduct and circumstance crimes. We have been talking about result crimes like murder: the attempt must be *intentional*, aimed toward and guided by the desired result. But maybe things are not so clear-cut. Horder (2022, p. 518) offers the following example of a reckless attempt, which raises a paradox. D is throwing stones at a tin can atop a wall, behind which are windows. If her rock breaks one of the windows, then this will be a clear example of criminal damage, where recklessness would suffice as mens rea. However, if D is apprehended before a window breaks, and charged with attempted criminal damage, she can defend herself by saying that she was merely reckless about the possibility of breaking the windows, but it was not her intention. This is because, surprisingly, there is no general crime of "reckless endangerment" of persons or property in English criminal law.

With conduct crimes (like dangerous driving), one cannot really "attempt" them — either one is already driving dangerously or one is not (yet) dangerous driving. Circumstance crimes are a bit tricky. *Khan* [1990] was convicted of attempted rape. He intended to have sexual

2 This is in contrast to complicity, which is a mode of responsibility. There is no such offence of "complicity to murder"; one is convicted of the principal crime ("murder"), as an accomplice. See Chapter 7 on complicity.

3 There is an interesting paradox about the minimum mens rea. For attempted murder, D must *intend* to kill V — nothing less will do. For murder, however, it might be enough for D to intend only GBH on V; if V nevertheless dies of the GBH wounds, then D's intention will be "stretched" to include V's death. This is called the "GBH rule." See Section 8.1. for discussion of the different kinds of "stretching.")

intercourse (not in itself illegal), but he was reckless about whether V was consenting or not (the key circumstance). Could this be called a reckless attempt? It's not clear. At any rate, *Khan* has since been superseded by the definition of rape in the *Sexual Offences Act* 2003, which requires that D "does not reasonably believe that [V] consents." (We discuss sexual offences in Chapter 9.)[4]

The temporal threshold of liability

The central philosophical and legal problem has to do with the perpetrator's timeline from the first idea to the final execution of the result crime: at what threshold does she become criminally liable? That's the question for the police surveillance team, as they wait for the best moment to intervene. There is a trade-off here: the earlier the better, in order to reduce the risk of harm (to people or property), increase the element of surprise, and save later surveillance costs; the later the better, in order to increase the evidence for the agent's intention and reduce deniability. If the attempts has failed or been abandoned, and the police discover evidence of the attempt, there will still be a question about the identity of the attempter, what she was planning, and how far along she was.

Criminal attempts are governed by the *Criminal Attempts Act* (CAA) 1981. Section 1(1) defines an attempt as an "act which is more than merely preparatory to the commission of the offence."[5] That's a bit vague, but maybe it has to be, and left to the jury to decide on the facts of the case. Sometimes the "window" of attempt, between the preparation and the execution, might be quite narrow. Imagine that I plan to burgle a house during the day when the owners are away. I prepare for the burglary, by acquiring some tools, watching the house to spot patterns of activity, I check for CCTV on the street, etc. These are all "merely preparatory," and if questioned it would be easy to deny that I was planning anything untoward. On the big day, I grab my tools, put them in the car and drive toward the house: still preparatory. I arrive at the house, take out my bag of tools and walk toward the house: still preparatory.[6] It's only when I put my crowbar to the door that I have launched the attempt, as in the case of *Boyle and Boyle* [1987].

The police surveillance team swoop in and arrest me. But what was I attempting? Technically I was attempting to *trespass*, and there might be no evidence of any intention to *burgle*.[7] After all, I might just be a stalker with the goal of inspecting the house owner's knickers rather than taking anything. So the police surveillance team might want to wait (i) until I successfully enter the property, whereupon they can arrest me for *trespassing* (more serious than

4 A similar question arose in *A-G's Reference* (No. 3 of 1992) (1994). The Ds threw a petrol bomb from a car, which smashed into a wall, towards the Vs. No one was hurt. The question referred to the Court of Appeal was whether the Ds could be convicted of attempting to commit not just criminal damage but *aggravated* criminal damage, contrary to s 1(2) of the *Criminal Damage Act* 1971. The aggravation in question refers to the endangerment of life. While the Ds intended to cause the criminal damage, they did not intend to endanger life — they were merely reckless about it. But the Court ruled that the endangerment was to be taken *within* the scope of the attempt.

5 In UK law, there is one big exception to the "more than merely preparatory" threshold: terrorism. Sec. 5 of the *Terrorism Act* 2006 states that someone will be liable if, with the intent of committing or assisting an act of terrorism, someone "engages in any act in preparation for giving effect to this intention." Given the severity of the terrorism threat, the police are justified in intervening earlier, at the preparation stage.

6 If contrast, if I was *conspiring* with you to burgle the house, then the temporal threshold is much earlier: as soon as we conspirators *agree*. We discuss conspiracies in the next section.

7 Section 9 of the *Theft Act* 1968 states that a person is guilty of burglary if he first enters any building or part of a building as a trespasser, with the intent to steal or to attempt to steal anything in the building (or with the intent to inflict grievous bodily harm on anyone in the building).

attempted trespass), or (ii) until I am leaving the property with my bag full of loot, whereupon they can arrest me for *burglary* (more serious than trespass). There might also be a scenario (iii) where the police arrest me empty-handed outside the property, but they find evidence inside that I tried to take a porcelain statue, but dropped it, and left it in pieces — in which case they can arrest me for attempted burglary.[8]

Making a prospective judgement about the defendant's future intentions in order to pre-emptively arrest them and protect the intended victim will often be controversial. In *Campbell* [1991], D was under police surveillance, suspected of planning to rob a post office. He was carrying an imitation firearm, with a hand-written demand note. The police arrested him just outside a post office, where he had been loitering. However, the Court of Appeal held that Campbell was still in the preparatory phase because he had not yet entered the exact *premises* where the attempt was to be launched. Is this somewhat arbitrary? Imagine if the police had arrested him inside the post office, but not yet at the counter — could that also be a location of mere preparation? Indeed, if he had been arrested at the counter, then perhaps the attempt proper had not begun until he had pulled out the firearm and the demand note — since up to that moment he could still turn out to be a bona fide post office customer, eager to buy some stamps. (And there is still the problem of deniability: maybe the gun and the demand note were for a theatre performance for neighbourhood kids.)[9]

In *Campbell* the defendant had not yet put himself in the place to commit the planned crime. In *Geddes* [1996], the defendant was in the right *place*, but the intended *victim* was not yet in that place, and so the attempt could not yet be launched. D entered a school (without any legitimate reason to do so) and hid in the boys' lavatory, where he was challenged. He ran off, dropping his rucksack, and was later apprehended. In his rucksack was a knife, rope and masking tape. A third party offered evidence that Geddes was sexually fascinated by young boys. The first court convicted him of trespassing and attempted kidnapping; D successfully appealed the attempted kidnapping conviction on the grounds that the intended victim had not yet appeared in the lavatory, and so there was nobody against whom to launch the attempt.

While Geddes was deemed to be still preparing under English law, he would probably have been found guilty under the American *Model Penal Code* Section 5.01 Section 1(c), which defines a person as guilty of an attempt when she

> purposely does or omits to do anything that, under the circumstances as he believes them to be, is an act or omission constituting a *substantial step* in a course of conduct planned to culminate in his commission of the crime. [emphasis added]

This might seem to be just as vague as "more than merely preparatory." However, while English law leaves it to the jury to decide whether the attempt was launched, the MPC (subsection 2 of the same section) offers a number of paradigmatic examples of a substantial step, for example, "(a) lying in wait, searching for," "(b) following the contemplated victim of the crime" or "(c) reconnoitring the place contemplated for the commission of the crime." So the MPC is considerably more expansive in its inculpation threshold. The advantage of the

8 There is also the problem of acts and omissions. The *CAA* clearly describes a more than merely preparatory *act*, and so far we have only been talking about acts. But there are certain crimes I can still attempt by doing nothing, precisely when I have a duty of care to do certain things. So a parent can attempt to kill her infant child by withholding nourishment. This would raise a problem of defining the threshold to mark the undeniable launch of the attempt proper.

9 The problem of pre-emptive arrest mirrors the problem of a pre-emptive lethal strike in self-defence cases. After all, almost every self-defensive action will be pre-emptive, unless the aggressor is already plunging his blade into the defendant. See Chapter 10 on defences.

MPC's threshold in *Geddes* is obvious: the English police would have to wait for the intended victim to enter the lavatory and for D to pounce — which would have been very traumatic for the victim.

One last point about another, informal threshold. Attempts can be divided into "incomplete" and "complete" attempts. The latter means that I have done everything that I can and want to do, and I just have to wait for the attempt to succeed or fail: it might depend on natural events (the wind might blow the assassin's bullet off course), it might depend on other people's decisions and actions (the intended victim might bend over to tie his shoelace). A complete attempt is more serious because it reveals an intention strong enough to sustain the plan through from the more abstract earlier stages to the concrete final stages. (The strength of the intention will also depend on the minimisation of risk.)[10]

A complete attempt offers more evidence than an incomplete attempt, and less room for deniability. In addition, if the police swoop too soon, they might prevent the attempter from voluntarily abandoning the attempt herself, either out of caution, or out of failure of nerve. English criminal law does not formally distinguish between incomplete and complete attempts, although if a complete attempt reveals a more culpable intention, this might be reflected in sentencing. If such a distinction could be carried out more consistently, and publicised, and if there were a significant punishment differential between incomplete and complete attempts, this could act as an incentive for voluntary abandonment before or during the attempt, or for an accomplice to inform the police.

Impossible attempts

The discussion thus far might suggest that the attempter is *on her way* toward a good chance of completing the attempt and bringing about the desired harmful consequence; she is objectively endangering someone; hence the criminal law's justified intervention even though she has not created any harm yet. But what if there was never any possibility of the desired harm ensuing at all? And as such no objective endangerment, regardless of what D thought, desired or intended? There are several different versions of the problem of impossible attempts.

First, recall the case of *Easom* [1971], discussed in Chapter 2 on intention. Under the police sting operation, a plain-clothes policewoman sat in front of Easom and placed an empty handbag next to her. Sure enough, Easom surreptitiously opened the handbag to look inside, and the policewoman arrested him for attempted theft. But if the handbag was empty all along, then it was actually impossible for him to take anything from the handbag (true, he might steal the handbag itself), and the court therefore acquitted him. As we saw, what the court should have said was that he brought an intention to steal "something" *to* the handbag, and then waited to see whether to execute the intention or not.

Second, let's return to the failed assassin, D2, whose bullet was blown off course by a sudden gust of wind. We called this a matter of luck. But of course there is no room for luck in the universe: not only did D2 fail, but she was *bound* to fail, given the way the world was organised, given the laws of nature, all beyond her control, at the moment when she pulled the trigger — the gust of wind not only blew, but *had* to blow, strongly enough at that exact moment to deflect the bullet. Of course, D2 did not know about the gust of wind ahead of time, and she did not know that her attempt was bound to fail, even though she would not deny that bullets sometimes get blown off course. However, we would not want her to be let off on the grounds

10 With the sniper's bullet, there is very little time between the complete attempt and the success or failure of the attempt. But of course the assassin might use a bomb on a timer, with several hours in between.

of impossibility. So the emphasis is more on what D2 knew about the future rather than what turned out to be the case. And she was confident enough about hitting her target to have a go — and she came very close.

Third, imagine another assassin, D3, skilled and experienced, who intends to shoot V3 dead. D3 reaches for a gun, aims it at V3, calmly pulls the trigger, but nothing happens, not even a click. Unbeknownst to D3, someone had sabotaged the gun, and so all along it was impossible to shoot. Does this mean that it was impossible all along for D3 to even *attempt* to shoot V? This is different from the physical determinism of the wind blowing D1's bullet off course, since it was in principle possible for D3 to check the gun earlier and to fix the gun or find another one. However, *given* that it had not occurred to D3 to check the gun beforehand, then at the moment of firing, it was just as impossible to shoot the victim as when the uncontrollable gust of wind deflected D2's bullet. The important point is that, despite the impossibility, D2 and D3 both *intended* to kill their respective targets. And the CAA 1981 Section 1(2) adds that "A person may be guilty of attempting to commit an offence to which this section applies even though the facts are such that the commission of the offence is impossible." It is enough for D to be judged on the basis of "the facts of the case had been as he believed them to be." So D2 believed her weapon was functioning properly, and formed her murderous intention on that basis.

However, this might be *too* inclusive. D4 believes in voodoo, and genuinely intends to kill V4 by stabbing pins in a doll representing V4. Here the impossibility is not just contingent, as with the gust of wind and the sabotaged gun, but more fundamental, based instead on the laws of nature. Perhaps the case would not go to trial on the grounds that D4, unlike the other Ds, is not particularly *dangerous* to the public. Dangerousness, after all, is one justification for intervening at the harmless early stage of an attempt. (However, it is true that D4 might discover that the voodoo does not work and *then* try something more conventionally dangerous to kill V4.)

There is one more kind of impossible attempt worth mentioning. In *Shivpuri* [1987], D admitted that he was knowingly smuggling either heroin or cannabis. In fact, he was mistaken, because the white powder turned out to be snuff, possession of which is not illegal. On appeal, the House of Lords confirmed that D was nevertheless guilty of attempting to smuggle a controlled substance because "if the facts of the case had been as he believed them to be," he would indeed be liable. As Padfield (2016, p. 189) puts it, however,

> *Shivpuri* represents subjectivism gone mad: if you take your own umbrella from my house, believing it is mine, you are now guilty of attempted theft. Are you being charged with attempted theft of my umbrella (I don't have one: so clearly nonsense) or attempted theft of your own umbrella (also clearly nonsense)?

6.2 CONSPIRACY

A conspiracy could basically be defined as a group attempt. Two or more people reach an "agreement" to commit a substantive offence in the future. (We're putting "agreement" in scare quotes since that will be the key term that needs to be defined — see next section.) Perhaps they will be carrying out the offence jointly, perhaps they will each causally contribute to its success in different ways and to different degrees. Perhaps they all know the full plan, perhaps each person only knows what she needs to know about her small segment. Perhaps the plan is scheduled later in the same day, perhaps sometime vaguely in the future.

Like attempts, the conspirators could in theory be charged for *both* the conspiracy *and* the subsequent joint offence; since they probably had to conspire first in order for the joint offence to be successful. Like attempts, conspiracies are normally taken as failures by definition. Also like attempts, we can talk about conspiracies prospectively, when the police seek to thwart them before they are carried out, or retrospectively, after the police discover the collapse of the conspiracy. As an inchoate crime, the culpability of the participants does not depend on harmful results.

An agreement does not need to be a formal written contract, of course; suffice that each party *take themselves to be* in agreement with a single plan, and that each is clear of her role. But here's the interesting part: the agreement itself already inculpates the participants, i.e. at the very moment of the agreement, whether or not the parties go on to carry out the agreed offence or not, and whether or not the parties carry out preparatory steps or "more than merely preparatory steps" (as per the *Criminal Attempts Act* 1981), or a "substantial step" (as per the *Model Penal Code*).

In terms of the execution timeline that we discussed with attempts, the threshold of liability is therefore much closer to the start. The thought is that any group (even a group of two) is inherently more *dangerous* than an individual, and this justifies an earlier intervention from the police. This is not only the fact that a well-organised group can do much more harm than an individual because of economies of scale and the distribution of tasks. (In general, bigger banks can only be robbed by groups.) But also in terms of group dynamics, there is greater normative pressure on individuals, making the conspiracy more likely than the individual attempt: one member encourages (or threatens) another into keeping her commitment; some otherwise reluctant members will feel less restraint because they can mentally shift responsibility onto the "ringleaders," while seeing themselves as an innocent cog ("just the driver"); finally, if the members are recruited from a criminal milieu, they will be motivated by their experience of the penalties imposed on others for backsliding.

But the earlier threshold risks unfairness. As we saw, when a single individual thinks out a plan, she has not yet *done* anything; when she prepares for the attempt and gathers information and materials, she has not done anything; when she reports her plan to a witness, she has not done anything; it is only with the launch of the attempt proper (however ambiguous that threshold is) that she fairly exposes herself to legal intervention. In the case of a single agent, we have a clearer distinction between thought and action. In the case of a group (even a group of two), there is the initial thought in one mind, but this thought receives the objective endorsement of agreement, giving the plan a kind of "intersubjective" reality prior to action, capable of objectively binding the participants.

The conspiracy charge offers huge advantages to prosecutors precisely because there is no need to prove that anybody took any preparatory or other steps, or that anybody knew much about the conspiracy, or that anybody had a particular role (since all are equally guilty). It is enough to prove that they were a free and knowing party to the "agreement." This is a positive and negative feature: positive in that it allows access to the senior gang leaders who are normally careful to avoid demonstrable complicity in the crimes committed by their minions; negative in that there has always been a risk of prosecutorial abuse.

The agreement

How exactly does English criminal law define a conspiratorial agreement? This is not altogether clear, and it's not defined in the relevant 1977 legislation (on which, see below). First of all, a conspiracy has to be distinguished from the case of two defendants pursuing two goals in parallel or in alignment, both aware of one another, but not in agreement. Instead, there has to be a single project which they both want to pursue in collaboration and coordination with each other. The Canadian case of *Sokoloski* [1977] is a useful example of a *non*-conspiracy. D purchased illegal drugs from E, and both were charged with conspiracy to traffic. They were acquitted because they were judged to be in two separate, albeit mutually aligned projects. D was buying, E was selling; D was motivated by the drugs, E was motivated by the money. D was indifferent about where he got the drugs from, if E had refused he would have bought elsewhere; similarly, E was indifferent about who was willing to buy his drugs.

Second, an agreement has to be distinguished from a tentative negotiation *toward* an agreement. A defendant might argue that the alleged agreement was only a provisional move in an on-going negotiation, e.g. she was waiting for the counter-offer — as such there was no agreement that they could even start carrying out. However, an agreement might legally still come into being even if some of the details (e.g. the exact day and time) have yet to be worked out. In *Walker* [1962], the parties *thought* they had reached an agreement to carry out a robbery. But when the conspirators started discussing the details, Walker withdrew because of irresolvable differences. The remaining conspirators were convicted, but Walker was acquitted on the grounds that he had not yet sufficiently agreed to the plan.[11]

Walker highlights a disturbing inconsistency in English criminal law. In principle, once D has agreed to the conspiracy, then she has *already committed* the inchoate crime and any subsequent withdrawal from the conspiracy will be legally irrelevant to her culpability. It's similar to the law of theft. Once D has stolen the object, then she is guilty even if she returns the object to its rightful place and owner right away (and even if the owner is entirely oblivious). In both cases, there is something quite mystical about this — the "moral order" has been harmed by the very conspiratorial agreement and the very act of theft, even if there is no concrete harm to anyone in both cases. Alternatively, both policies are justified in purely consequentialist terms (see Chapter 11 on punishment). That's why the court, in order to acquit Walker, had to interpret him as being insufficiently committed *throughout*.[12]

Conspiracy is thus again to be contrasted with attempts. D can abandon her planning and preparations at any point because she has not yet committed any offence; and the widespread knowledge of the threshold of liability is supposed to provide an incentive for just such abandonment. Conspiracy can also be contrasted with complicity: D the secondary party can withdraw from the planned enterprise so long as she is also able to withdraw any assistance she has already provided, e.g. by withholding the tools that she promised. This is because the illegality of the complicity only begins when the principal commits the offence; by that stage, if the secondary party and her assistance are simply absent, then the principal is legally alone and then the secondary is not involved. (In the case of complicity by encouragement, however, this would be harder to "withdraw" later.) This is ironic, because (i) if the principal carries out the planned crime (without the secondary), this legally erases the prior conspiracy, and the secondary is innocent. But (ii) if the police discover and disrupt the plan before the principal can carry it out, then the whole issue becomes a failed conspiracy, and the secondary *would* be liable because of her original commitment (the promise to provide tools) and the impossibility of withdrawal. So if the secondary really did want to withdraw, she would have to pray that the principal carry on and succeed! (We discuss complicity in Chapter 7, next.)

If D1 and D2 are going to be charged with conspiracy to commit crime C, then the agreement has to include a reference to C with enough specificity. For conspiracy to *murder*, for

11 The word "sufficiently" designates a threshold of commitment, which need not be full-hearted. Interestingly, the commitment does not depend only on the one member's act of will; it also depends on the other members *taking* her words *as* a sufficient commitment. Given the non-explicit and unwritten nature of much of the negotiation, there is plenty of room for mistake — in the literal sense of "mis-take."

12 Any member's prior withdrawal could be recognised as mitigation in the sentencing stage, however. In addition, she might be acquitted if she not only withdraws but reports the entire conspiracy to the police, and therefore she can effectively be rewarded as a police spy.

example, it is not enough for D1 and D2 to conspire to poison V's soup; they have to intend that V die as a result of the poison. There is an interesting question here about the implicit meanings within agreements. For example, D1 might suggest poisoning V's soup and D2 might agree, and there might be a wink-wink nudge-nudge sufficient for both of them to understand that they were actually talking about murder. If both of them had a criminal background, they would be conversant in the right euphemisms and hints, and each would have sufficient reason for considering the other to be seriously committed. And as with attempts, this would raise questions of plausible deniability, especially in the event of a prospective enquiry: the police would then need to seek wider evidence of murderous intention, as well as plausible motivations in order to prove beyond reasonable doubt that a conspiracy to murder existed.

There might be a problem with a first-time criminal conspirator, who "agrees" but does not *really* understand what she is agreeing to. For example, a 15-year-old who wants to become part of an urban gang for reasons of prestige and opportunity might "agree" to participate in a crime as an initiation ritual. By the time the police thwart the conspiracy and arrest her, it might well have been the case that she would have withdrawn as the reality of the planned substantive crime, and her involvement with it, dawned on her. As such her age and vulnerability might *morally* — although not legally — vitiate her agreement.

Finally, consider the tragicomic case of *R v G and F* [2013]. D1 had met D2 through an online paedophile chat group, and soon started texting one another. In their texts, they started "planning" the kidnap and sexual torture of a 13-year-old boy. However, the pair never met in person, the plans were always vague, and by the time the police discovered the texts, more than a year had elapsed without any action. They were charged with conspiracy, but during the trial it turned out that they had never really intended to act on their "plans" or "agreements"; it was all a harmless fantasy. So while in theory all that a conspiracy charge needs is an agreement, in practice it also needs some further demonstration of serious intention, some progress (e.g. in the form of specific preparations), to provide sufficient semantic weight to the agreement. This is an interesting case of time revealing greater innocence rather than greater guilt: if the police had discovered the texts sooner, and the absence of concrete plans and preparations was not yet clear, then the police might have more justification in taking the texts as evidence of a dangerous conspiracy.

The relevant legislation

The *Criminal Law Act* (CLA) 1977 governs conspiracy in the United Kingdom. There are a couple of philosophically interesting things here. Section 1(1) states:

> Subject to the following provisions of this Part of this Act, if a person agrees with any other person or persons that a course of conduct shall be pursued which, if the agreement is carried out in accordance with their intentions, either —
>
> (a) will necessarily amount to or involve the commission of any offence or offences by one or more of the parties to the agreement, or
> (b) would do so but for the existence of facts which render the commission of the offence or any of the offences impossible,
>
> he is guilty of conspiracy to commit the offence or offences in question.

Three easier points first. First, note the draconian inclusivity of this provision: it might only be one or more of the parties who actually commit the planned offence, but *all* members will be charged as conspirators of equal status. (In practice, the differing involvement might be reflected in a variety of sentences.)

Second, we have the "agreement." Note the reference to the conspirators' *intentions.* This is important because it means that *recklessness* is not enough. This was tested in the case of *Saik* [2006]. D worked in a currency exchange office, and received an order to change a large amount of pounds sterling. He *suspected* that the money was the proceeds of crime, but without any legal duty to report his suspicions he went ahead and changed the money anyway. It turned out the money *was* from crime, and he was charged with being a member of a pre-existing conspiracy by virtue of his "agreement" to change the money. However, his appeal was successful because mere suspicion was not enough for agreement. All he had agreed to was to change the "money" (that's the description under which he acted); he had not agreed to change the "stolen money" (i.e. he did not *treat* it as money that he knew was stolen, he thought its origins were none of his business).

It's worth mentioning subsection (b) *before* (a). Subsection (b), "would do so but for ..." is a bit of a mouthful, but it brings us back to the impossibility question that we considered in our earlier discussion of attempts. D1 and D2 agree to commit crime C using a gun. Because of a contingent fact (the gun is broken), unknown to D1 and D2, it will in fact be impossible to commit C. However, to paraphrase from the *CAA*, if the facts (about the gun) had been as they believed them to be (the gun working), then they would have been able to carry out their plan, and that's the legally important question.[13]

The "necessarily" clause

Now let's look at subsection (a): "... will necessarily amount to or involve the commission ..." The problem here is the word "necessarily." This has to do with the quality of the conspirators' intentions. The best way to explain it is to take a schematic example, which comes from *Reed* [1982, p. 120]. D1 and D2 plan to drive from London to Edinburgh in eight hours. They both have drivers' licences, the car is insured, and there is nothing illegal about them being on the road. And the plan is quite plausible. However, it may well happen that they are delayed on the congested roads out of London, so that if they still want to make it within the eight hours, they would *later* have to make up the time by breaking the speed limit. They have a conditional intention.

So there are two possible journeys: (i) make it in eight hours comfortably, or (ii) make it within eight hours by breaking the law. That means that their eight-hour plan, if they are lucky driving out of London, does not *necessarily* involve breaking the speed limit, and so at the start of their journey they cannot be described as having formed a criminal conspiracy to break the law. If, on the other hand, the plan had involved a journey time of no more than six hours, then given the reality of the speed limit and the distance to Edinburgh, this would necessarily mean conspiring to break the law.[14]

The conditional intention underlying the conspiracy to break the speed limit if necessary to carry out the eight-hour plan should be contrasted with the details from the *Reed* case itself,

13 Subsection (b) was actually brought in to fix a problem revealed in the case of *Nock* [1978]. Nock and his co-defendants were accused of conspiring to produce cocaine from a batch of white powder that had been obtained by one of the co-defendants. Unbeknownst to Nock, their plan was chemically impossible because of the nature of the powder, and for this reason they were acquitted of conspiracy. However, note again the different kinds of impossibility. Broken guns can be fixed; and perhaps fixed quickly enough for the conspirators to carry out their plan after they discover that it is broken. But if there's no way of making cocaine from *this* powder, then one has to start a new plan to find the right powder from elsewhere.

14 This is actually an odd example when one considers the realities of detection. Either the police will detect the couple as they are speeding, and will penalise them without any discussion of a conspiracy; or they will stop them on their way out of London, when they are not speeding, and accuse them of ... what, exactly? Of planning to speed? D1 and D2 would just deny it. What sort of evidence could the police possibly gather to refute their denials?

which are interesting enough in their own right. D1 and D2 were members of a secret society which targeted suicidal individuals. For a given individual, their plan comprised two stages. In the first stage, they would visit the "client" to confirm the situation. They would offer comfort, and urge the client not to do it. However, if the client continued to insist on eventually committing suicide, then — in the second stage — D1 and D2 were ready to give practical advice about and assistance with the suicide. When the police discovered the plan, D1 and D2 had not yet actually launched any second-stage efforts with any clients, and so had not causally assisted any suicide. So they were rightly convicted of conspiring to aid and abet suicide and other counts of conspiracy and aiding and abetting suicide, contrary to the *Suicide Act* 1961.[15]

This then becomes a two-agent version of *Easom*'s [1971] conditional intention to steal the contents of the handbag (discussed in Chapter 2). Easom had argued that he approached the handbag without any intention to steal a *particular* thing (being ignorant of whether there was anything worth stealing), and for that reason he was acquitted. We argued that Easom should have been described as bringing a settled intention to steal *something*, subject to a conditional execution of the intention. D1 and D2 in *Reed* tried to offer the *Easom* ignorance account: they arrived at the client's house with no intentions, and therefore no conspiracy. They would only *form* the intention to conspire if the client revealed their resolve to commit suicide, and that had not yet happened. Instead, D1 and D2 were interpreted as having brought *two* settled intentions to the client's house: (i) an intention to offer comfort and (ii) an intention to encourage and assist suicide, and the *execution* of one or the other intention was conditional. And this second intention was enough for the court to consider it a conspiratorial agreement, such that if "the agreement is carried out in accordance with their intentions," it "will necessarily amount to or involve the commission of any offence" (as per Section 1.1. of the *CLA* 1977).

There remains a fundamental difference between *Easom* and *Reed*, however. In *Easom*, the contingency concerned a fact: either there was something valuable in the handbag or there was not; and that fact was obtained *before* Easom opened the handbag. With *Reed*, there was no fact of the matter about whether the client was going to commit suicide or not, because that fact lay in the future, and an act as radical as suicide is essentially unpredictable. Whatever the client might *tell* D1 and D2 about her plans or intentions for the future, she remains free to change her mind. That is not enough to get D1 and D2 off the hook, but it does make it more complicated to say what they have done wrong. We will return to the issue of encouraging suicide in the section on incitement, below.

Intention and knowledge

Recall the clause from the CLA: "If the agreement is carried out in accordance with their intentions." In the paradigm case, D enthusiastically joins the conspiracy, and has two

15 We're picking up on a discussion of suicide in Chapter 5, on causation. The *Suicide Act* 1961 is unusual, for three reasons. (i) The prior crime of suicide had always been a matter of absurdity and cruelty, and it was sensible to decriminalise it. At the same time, the Act explicitly prohibits encouraging or assisting the suicide of another, and this is also sensible, given the issues of temporary vulnerability and compromised autonomy involved in the great majority of suicidal ideation. But there remains something illogical about prohibiting the assistance of a legal act. (ii) The encouragement or assistance prohibited by the Act is inchoate, in that the offence is committed whether or not the person actually goes on to commit suicide. In contrast, before 2007 (and the passing of the *Serious Crime Act*), one could be complicit only if the principal offence had actually been carried out. (iii) The 1961 Act was amended in 2009 to describe the prohibited acts as those "*capable* of encouraging or assisting the suicide," (sec. 59). If the encouragement or assistance *fails*, however, and the "target" individual is still alive, one can imagine many problems for the prosecution to establish that the act was indeed "capable."

relevant intentions: the first concerns her own acts as they contribute to the plan; the second concerns the success of the plan itself. But what happens if D has the first but not the second? What if D believes the conspiracy is foolish and doomed to failure? What if D is motivated entirely by the payment offered for her contribution, but is indifferent about whether the conspiracy succeeds or not?

Such was the situation of *R v Anderson* [1986]. Anderson and Andaloussi had met in prison, and Anderson was released earlier. Anderson agreed to join an existing conspiracy to break Andaloussi out of prison. Anderson agreed to his role, which was to acquire some diamond wire (to saw through steel bars), and to arrange for it to be smuggled into the prison — for this he would be paid £10,000. The plan was discovered, and Anderson was convicted along with the other members of the conspiracy. Anderson appealed, arguing that what he had done was a legally discrete event: certain tasks (acquiring the wire and arranging the smuggling) in exchange for money (and he was ready to plead guilty to attempted smuggling). What Andaloussi would do with the wire when he received it was his business — another legally discrete event. Although he knew about the escape plan, he thought it would fail, and he was indifferent about whether it would fail. He was planning to be gone, with his money, before Andaloussi would make his attempt.

The House of Lords rejected his appeal, with Lord Bridge stating:

> The appellant, in agreeing that a course of conduct be pursued that would, if successful, necessarily involve the offence of effecting Andaloussi's escape from lawful custody, clearly intended, by providing diamond wire to be smuggled into the prison, to play a part in the agreed course of conduct in furtherance of that criminal objective.

If we take Anderson at his word, then, he had the knowledge but lacked the intention — but the court is saying that mere knowledge was enough for conspiracy insofar as Anderson intentionally did something that he knew would likely contribute to the project. This seems to be going against the standard account of conspiracy, and indeed aligns it with complicity. To put it crudely: a conspiracy plan fails by definition and complicity plan succeeds by definition — and the plan can be identical. As we will see in the next chapter, the dominant "Youden" definition of complicity is where the accessory-defendant (D) must *intentionally* assist the principal (P) in the *knowledge* that her (D's) actions are *likely* to assist P to commit a crime, the essential features of which are at least familiar to D.

It turns out that *Anderson*, even if it is formally a binding precedent on subsequent conspiracy rulings, has not been too influential because of all these complications.

6.3 INCITEMENT

Before 2007, it was a traditional offence ("in common law") where someone incited (i.e. encouraged) another to commit an offence. This was an inchoate offence and implied failure; successful incitement was deemed to be a conspiracy. Most types of incitement were formally abolished by the *Serious Crime Act* (SCA) 2007 (sec. 59), which replaced it with "encouragement," which could be inchoate, like incitement. (We discuss the SCA in the next chapter, on complicity.) We're going to look at some of the few statutory versions of incitement that remain.

One of them we have seen: encouraging someone to commit suicide, which is prohibited by the *Suicide Act* 1961. Another is to be found in Section 8 of the *Sexual Offences Act* 2003, which prohibits the incitement of a child under the age of 13 to engage in sexual activity. Then

Section 17 of the *Public Order Act* 1986 prohibits the incitement of racial hatred. And finally Section 4 of the *Offences Against the Person Act* (OAPA) 1861, reads:

> 4. Conspiring or soliciting to commit murder
> Whosoever shall solicit, encourage, persuade, or endeavour to persuade, or shall propose to any person, to murder any other person ... shall be guilty of a misdemeanour, and being convicted thereof shall be liable to imprisonment for life.

Let's briefly look at this last, OAPA, version. Perhaps the most obvious form of OAPA incitement is for D a mafia godmother to pay a hitman (P) to kill V (or to order the hitman to do so if he is already in D's employ). If the hitman successfully kills V, then the godmother would already be guilty of murder, as an accessory. It might seem to understate the godmother's culpability to call her a mere accessory, when she was the but-for causal origin of V's death, assuming that P had no other reason to kill V. However, under the principle of equivalent culpability, the godmother would still be convicted of murder, alongside P, as if she had been a joint principal. (We discuss complicity in the next chapter.) However, if the hitman chooses not to kill V, then the godmother could not be complicit in something that did not happen. So the OAPA incitement is designed to catch the godmother in such an event. But again we have the problem of understatement: calling the godmother a mere inciter does not seem enough, as if she had merely been trying to persuade her friend to run an errand. The possibility of life imprisonment makes up for the label, certainly. But surely in the case of (failed) incitement to murder, there might be grounds for describing the godmother's incitement as "attempted murder," precisely since it was based on the reasonable expectation that the money would indeed suffice to get P to carry out her wishes.

Paying a hitman is relatively clear, since the hitman has a role and a price, and these can be corroborated during the police investigation: the godmother "buying" a hitman and sending him off to kill V is, in terms of causal chains, not unlike the godmother buying a bomb and setting it to explode under V's car. But soliciting, encouraging or persuading *without* money or commands seems far too unclear to establish responsibility.

Imagine a husband and wife, and the husband is having an affair with his lover. The lover incites the husband to kill the wife, and gives him reasons to do it: he can inherit her money, and then he can live with her (the lover) in bliss. The husband is horrified, and reports the lover to the police. The police interrogate the lover, and of course she says that she was only joking. How on earth would the police prove otherwise?

But even if the police have a surveillance tape of her incitement, there remains a problem. Technically, the lover has incited the husband to murder his wife and would be guilty under the OAPA definition, but it turns out that (much to the lover's surprise) there was never any possibility of him agreeing. With impossible *attempts*, as we saw earlier in this chapter, we were prepared to inculpate the agent who pulls the trigger of a gun that turns out to be empty; in such a case it is very clear what she was trying to do, and — given how guns with bullets normally work — how close she came. But with the lover's failed incitement of the shocked husband, she seems a million miles away from achieving her desired outcome, and so it might not be appropriate or fair to punish her.

CHAPTER 7

COMPLICITY

Complicity is one of the most complicated areas of criminal law, but for that reason it is also one of the most philosophically interesting. We have already seen some of the complexities of joint action in our discussion of conspiracy and incitement, both of which were normally defined by failure. Complicity, on the other hand, starts with the success of the criminal enterprise and works backwards, asking who was complicit in what way, to what extent, on what basis, and from what moment. And suddenly there seem to be as many different types of complicity as there are types of human relationship! Lepora and Goodin (2013) use their Chapter 3 to describe and distinguish some of the following: assisting, colluding, encouraging, informing, bribing, ordering, begging, persuading, cajoling, threatening, blackmailing, failing to prevent, turning a blind eye. In addition, the *Accessories and Abettors Act* (AAA) 1861 — which is still law in England — uses the four verbs of aiding, abetting, counselling and procuring, and these four verbs have provoked considerable discussion themselves.

For the purposes of this chapter, we're going to stick to two verbs only: *assisting* (which is the easiest to grasp), but also *encouraging*. Note that a single act can sometimes both assist and encourage, of course. We feel ourselves justified in limiting ourselves to these two verbs because (i) the *Serious Crime Act* (SCA) 2007 ss. 44–46 use only those two verbs in their discussion of complicity; and (ii) the Supreme Court in *Jogee* [2016] summarised the history of complicity, and spent most of its discussion on those two verbs. (We will be discussing both the SCA and *Jogee* later in this chapter.)

Schematically, we have D (the defendant) assisting P (the principal) to commit a crime against V.[1] "Assisting" (and "participating") are meant to be legally and morally neutral: it remains to be seen whether D is an "accessory" (a.k.a. "accomplice") and therefore "complicit." As elsewhere in this book, for the sake of clarity of pronoun use, we will refer to D as female and P as male. P has committed a crime, the so-called principal offence, and is straightforwardly arrested, charged and convicted. Now our attention turns to D — she is a defendant who stands accused. What is her relationship to P and to P's crime?

Complicity sits between innocent participation and joint principalship. (i) D could have participated in P's crime unknowingly. If D owns a crowbar, and P takes the crowbar to use in his burglary without D's knowing, then D's property has been involved but D will not be complicit; (ii) If D assists P with the preparations and with the burglary itself, it would make more sense to convict them of joint principals involved in a single crime. (This applies even if they are carrying out different action components of a single crime: if P breaks open the door, and D goes in to steal the goods.) As usual, there are fuzzy boundaries.[2]

1 Sometimes this person is called the Secondary Party, or just "S." Sometimes she is called D2, alongside D1 who is the principal, as if they were both defendants on trial.

2 Consider the recent case of *Grant* [2021], as an example of some of the questions about whether D was an accomplice or a joint principal. D, P and others set out by car to search for V and inflict GBH on him. In the boot of the car were various weapons intended for that purpose: knives, a sledgehammer and a baseball bat. As they drove, P suddenly caught sight of V and drove the car straight into him, killing him. The question was whether P's vehicular murder of V was an "overwhelming supervening act" (in the language of *Jogee*), that would render the original personal attack plan obsolete. D's appeal was rejected, since it was enough that he had signed up to a plan (i) with P, (ii) to inflict GBH on V, and (iii) in accordance with the "GBH rule" (see Section 8.1. in the next chapter), D had the *mens rea* for murder. The situation would have been different if D and P had planned to simply beat up V with their fists.

DOI: 10.4324/9781003351887-7

So P visits D on Friday and asks to borrow her crowbar. D might shrug her shoulders and say "Sure, go ahead." P is planning to use the crowbar for a burglary on Saturday night. In order to be complicit, however, D has to *know* something about a burglary, even if not the precise day, time or location. If P does not tell her, D remains innocent, and her crowbar-lending remains legally innocent.[3] But if P is a career burglar, and D knows this, then she might know enough to risk complicity when she lends the crowbar. For she is no longer acting under the description of "lending her crowbar to my friend P" but rather "lending my crowbar to career burglar P, in the knowledge that the crowbar might well be useful for an upcoming job." So it's all about what D should believe. And as elsewhere, D's motivation for lending (maybe she's returning a favour) and her attitude to the crime (she might be indifferent to whether P succeeds or not) will normally be irrelevant.[4]

On the wider description, her action is not just the moment of handing over the crowbar, the action effectively continues until he returns the crowbar to her after the burglary on Sunday morning. (And while her crowbar is being used for the burglary, it is as if she is there too, at the scene of the crime.) We are assuming, of course, other background knowledge: D knows what a crowbar is for, knows what a burglary is, knows that burglaries are illegal, knows that *this* crowbar would be useful in someone else's burglary etc. …

Let's assume P, during his visit on Friday, comes right out and says it: "I need your crowbar for a burglary tomorrow night." D lends him the crowbar and risks complicity. We say "risks." On Friday she is not yet complicit because P has not yet broken the law: all that has happened was a consensual loan. It is only when D actually launches the burglary (on Saturday night) with D's crowbar that P becomes the principal and D becomes the accessory.[5]

3 In this case D would be innocent, and P would take full responsibility. If D has an excuse for assisting P, she might well be acquitted as well. Imagine P is a bank robber, who points a gun at the teller D, and demands that she hand over the cash. Technically D would then become an accessory to the robbery, but she would claim duress. (Chances are that she would not even be charged, and so would not have to claim a defence.)

Note: in some prima facie complicity scenarios, P might be an "innocent agent," and D would act "through" him. If D poisons some tea, hands it to P with instructions to deliver it to V, who drinks it and dies, then this is no longer complicity: P will be innocent, and D will take full responsibility for the murder.

4 As Devlin J put it in *National Coal Board v Gamble* [1959]:

> if one man deliberately sells to another a gun to be used for murdering a third, he may be indifferent whether the third man lives or dies and interested only in the cash profit to be made out of the sale, but he can still be an aider and abettor [i.e. complicit].

Compare this to *Jogee* [2016] para 10:

> there can be cases where [D] gives intentional assistance or encouragement to [P] to commit an offence and to act with the mental element required of him, but without [D] having a positive intent that the particular offence will be committed. That may be so, for example, where at the time that encouragement is given it remains uncertain what [P] might do; an arms supplier might be such a case.

This is not entirely clear. How exactly should D give "intentional assistance" in order for P to commit the offence, while lacking a "positive intent" that the offence be committed? The reference to uncertainty suggests a conditional intention, so that D is saying "*if* you want to commit the offence, this gun will be useful"? Horder (2022, p. 487) interprets this as over-ruling Devlin, and acquitting the indifferent gun supplier.

5 There is a metaphysical question here, perhaps only of interest to philosophers! When P launches the burglary with D's crowbar on Saturday night, does that make D an accessory only *from that moment on*? Or does that retroactively make D an accessory from the moment she intentionally lent him the crowbar, i.e. on Friday? If the latter, this is not retroactive causation, but a retroactive change of meaning, which is

If P changes his mind and cancels the burglary, then D can no longer be an accessory. So this is another instance of moral luck, and D might even be grateful when P returns the crowbar to her, unused.

So far we have been discussing D lending the crowbar to P, that is, where D is under no obligation. What about the facts of *Lomas* [1913]? The case begins with a loan in the other direction: D had borrowed a crowbar *from P.* And then P asked for his property back. At the same time, D was aware that P was a career burglar, and would use the crowbar in future burglaries. D returned the crowbar and P did indeed go on to use it in future burglaries. Was D complicit?[6] The court decided that he was not, the thought being that D was merely restoring the earlier situation where P was in lawful possession of his own crowbar (D's action was describable precisely as obligatory restitution), and therefore P was entirely responsible for what he went on to do with his crowbar. Child et al (2022, p. 248) disagree: although D was legally obliged to return the crowbar to P, she was not physically compelled to do so; she knew enough of what P was planning to do with the returned crowbar, and so in returning it she should have been understood as intentionally assisting P's burglary. In response to Child et al, however, it is not clear what D is supposed to do with the crowbar if she retains possession of it without the owner's consent: is she *never* to return it to him?

Back to our paradigm account of D loaning her crowbar to P on Friday. P has told D explicitly that he wants to use her crowbar for a burglary on Saturday night, and so D intentionally *loans* the crowbar with that knowledge. Question: can we say that D intentionally *assisted* the burglary? On Friday, the burglary lies in the future, and the future is indeterminate. It would be easier to say that D intentionally assists the burglary when she drives P to the site of the burglary and waits in the car for him to finish. So with the crowbar loan, perhaps the better question is: how confident is D that P will carry out his plan? How well does she know him — does he normally do what he says he will do? How realistic does she think the plan is?

It seems to be clear that one cannot be *reckless* about one's complicity. In his article "Reckless complicity" (1997) Kadish offers the following example: a father has a 17-year-old son who has recently passed his driver's licence. The father knows the son to be generally impulsive and careless. The father asks the son to take the family car to the petrol station to fill it up, knowing that (i) there is a risk that the son will take the car for a dangerous joyride, during which (ii) there is a risk that the son will hit and harm another road user. The son does indeed go for a joyride, and does indeed kill a pedestrian. Kadish's question is whether the father's reckless loan of the car keys should make him complicit in (i) the son's dangerous driving, and perhaps also to (ii) the son's killing of the pedestrian.

The current criminal law, both in the American context in which Kadish was writing and in the English context, would seem to say no. But perhaps he should? The case for complicity is strengthened by two other facts. First, the father *enabled* the dangerous driving and the killing, i.e. but for the loan of the car keys, the son would almost certainly not have killed anyone that night (we discuss "enabling" below); second, there is an asymmetry under current law in allowing a lower *mens rea* threshold (recklessness) for the son's killing, but not for the father's loan of the car keys (intention). The standard response to Kadish's proposal in the academic

---

not unusual. Compare: I stab Jones on Friday, and he ends up in the intensive care ward in the hospital. While Jones lives, my Friday stabbing was an act of attempted murder. If Jones dies on Saturday, then my Friday stabbing becomes an act of murder.

6 This is similar to the situation in Plato's *Republic*, where Socrates argues that D would be justified in withholding P's sword if P had gone mad.

literature is that it would over-criminalise, since too many people in too many situations are well aware of the risk of their actions possibly assisting the future commission of a crime.[7]

7.1 THE PRINCIPLE OF "EQUIVALENT INDICTMENT"

Complicity is not a discrete crime, in the way an attempt is; under English law it is a mode of responsibility. If D assists P's burglary and D is convicted, she will not be convicted of "complicity" but of "burglary" alongside P. The advantage of this convention for the prosecution is that they do not need to be too worried about who, between D and P, was the accessory and who the principal. Call this the "principle of equivalent indictment." This principle originally comes from the *Accessories and Abettors Act* (AAA) 1861, sec. 8, which reads: "Whosoever shall aid, abet, counsel, or procure the commission of any indictable offence ... shall be liable to be tried, indicted, and punished *as a principal offender*" [italics ours].[8] This is convenient for the prosecution, but the all-or-nothing involvement can lead to unfairness. In practice, the accessory might get a lesser sentence than the principal, depending on her culpability, e.g. how much of a causal contribution she made. (The exception would be for the crime of murder, where both accessory and principal will be given the mandatory life sentence.)

In a bid to deal with this unfairness, and with the moral luck of making D dependent on P actually committing the crime, Parliament passed the *Serious Crime Act* 2007, where sec. 44–46 provide for several new crimes that could be called "inchoate complicity."[9] Recall our discussion of inchoate offences in Chapter 6. The central idea is that D has committed a crime in *attempting* to X even if her attempt is unsuccessful and harmless; or in *conspiring* to X even if her fellow conspirators never carry X out. In a similar way, inchoate complicity describes a situation where D "(a) does an act capable of encouraging or assisting the commission of an offence; and (b) he intends to encourage or assist its commission." In other words, D's offence is not derivative, i.e. does not depend at all on whether or not P goes on to commit the principal offence.

One aspect of the principle of equivalent indictment takes us to a problem of collective harmful action. Christopher Kutz, in his full-length philosophical study *Complicity* (2000, Chapter 3), offers the example of the Allied bombing of Dresden. In February 1945, more than 1200 bombers attacked Dresden in two waves, starting a firestorm which laid waste to the city. Given the enormous number of civilian casualties and the limited military importance of the target (especially at that late stage in the war), the act was probably a war crime. If it was a war crime, then to what degree would an *individual* pilot be complicit in it? Given the huge number of planes, it is plausible to say that it would have made no real difference to the criminal outcome if a single pilot dropped or refused to drop his bombs. What is essential to complicity in such large-scale collective action is not the causal contribution, concludes Kutz, but "participatory intention."[10] This is different from SCA 2007's inchoate complicity, which

7 For discussion of Kadish's example and "reckless enabling," see Cowley (2020).

8 Paradoxically, this means that if a woman helps a man commit rape, then as an accessory she can be convicted of rape, even though the *Sexual Offences Act* 2003 defines rape as requiring a penis.

9 The SCA was a legislative response to a Law Commission *Report no. 305* "Participating in Crime" (2007). This Report contains an excellent summary of the criminal law surrounding participation, and makes concrete proposals for new legislation, one of which was the creation of what we are calling inchoate complicity. The problem is that the government ignored most of the other proposals, and this made the SCA 2007 less coherent than it could have been. In practice it has not been used very much, with a famous exception of encouraging a riot in *Blackshaw* [2011].

10 The same argument applies in audience-encouragement cases: where there are many spectators who encourage the perpetrator it will often be impossible to prove that any single one of them made a

is focused on an intentional discrete act that has to be "capable" of assisting or encouraging another person's discrete criminal act. Instead, it is about finding oneself in a situation where the only way to avoid complicity is to withdraw oneself entirely from one's role and responsibilities — in the military context, that means an attempted conscientious objection, and if that fails then desertion. (Could the sceptical pilot not discretely drop his bombs in a field outside Dresden? Perhaps. But he would still be complicit insofar as he takes off with the other pilots and therefore encourages them to carry out their mission.)

In the SCA case, it is explicitly unnecessary for an accessory to *causally* contribute to the "target" offence; in the Dresden case, the bomber pilot's *effective* causation is negligible. It might seem counter-intuitive to remove causation from the equation and still call it complicity. But in fact causation is not required in ordinary cases of complicity. Let's look at causation in a bit more detail.

Knowledge vs. endorsement

Back to our example of D lending her crowbar to P. Under English law, the focus is on what D *knows* about P's plan. But there's a slightly different take on it in America. Here's the *Model Penal Code* (MPC) Section 2.06(3):

> A person is an accomplice of another person in the commission of the offense, if, with the purpose of promoting or facilitating the commission of the offense, he solicits, or aids, or attempts to aid, or has a legal duty to prevent but fails to make proper efforts to do so.

So P explains to D that he needs her crowbar for tomorrow's burglary, and once P commits that burglary, D becomes an accomplice, given her knowledge of the plan. But under the MPC, the prosecutor would have to demonstrate not only that D knew the details of P's crime, but also that she had the "purpose of promoting" it; in other words, that she endorsed it, that she wanted it to succeed. If she was indifferent about whether P succeeded or failed in the burglary, then she could not be complicit.

The cynical view is that the MPC is designed to protect licensed gun salespeople from complicity charges even when they are quite knowledgeable about their customers' criminal plans. As long as the salesperson does not endorse the plans, and her purpose is only to make money on the sale, then she cannot be complicit. In addition, the gun salesperson differs from the indifferent crowbar-lender because the former sells the weapon and thereby surrenders any claim to it: it becomes the customer's property, and thereby the customer's responsibility. In contrast, when D freely lends a crowbar to P, then the crowbar remains D's property, and in this sense D's endorsement of the principal crime is more tangible, especially when compounded by P returning after the job to thank D and return the crowbar.

7.2 THE ROLE OF CAUSATION IN COMPLICITY

In most of the discussion above we have been assuming a clear causal contribution: D lends her crowbar to P and P uses the crowbar in the burglary. As such the main question is how much D knew. In what follows we're going to assume that D knows all about P's plans, and that such knowledge infuses her intentional loan. Intuitively we would want to say that D

difference to the perpetrator's conduct or the outcome. But it will be enough to look at their participatory intention.

can *only* be complicit if her assistance *actually* ends up causally contributing to P's crime. The bombing of Dresden already showed that this was not necessary, although that is a very specific context. But even in our ordinary two-person burglary, actual causation is not necessary. Let's compare two ways in which D's contribution might *fail* to assist P's crime:

(i) *Forgotten assistance.* P takes the crowbar from D on Friday, but then *forgets* to take it with him to the burglary on Saturday night. P finds a way to get into the house and carry out the burglary anyway, but without making D an accessory (i.e. even if D had fully intended to assist P's burglary).
(ii) *Redundant assistance.* P takes the crowbar from D on Friday, takes it with him on Saturday night, but discovers an open ground-floor window that he can crawl through without using the crowbar. In this scenario, however, D would *still* become an accessory, precisely because her crowbar was there at the scene of the crime, ready to be used if necessary.

In the first scenario, P is annoyed to have forgotten the crowbar, but soon forgets it as he concentrates on the burglary: as such the crowbar is both physically and psychologically absent from the crime. In the second scenario, P is conscious of the crowbar in his bag, he's getting ready to use it as he walks around the house — and he might well have used it if all the windows were locked, which was very likely. So we are back to a moral luck situation, since in both scenarios, D lent the crowbar with the same intention.

Another question about causality has to do with the significance and relevance of different intentional causal contributions to P's burglary. On Saturday morning, P informs his father that he is planning the burglary for that evening, and the father replies: "I'll make you a good lunch to give you lots of energy." And sure enough, P finds himself that evening with lots of energy, and this helps him with the burglary. This example might seem trivial, but the father's intention would seem to be "participatory" enough to inculpate him in Kutz's sense. Otherwise, we might reject the lunch-making as complicity on the grounds that it did not assist P with any *criminal element* of his plan — it assisted him with whatever he went on to do that Saturday evening. Whereas D's provision of a crowbar would seem to assist P in breaking open a window, which is a criminal element. However, the border is fuzzy here. What if D provides P not with a crowbar but with a car? The car will certainly be useful for P to get to and from the scene of the crime, and as such makes a causal contribution, but it does not assist P with the actual crime.

Facilitating and enabling

Recall this distinction from Chapter 5 on causation (Mellema 2016). If D *enables* P's commission of the crime, then D's assistance is a necessary condition for that crime. Without D's assistance, P would not have been able to commit the crime, or at least not *that* crime. The most obvious examples of enabling assistance involve rare technical expertise, such as computer hacking. If P does not have that expertise and D does, then P simply cannot override the target object's defensive security system, and will need to look for a more accessible target or another expert accessory. In contrast, if D only *facilitates* P's commission of the crime, she makes it go more easily, cheaply, quickly than it would otherwise have gone. It is still a causal contribution in the sense that it makes a difference, but throughout it is clear that P is determined and able to do it anyway, without the facilitation if need be.

The important point about this distinction for complicity is that the enabler *controls* P's crime, in the sense of having the power to prevent it. If, however, despite such self-conscious power, D nevertheless provides the assistance, that would seem to represent much more endorsement, and therefore much more culpability. (Again, however, more or less culpability would not amount to more or less complicity because of the all-or-nothing principle; but it might lead to more or less punishment.)

Note that the withdrawal of a putative facilitation might reveal it to have been enabling, to the surprise of both D and P: if the cost to P of acting alone (to commit *that* particular crime) is already onerous, then D's cash facilitation might turn out to have been a necessary condition, as P realises when D stomps away in a sulk. Similarly, in our standing example, if D lends P a crowbar to assist with his planned burglary, then the status of D's assistance as enablement or facilitation might depend on a number of contingencies, some of which might not be ascertainable until P reaches the scene of the crime. Neither D nor P might be aware, at the moment of lending, whether D was enabling or facilitating.

Redundant assistance

Let's return to the case where P brings D's crowbar to the target house, and finds he doesn't need it because a window is open. We argued that D would nevertheless remain complicit because the crowbar was there and because P intended to use it if necessary. (Whereas if P had forgotten it, he could not intend to use it.) But this does not quite seem robust enough to make D complicit. Certainly, D's lending of the crowbar would have *encouraged* P, and maybe given him peace of mind as he approached the house; certainly D's lending of the crowbar was "*capable*" of assisting P (as per the SCA 2007 definition of "inchoate" complicity). But some might worry that there are too many hypotheticals to make D complicit.

Consider a different case of complicity. D acts as a lookout during a bank robbery. She stands at the street corner, with her finger on her phone, ready to give advance warning to the principals in the bank. As it turns out, no police arrive and no passers-by notice, and so D's looking-out turns out to be redundant. The bank robbery would have taken place in exactly the same way without her. And yet a passer-by might have noticed; and the police might have received a tip-off. Every bank robber knows that. And the objective risk is sufficiently high to make D useful — and therefore complicit. But notice that we can describe her as "useful for managing the risk," *rather than* "useful in giving warning." In that sense, she provided assistance that was much appreciated (and gave the nervous principals a bit more peace of mind during the job).

We also have to consider the question of impossibility, recalling our discussion of impossible attempts in Chapter 6. There we said that someone stabbing a voodoo doll could technically be convicted of attempted murder, although the CPS might not see the value in prosecuting her. What if someone intentionally performed magic to "facilitate" P's burglary? In such a case it would be hard to consider her an accessory. In terms of contingent impossibility, what if D offered P a gun to murder V, but, unbeknownst to either, the gun was broken. V takes aim, squeezes the trigger, and nothing happens. Assume that P has been under surveillance, and is promptly charged with attempted murder. What about D? It would seem that D would be guilty of complicity in attempted murder: for all that D knew, she was intentionally assisting P's murderous plan by providing the necessary tools.

One final case of redundant assistance, a classic cited in many criminal law textbooks, is *Tally* [1893] from Alabama, US (as discussed in Kadish (1985)). The Ps are pursuing V across the country, with the intent to kill him. V's family learn of the Ps' plans, and arrange to send a telegram to V to warn him. Tally happens to be a judge, and so has some authority. In an effort to assist the Ps' murderous plans, Tally orders the telegram operator not to send the warning telegram. (The Ps, meanwhile, have no knowledge of Tally's efforts.)

The Ps catch up with V, kill him, and are apprehended and convicted of murder. The police learn of Tally's interference with the warning telegram, and charge him as an accessory in the murder. But what did Tally do, exactly? He prevented V from being warned, and he was therefore closing off a potential escape route. But here's the thing: it is not at all clear that (i) V would have received the telegram even if it had been sent; nor that (ii) V, having received the telegram, would have been able to evade the Ps. So there was a strong likelihood that Tally's complicity was redundant. Nevertheless, Tally was found guilty precisely because of the proximity of the possible world in which V would have tried and failed to save himself *because of* Tally.

7.3 TWO-CRIME SCENARIOS

Let's consider another schematic example here. D and P are joint principals in the robbery of a small bank. So at first glance this does not seem to be a complicity scenario (but we will call them D and P for reasons that will become clear). They plan the robbery together, and carry it out together; if they are apprehended, there will be no doubt about their joint principalship in a single action. Now P is carrying a loaded gun with him, and uses that to intimidate the bank staff, customers and a security guard into co-operation. At one moment, however, a security guard lunges at P, and P shoots him dead, and both D and P flee. D and P are later apprehended. Both are convicted of the robbery (Crime A) as joint principals — that much is clear. P is also convicted of murdering the guard (Crime B) — that too is clear. The question then becomes: was D an accessory to the guard's murder?

D and P were engaged in the common venture of the bank robbery.[11] But how much was the guard's murder (Crime B) *part of* the common venture? That is, how much was it tacitly *understood* by D and P, when planning the robbery, that one of them might shoot the guard if necessary to safeguard the success of the venture? If P was carrying a loaded gun to the bank, and D *knew* that P was carrying the gun, and D continued her participation in the common venture with such knowledge, this would be strong evidence that D had "pre-endorsed" its possible use — and therefore would be complicit in crime B if and when P carried it out. (Loaded guns are only used for shooting, so there was no plausible alternative use for the gun that D could have imagined.)

Contrast this with the following case. D and P are robbing the bank, and P notices an old rival among the customers cowering on the floor. P shoots the rival dead. Here we would say that crime B was not part of the common venture, neither in terms of foresight and planning, nor in terms of the need to safeguard success — it really was entirely P's business. So D would still be liable as a joint principal of the robbery, but not be an accessory to the murder.

There remain a number of uncertainties: how explicitly did D and P discuss the hypothetical murder? How much could D foresee P using the gun? What was D's prior attitude toward the hypothetical murder? Indeed, did P reassure a reluctant D that the gun was "only for show"? What if D and P had different evaluations of the risk posed by the guard — P was

11 Sometimes this would be described as a "joint enterprise," and this term has been associated with a lot of controversy. For the moment we're going to avoid it because it is importantly ambiguous.

a trigger-happy amateur while D was more experienced and would not have fired it? What if D had assumed that P would only shoot to disable the guard rather than kill him?

To get some grip on all these complexities, it is worth briefly summarising the legal history. Traditionally (in common law), any discussion of D's liability for crime B in a common venture focused on the prior understanding (implicit or explicit) between D and P. The case of *Chan Wing-Siu* [1984][12] changed this. From now on, if D could be shown to have *foreseen the mere possibility* (i.e. not the likelihood) of P committing crime B (whether or not it was even connected to Crime A), and despite such foresight D continued with the common venture, then D would be held complicit in Crime B. Needless to say, "foreseeing the mere possibility" is a much lower threshold than a prior understanding (between D and P). John Smith (1997) coined the term "parasitic accessorial liability" (PAL) to describe it, and for the sake of clarity, we will use it too.

What does "foreseeing the mere possibility" mean in practice, and why did it prove so controversial? The big advantage of PAL is that it allows a much more effective prosecution of urban gang criminality. The problem with gangs is that you have a group of people, a dead body, and enough group loyalty or fear that nobody is willing to testify about who did what to whom. But now imagine the following description. Imagine that one gang (the Jets) attacks another gang (the Sharks) violently. Already we have Crime A, assault. During the attack, one of the Sharks is killed, but it is not clear which Jet did it. Using PAL, the prosecutor can assume that *every* Jet had foreseen the mere possibility that a Shark would be killed, but had continued their participation in Crime A of assault. This makes every Jet an accessory to the murder. This is a very powerful weapon for the prosecution, but its controversy lies in the fact that it seems to amount to "guilt by association" — and after 1984 it led to a large number of appeals and academic criticisms.

The situation was perhaps resolved with the *Jogee* decision in 2016, which effectively rejected PAL by declaring it a "wrong turn," and restored the original common law version of "common venture."[13] The Supreme Court in *Jogee* uses a schematic two-crime bank robbery case like ours:

> The bank robbers who attack the bank when one or more of them is armed no doubt hope that it will not be necessary to use the guns, but it may be a perfectly proper inference that all were intending that if they met resistance the weapons should be used with the intent to do grievous bodily harm at least.
>
> (92)

The key word here is "intending," a much higher *mens rea* threshold than mere foresight of possibility, although *Jogee* leaves open the possibility that the jury might infer the requisite intention from evidence of D's foresight alone:

> if [D] continues to participate in Crime A with foresight that [P] may commit Crime B, that is evidence, and sometimes powerful evidence, of an intent to assist [P] in Crime B. But it is evidence of such intent (or, if one likes, of "authorisation"), not conclusive of it.
>
> (66)

There is a question of how *Jogee* is playing out in subsequent cases. At the time of writing, there is some evidence that it will not make much difference: juries can and will still *find* intention

12 This was a Hong Kong case. At the time Hong Kong was a British colony, and so some criminal appeals went to the UK Privy Council.

13 Curiously enough the facts of *Jogee* [2016] did not really invite a PAL interpretation. But the UK Supreme Court used the case to provide a thorough summary of complicity law and in the process to overturn PAL. Australia had adopted PAL in the 1980s, re-examined the issue after *Jogee*, but decided in the case of *Miller* [2016] to retain it.

when presented with enough evidence of foresight. And there has been much disappointment among prisoners still serving mandatory life sentences for PAL liability. PAL was simply too useful when dealing with gang conflicts, and governments of all stripes are reluctant to appear soft on crime.[14] Of course, there are larger criminological debates about how best to control the social problem of gang violence, whether by special legislation[15] or through coordinated interventions within the education, social welfare, urban planning and healthcare systems. The criminal law is a notoriously blunt instrument.[16]

7.4 AFTER-THE-FACT COMPLICITY

So far we have been taking assistance provided before or during the principal offence. Certainly the question of causal contribution would only make sense before or during. And yet the category of "complicity after the fact" exists in several American states, and existed in English law up until the middle of the last century.

The classic example is the getaway driver. Imagine D drives P to the house to burgle (before-the-fact), waits in the car as a lookout (during-the-fact), and then drives P away with the loot (after-the-fact). The conceptual question is whether D *as the getaway driver* is assisting P's past crime, or whether she is assisting P in his present desire to get away and avoid capture. English law now chooses the latter option, and would convict D of hindering the apprehension of a known offender, and/or of handling stolen property.[17] This is slightly curious, however, since English law does not acknowledge any duty to prevent or report crime or to assist the police pursuit of offenders. In light of this, in the example, when P comes to D's car after the burglary, D might want to argue that he is just harmlessly "offering a mate a lift." The fact that P has just committed burglary, and D knows that he has, should be irrelevant to what D is now doing if D has no general duty to report the crime. Certainly, if D's car were to be pursued by a police car, then D would have to decide whether to pull over or whether to hinder the apprehension of P by trying to evade the police. But until the appearance of the police, D's efforts are not necessarily hindering police work at all.

14 The Centre for Crime and Justice Studies published a Report entitled *The Usual Suspects* (2nd ed.) in November 2022. The Report "uses national data to assess the use of joint enterprise laws in prosecutions for serious violence in England and Wales over the last fifteen years." The Report concluded:

- "Over a thousand secondary suspects were convicted of murder or manslaughter in the ten-year period to 2020.
- Those from minority ethnicity communities, particularly the Black community, are consistently over-represented in multi-defendant prosecutions and convictions for homicide.
- The Supreme Court ruling had no discernible impact on the numbers or demographics of people prosecuted or convicted of murder and manslaughter in multi-defendant cases."

See: https://www.crimeandjustice.org.uk/publications/usual-suspects-second-edition

15 E.g. the *Serious Crime Act* 2007 and the *Policing and Crime Act* 2009. See also the Home Office statement on 12 July 2017: "Government announces further funding to tackle gang related violence," available at: https://www.gov.uk/government/news/government-announces-further-funding-to-tackle-gang-related-violence

16 For more discussion of *Jogee*, see Cowley (2019b), and the other contributions to the volume by Krebs (2019). See also the extensive discussion about the new state of complicity law following *Jogee* in Horder (2022, pp. 489–507).

17 Section 4(1) of the *Criminal Law Act* 1967 reads:

> Where a person has committed a relevant offence, any other person who, knowing or believing him to be guilty of the offence or of some other relevant offence, does without lawful authority or reasonable excuse any act with intent to impede his apprehension or prosecution shall be guilty of an offence.

There might be the following argument for tying D more directly to the robbery as an accessory. Let's take D who is *only* the getaway driver. Even though D as the getaway driver cannot make a causal contribution to a burglary that has already ended, P's awareness during the burglary, that D would be waiting as agreed, may well have been a necessary condition for P going through with the burglary at all. In such a case, D would effectively be an enabler: since the agreement was made before the burglary, D controlled that particular burglary in that her prior withdrawal would have led to P's cancellation of that particular burglary — and D's refusal to withdraw before the planned crime means that she was already inculpated beforehand, already indirectly assisting the rest of P's plans through her reassurance that the post-burglary getaway problem was sorted.[18]

This is to be contrasted with P committing the burglary with the plan of returning home in his own car. When he reaches the car with the loot, he finds that his car won't start, and so he contacts a friend to come for him. That friend would not be complicit in the earlier burglary, although — depending on how much he discovered of P's activities — she might still be liable for impeding P's apprehension by the police, and possibly for handling the stolen goods.

As we saw, Christopher Kutz is more interested in institutional than interpersonal contexts, and in Kutz (2007) he offers the following interesting example of complicity after the fact. The United States invaded Iraq in 2003, and soon after started torturing detainees for information, in clear violation of their legal commitments to the relevant Geneva Conventions. At some point *after* the torture had begun, White House lawyers thought it would be important to articulate contrived legal justifications to protect the executive in the event of future revelations. Kutz argues that the lawyers were complicit in the torture, despite their lack of causal contribution to it. There are actually two claims here:

(i) the lawyers were complicit in protecting the White House from any *present and future* torture, torture that the White House might plausibly be more inclined to sanction, knowing that it was legally more protected — and as such the lawyer's complicity might plausibly amount to a potential causal contribution.

(ii) But Kutz argues that the lawyers were also complicit in the *past* torture, despite obviously being unable to make any causal contribution to it. In seeking to justify it retrospectively, they were allying themselves to the past offence, and thereby conceptually linking the memo-writing to the torture, regardless of the precise chronology. Future observers, more interested in the meaning of the memo-writing than in its causal influence, would reasonably see the lawyers as complicit — even if no court of law would.

7.5 ENCOURAGEMENT

For the sake of clarity on an already difficult topic, we have been speaking about assistance for most of the chapter. But D can also be complicit by encouraging D to commit the principal crime. Encouragement is enormously varied; think of the list of verbs offered by Lepora and Goodin (2013) at the beginning of this chapter. And the causal effect of the encouragement is much harder to assess. With assistance, it's usually clear what the driver or the crowbar contributes to the crime.

18 There is also a question here, perhaps, of when the burglary is *complete*: as soon as P has grabbed the loot or only once it has been securely stored away in D's car? If the latter, then D would effectively be assisting P *during* the burglary.

The problems of understanding encouragement were already foreshadowed in our discussion of incitement in Chapter 6. Incitement is an inchoate offence, and so it is normally a failure by definition. As a form of complicity, encouragement presupposes the success of the principal offence. Once that offence is committed, and then discovered, the police investigation will look back in time to see who might have encouraged the principal, and how. We will first discuss a generic case of encouragement as verbal persuasion, before considering a more tractable case of encouragement as payment (which we will call "instigation"), below.

In our discussion of incitement we imagined a husband married to a wife, but having an affair with his lover. The lover incites the husband to murder the wife, and she offers him reasons: e.g. so that we could live in bliss, and so that you (we) could inherit her money. When the husband refused, we asked what it meant for the lover to incite him. If the husband goes ahead and murders the wife, we can ask what it meant for the lover to encourage him to do so, where such encouragement is serious enough to be treated as complicity. The first problem is proving a causal influence, since of course the lover will deny that she was serious. In addition, it will be very difficult to tell whether the husband was persuaded by the lover, or by others, or whether it was an idea that he came up with on his own. The husband himself may not know what persuasive forces were at work in his mind.

We saw with assistance that the redundant crowbar can still inculpate the crowbar-lender, as long as the crowbar was close at hand during the burglary, ready to be used if necessary. So there might be a possibility to inculpate the persuader even if her words did not add any motivational force to what the principal was planning to do anyway: suffice that her persuasion was there, close at hand, ready to be used if necessary. But again, who can tell, with any accuracy that would stand up in court, what sort of motivational force her persuasion had or *might have had*? So much will depend on the principal's state of mind to receive and accept the persuasion.

But even if the police had evidence of her persuasion attempts (let's say surveillance tapes), there's still a problem. If the lover provides the husband with good reasons to kill the wife, then at some point the husband takes those reasons and makes them *his* reasons. When he is arrested, he informs the detective about those reasons as *his* reasons (e.g. "so that I would inherit the money," "so that I could be with my lover"). Importantly, what he will *not* say "my lover made me do it!" Maybe the lover provided him with reasons which would not have occurred to him otherwise; or maybe he got the reasons from a detective novel; or maybe he got the reasons from his friend Spikey down the pub; maybe he just can't remember. The whole point of a competent adult is that he can make up his own mind, endorse certain reasons, act on the basis of those reasons, and take full responsibility for his actions. Following this line of thought, the lover is *entirely* out of the culpability nexus, and encouragement could only rarely be taken as a legitimate form of criminal complicity.

This leads us to a second problem: the risk of opening up the conceptual space *too much*. We need some kind of limit to the type and degree of encouragement that is to count as complicit. Otherwise there might be many who causally contributed to the husband's decision to murder his wife. One limit comes from the "bystander principle." If a high street shop is robbed in daylight, and witnessed by bystanders who are there accidentally, then they cannot be guilty of complicity by their mere presence alone, even if their *inaction* effectively "encourages" the robbers to continue the job. It is only when they overtly encourage the robbers, in utterance or gesture, that we can speak of complicity.[19]

19 This principle was seemingly confirmed in the case of *Clarkson* [1971], a case cited by most legal textbooks — but we suggest this is controversial. D1 and D2 and D3 were privates on a British army base who stumbled on a gang-rape of V by four of their colleagues. D1 and D2 and D3 stayed and watched,

A third complication has to do with the *authority* of the encourager. *Gillick* [1971] is an interesting case here, not only because of the role of authority, but also because of the distinction between different descriptions of what the encourager was trying to encourage or discourage. A mother challenged the legality of Department of Health guidance which allowed GPs in exceptional circumstances to prescribe the contraceptive pill to 15-year-old girls. Was a GP in such circumstances complicit in a girl's subsequent underage sex with her boyfriend? A GP might argue that the girl was clearly going to have sex anyway, and that he saw his role as discouraging *unprotected* sex and the accompanying risk of pregnancy, which would not be in the girl's best interest — and the House of Lords concurred. But one can also imagine a girl reasonably taking the GP's agreement as encouragement *to have sex* (and break the law), given the moral authority that doctors usually have. A lot would depend here on the actual nature of their conversation.[20]

One final complication, and that is the possibility of encouragement by omission, especially in the context of a clear duty of care. We're thinking of the case we discussed in Chapter 4 on Negligence, of two parents: the father (P) is systematically abusing their young daughter (V), while the mother (D) is either wilfully blind or too afraid to intervene, with the result that P is effectively encouraged to continue his abuse. At the same time, she is not a mere bystander because of her explicit duty of care to the daughter and because of the long-term nature of the abusive assaults (i.e. the more often they occur, and the more obvious the consequences on the daughter, the less easy they are to ignore or explain away). As in our discussion in Chapter 4, however, we have to be careful of blaming the mother entirely, since, likely as not, she will also be a victim of P's abuse. Not only would she have the defence of duress, but it would make more sense conceptually for the law to take both mother and daughter as victims to the unencouraged perpetrator. (On this see Herring, 2007.)

Instigation

There is one type of encouragement that can be more easily documented, and where the motivational force can be more easily determined, and we're going to call this "instigation." (Using the terms of the *AAA*, it would be called "counselling.") Again recall our discussion of the godmother in Section 6.3. on incitement. The godmother (D) hires a hitman (P) to murder her business rival (V). If the hitman refuses, then her efforts will amount to inchoate incitement. If the hitman agrees, then her efforts will amount to instigation (encouragement). The

without trying to prevent or report the crime, but also without encouraging it in utterance or gesture. The four rapists were convicted of rape, and the Court of Appeal quashed the convictions of D1 and D2 for complicity. (There was sufficient evidence that D3 *had* encouraged the principals.)

We suggest that this was a special case because of the role of *humiliation* in sexual offences. D1 and D2 were not mere bystanders, for their presence (as men) compounded the egregious wrong and despair suffered by the (female) victim. For a more complete argument, see Cowley (2019a).

20 Nowadays the GP's exception would be covered by Section 73 of the *Sexual Offences Act* 2003, which reads:

> (1) A person is not guilty of aiding, abetting or counselling the commission against a child of an offence to which this section applies if he acts for the purpose of—
>
> (a) protecting the child from sexually transmitted infection,
> (b) protecting the physical safety of the child,
> (c) preventing the child from becoming pregnant, or
> (d) promoting the child's emotional well-being by the giving of advice,
>
> and not for the purpose of obtaining sexual gratification or for the purpose of causing or encouraging the activity constituting the offence or the child's participation in it.

hitman is apprehended and straightforwardly convicted of murder. The police then investigate D's relationship to P and to P's crime.

We call this instigation because "encouragement" (and "counselling") and indeed "complicity" seem to under-describe the godmother's specific culpability — for she was not only the enabler, she was also the prime causal impetus. Without her payment, it is virtually certain that the hitman would not have killed V, since we assume that he has otherwise no reason to do so, that he does not know V and is indifferent about V's fate. All of this is relatively easy for the police to discover, together with the payment. So it's very much a case of the godmother *herself* murdering V via the hitman, as if the hitman was no more than a tool. Nevertheless, the godmother's hands look clean, and that's the point.[21]

Now, because of the principle of equivalent indictment, she would end up being charged with murder and punished with the mandatory life sentence, so justice is still served. But the point about underdescription still stands. Indeed, "instigation" might itself be too weak; perhaps a new category of "contract murder" should be created. Alternatively, the godmother could be taken as a joint principal, engaged with the hitman in a *single* act involving payment-for-murder, even if the payment was far away (in time and space) from the murder.

21 Note that the instigator can only be guilty of instigating what actually ended up happening, even if it was less than what she wanted to happen. In *Richards* [1974], D hired P1 and P2 to assault V so severely that V would need hospital treatment. P1 and P2 did indeed assault V, but V's injuries were not that serious. P was convicted under Section 20 of the *Offences Against the Person Act* 1861, while D was convicted as an accomplice under Section 18, which is more serious. D successfully appealed.

CHAPTER 8

HOMICIDE AND ASSAULT

This chapter and the next mark something of a new approach to our subject. Chapters 2–5 explored three different degrees of *mens rea* and the related discussion of causation. Chapters 6 and 7 were about indirect modes of liability, i.e. inchoate offences and complicity. In principle, therefore, the book so far concerned all offences. In contrast, this chapter will look at the specific offences of homicide and assault; and the next chapter (Chapter 9) will look at sexual offences. We have chosen to focus on these areas of criminal law since they raise important philosophical issues. In Chapters 10 and 11 we then return to the more general approach, in our discussion of defences and punishment respectively.

In fact, we have already mentioned homicide quite a lot in previous chapters. After all, one clear way to distinguish intentional action from recklessness is to focus on the distinction between murder and manslaughter. We also talked about whether Blaue, in assaulting V, ended up causing V's death (Section 5.2). We considered attempted murder (Section 6.1.), and complicity to murder (Chapter 7). So some of the issues in this chapter will be familiar, but it is worthwhile laying them out more systematically, especially when murder is widely perceived as the most serious of all the offences.[1]

Before we continue, two points about terminology. English law distinguishes between "assault" and "battery." Battery involves some kind of unlawful and unwanted physical contact with the victim; it might be a punch, but it might also be mere touching. In contrast, a person is assaulted if they merely *apprehend the possibility* of imminent battery, and typically, they feel fear or distress upon the apprehension. This means that a person can be battered without being assaulted (i.e. battered by surprise), just as they can be assaulted without being battered (if the attacker is prevented from carrying out his planned battery). The distinction between assault and battery can be useful, as we will see, but it is also confusing for the layperson — for most of us, the word "assault" usually implies some sort of physical contact. So in this chapter, we're going to use "assault" throughout. When necessary, we'll follow the suggested Law Commission distinction between "threatened assault" and "assault."[2]

The second source of terminological confusion is the distinction between the (ordinary) assault and the *consequences* of the assault — whether it be wounding, (actual) bodily harm, or grievous bodily harm (GBH). Some of the consequences are listed in the *Offences Against the Person Act* (OAPA) 1861, especially Sections 18, 20 and 47 (in declining order of seriousness). Notoriously, the definitions in the *Act* are out-of-date, inconsistent and overlapping. But they are not necessary for our philosophical discussion, and so we are not proposing to analyse them further. The only important distinction for our purposes will be between assault causing GBH, assault causing non-grievous harm, and ordinary assault causing more trivial harm (sometimes called "horseplay").

1 It's true that terrorism and genocide are offences that are more serious than the murder of a single victim. However, terrorism and genocide are almost always committed by groups, even nation states, and this hugely complicates the business of preventing and prosecuting such offences, let alone understanding them. Our focus in this book has been much more at the level of the individual in society (perhaps with the complicity of another), harming a single victim (or a small number). This focus allows greater clarity of the philosophical issues.

2 The Law Commission, in their (2015) *Report no. 361: Reform of Offences Against the Person.*

DOI: 10.4324/9781003351887-8

8.1 MURDER

There is an important sense that homicide — whether murder or manslaughter — really is special because it is essentially irredeemable. This has to do with the fundamental and widespread touchstone of our civilisation, the sanctity of human life. One way of articulating this sanctity is to stress the irreversible finality of death, and of bringing someone else's life to an end. Every other crime, even if it involves irreversible injury and loss to the victim, can in theory be accepted, or at least accommodated, by the victim as she seeks to start her life anew, and perhaps even forgive her assailant. For every other crime, the surviving victim can at least draw satisfaction from the trial and imprisonment of her assailant.[3] Because of the finality of death, however, there is an important sense that there is *nothing* that the killer can do to make up for the killing, no matter how much just punishment she undergoes, no matter how much genuine remorse she feels. This irredeemability is contained in the intuition that once a person becomes a murderer, they have crossed a line and remain a murderer forever; even if they serve their time, they will never be an ex-murderer. The particular evil of murder is also contained in the experience of the victim's family — there is a world of difference between one's daughter being killed by an earthquake and being killed intentionally by another person.

Recall the two assassins (one successful, the other unsuccessful) and the two girl racers (one who kills a pedestrian, one who does not), discussed in Section 1.3. It might seem that each member of the pair was "doing" the same thing as the other, when in fact the consequence of death (even if a matter of pure luck) radically changes the nature of the action: the successful assassin and the unlucky racer have done something different, they have *killed.* Or consider Bernard Williams's famous lorry driver from his paper "Moral luck." He is not culpably reckless or negligent in any way: he is driving under the speed limit, he is sober, he is an experienced driver, his brakes have recently been inspected etc. — and yet he kills a child. Even if innocent in the eyes of the law, he feels terrible, and we expect him to feel terrible, because he has *done* something terrible. Even if he was just as legally innocent as the spectators at the scene, his experience is radically different from theirs because he was at the wheel.[4]

The basic definition of murder is clear enough: D must intentionally kill V. As we saw in Section 2.1., the precise motivation does not matter, just as the precise contours of the intention do not matter, i.e. whether D killed V out of personal animus, or because V was preventing D's plans, or because V was in the wrong place at the wrong time.

Section 2.3. introduced the "oblique" intention, with the example of the person who plants a bomb on an aircraft, in order to cash in on a fraudulent insurance pay-out for the destroyed cargo. In doing so, the bomber foresees that the pilot will be killed by the bomb that she intentionally plants, although she does not *intend* to kill the pilot. She would have been only too pleased if the pilot could have ejected and parachuted to the ground. On this basis, she might be tempted to plead guilty only to manslaughter. However, because of the "virtual certainty" of the pilot's death, and her knowledge of its virtual certainty, English law (as confirmed in the case of *Nedrick* [1986] and *Woollin* [1998]) considers her intention to have

3 There is a borderline question: what if D injures V to such an extent, that she enters a coma or suffers irreversible brain damage? In the coma case, at least there remains some hope, however minimal, that V would recover. The brain damage case is interesting, because it could be described as the death of the *person* V, even if not the *body* of V, and therefore there would be an argument for consider D's offence murder rather than assault. However, in sanctity of life terms, V has survived, and therefore it was not murder.

4 The example is in his essay "Moral Luck," in his collected volume also entitled *Moral Luck* (1981).

"stretched" to include the pilot's death. Therefore she will be guilty of murder. (Stretching intention in this way results in "constructed" liability.)[5]

It is worth considering two other examples of stretching intention to include unintended side-effects. The first is known as the *GBH rule.* D intentionally causes V GBH but does not intend to kill him. GBH generally involves injury serious enough to break bones or deeply penetrate the skin.[6] It might genuinely not have occurred to D that V might die; indeed, often a gangland punishment beating (such as the IRA's notorious practice of "kneecapping") is calibrated precisely to avoid killing. However, on this occasion D goes too far with the GBH and the victim dies from it. If the GBH had been serious enough for the death to have been "virtually certain," then it would be taken as intended like the case of the bomb on the plane. However, according to the GBH rule, even if the death is not virtually certain — indeed, even if the death is quite unlikely — then D's intention to commit GBH will be stretched to include the resulting death, and she will be guilty of murder. The argument behind this is that even if the death was unforeseeable, it was hardly a *complete* accident; to commit GBH on someone already requires a certain degree of cold-blooded contempt for V's welfare, a contempt that would seem qualitatively similar to the mindset required for murder.

D might still object: "It was just a punishment beating! The death was an accident! It was just bad luck that he died from his wounds!" Like the plane bomber, she might be tempted to plead guilty to manslaughter, but not to murder. One response to this would be to say that D's right to complain about being held responsible for bad luck will be "outweighed" by V's right to complain about dying through the GBH.

The second way of stretching intention is called "transferred malice" ("malice" is an old word for "intention"). D intentionally attempts to kill V1 by shooting at him. V1 ducks, and the bullet hits V2, killing him instantly. Now D did not intend to kill V2, and indeed she might have taken all sorts of precautions to avoid killing anyone else. But the law will describe her as intending to kill "some person," and V2 fits that description; so the intention is "transferred" from V1 to V2, according to the fiction that D had intended to kill V2 all along. Without this doctrine, then it might only be possible to charge D with the attempted murder of D1 (resulting in a much lesser sentence), leaving V2's death as a mere natural catastrophe.[7]

To understand how important transferred malice is, we may consider the random victims of a terrorist atrocity. The terrorist sets the bomb to go off at 12 noon the next day, and she has no idea who will be in the marketplace, and who among them will be killed or injured: if a particular person, Smith, is killed, then the terrorist could sincerely deny that she had intended to kill *Smith* ("I've never even met Smith!"). And yet clearly she had intended to kill "some people," and these people would be individuated at the moment of the blast.[8]

5 Note the two medical exceptions to the rule about oblique intention. In Section 5.4. we discussed *Bland* [1993]. Here the doctors intentionally withdrew artificial nutrition and hydration (ANH) from the comatose patient, and were virtually certain that he would die from the withdrawn ANH. In Section 10.3. we will discuss the case of *Re: A (conjoined twins)* [2000], where the doctors intentionally separated the twins, and were virtually certain that the weaker twin would die.

6 For the Crown Prosecution Service's definition of GBH, see: https://www.cps.gov.uk/legal-guidance/offences-against-person-incorporating-charging-standard

7 A fascinating but difficult case is *AG's ref No 3* [1994]. D stabbed his pregnant girlfriend. The girlfriend gave premature birth to a baby, V, who died three months later. The question is whether D could be charged with the murder of V under the transferred malice rule. The trial judge held that he could not, because the human foetus is not recognised as a person in law, and therefore the malice could not be transferred to it at the moment of attack. The Court of Appeal agreed that D was not guilty of murder, but found him guilty of manslaughter via UDAM — "unlawful dangerous act manslaughter." For the 3-month-old baby died as a direct result of the unlawful dangerous stabbing before its birth. We discuss UDAM below.

8 It is worth briefly mentioning one more stretched form of intention: the felony murder rule. This existed in English Law until abolished by the *Homicide Act* 1957. It still exists in most American jurisdictions. The

Proposal: first- and second-degree murder

In 2006, the Law Commission proposed a distinction between first and second-degree murder.[9] Their main concern was that the mandatory life sentence, considered politically necessary by Parliament, was unfair for certain murders. So they proposed that the less serious murders, called second-degree, would receive a discretionary sentence (that could still be a life sentence). The Commission's proposal was not accepted by Parliament, but it is still worth examining. Section 1.67 of the *Report* reads as follows:

> (1) First degree murder (mandatory life penalty)
> a. Killing intentionally.
> b. Killing where there was an intention to do serious injury, coupled with an awareness of a serious risk of causing death.
>
> (2) Second degree murder (discretionary life maximum penalty)
> c. Killing where the offender intended to do serious injury.
> d. Killing where the offender intended to cause some injury or a fear or risk of injury, and was aware of a serious risk of causing death.
> e. Killing in which there is a partial defence to what would otherwise be first degree murder.

First-degree murder would still include cases where D was aware of V's death as virtually certain (the bomb on the plane), but the second degree would allow the judge a much more nuanced assessment of culpability and circumstances. So (2) a. would include the kneecapping-gone-wrong, where the offender plausibly had no awareness of any serious risk of causing death. (2) b. would include a case where D throws V into the water as a prank, while being aware that D can't swim. Category (2) c. refers to the partial defences of "diminished responsibility" and "loss of control," and we discuss them in Chapter 10 on defences.

8.2 MANSLAUGHTER

A possible definition of manslaughter would be unintentional killing. However, there are again problems at the borders. At the upper border, we have already seen some cases of unintentional killing promoted to murder; below the lower border, some unintentional killings (such as Williams's lorry driver) will be freak accidents. This section is about how to capture those unintentional killings within the offence of manslaughter.

We can start with the slightly confusing distinction offered by English law, between "voluntary" and "involuntary" manslaughter. Voluntary manslaughter involves intentional killing which would be a case of *prima facie* murder, but which is reduced to manslaughter after D's successful presentation of the defence of "diminished responsibility" or of "loss of control." Again, we're going to leave these to Chapter 10, on defences. Instead, we're going to look at four types of *involuntary* manslaughter — but the word "involuntary" should not suggest that D had lost all control of her movements, as if she were suffering an epileptic fit.

---

basic idea is similar to the GBH rule, but wider: if D commits a felony (e.g. a bank robbery) and D kills V during the course of the felony, then D will be automatically guilty of murder, even if D had no intention to kill anyone, even if D's gun went off accidentally during the robbery.

9 Law Commission (2006) *Report 304: Murder, Manslaughter and Infanticide.*

Gross negligence manslaughter

We already discussed the first type in Section 4.1, with the case of *Adomako* [1993]. Adomako was the anaesthetist who failed to notice a dislodged oxygen tube in a routine, low-risk operation on a young, healthy patient, and as a direct result the patient died. Here the important distinction is between ordinary and gross negligence: ordinary negligence is a tort matter, usually resulting in a compensation pay-out; gross negligence is a criminal matter, resulting in a stigmatic criminal penalty (although in the case of Adomako, his prison sentence was suspended). It's not only a question of the degree of negligence — Adomako's failure to notice the tube was so simple and so stupid — it's also a sense that the family of Adomako's victim would be entitled to greater "satisfaction" than mere money, especially since compensation pay-outs are normally covered by the doctor's or the hospital's malpractice insurance policy. There is a sense that Adomako *did* something much worse than in cases of ordinary medical negligence.

The recent case of *Broughton* [2020] introduces another element. D supplied his girlfriend V with a drug during a music festival. V autonomously consumed the drug and died. In accordance with *Kennedy (No. 2)* [2005], D was not directly liable for the death, since V made the free, deliberate and informed decision to consume the drug, at her own risk (see discussion in Section 5.3). However, once it was clear that V was suffering, D failed to summon immediate medical assistance, and was charged with gross negligence manslaughter. D had a duty of care to V in virtue of their intimate relationship, and his breach of that duty of care prevented her from accessing timely medical assistance, and therefore caused her death. D appealed, arguing that it could not be proven that timely medical assistance would have saved V's life. In other words, it could not be proven that his breach of the duty of care was a necessary condition for the harm caused.

There are two interesting questions here. The first is about the burden of proof. The prosecution argued that this test was too onerous, and that it was enough that D had deprived V of a significant chance of survival. In other words, D's failure should be taken as having caused the death unless the *defence* can prove that it made no difference. In the end, the Court of Appeal put the burden on the prosecution, and granted the appeal. Second, there is a question of whether D's *attitude* should be relevant. Normally D's attitude is not relevant, as we discussed in Chapter 2. But his failure to summon timely medical assistance betrayed a callous indifference to V's welfare, and this might be enough to hold him more culpable, when all other considerations are equal. (There is a larger question about the callous indifference of those who distribute illegal class-A drugs.)

Unlawful Dangerous Act Manslaughter (UDAM)

This is a case of constructive liability, similar to the GBH rule. As we saw, under the GBH rule, if D intends to commit only GBH on V, but V ends up dying from the GBH, then D will be charged with murder. Under UDAM, if D was carrying out *any other kind* of dangerous and unlawful act against V, and V dies as a direct result, then D will be charged with manslaughter.

So in *Watson* [1989], D1 and D2 burgled the house of V, an 87-year-old man. There was a verbal confrontation, so the Ds should have noted V's age and frailty, before they ran off. Within 90 minutes of the burglary, V died as a result of the stress. Here we have the unlawful act of burglary, the evident danger posed to this particular V, and so the court could attribute the death to D1 and D2. Importantly, the dangerousness is objective: it does not matter what D thinks about the act or about the V, it is for the jury to determine whether a reasonable person would have considered the act dangerous, given the specific V, and given the circumstances. Importantly, it does not have to be a danger of *death*, but a danger of any kind of harm.[10] So in *Newbury* [1977] two 15-year-old boys threw a paving stone off a pedestrian bridge, aiming for a train passing underneath. The stone killed the train driver. The court accepted that the two boys were genuinely unaware of the danger that the stone presented to the driver — their intention had only been to have some fun watching the stone smash off the train. Nevertheless their conviction for manslaughter under UDAM was upheld, on the basis that a reasonable person would have been aware of the danger of harm.

In contrast, in *Dawson* [1985], V was a 60-year-old petrol station attendant who looked fit enough for his age. A group of robbers invaded the petrol station with a replica gun, but the attendant sounded an alarm, and the robbers ran away. Later they were apprehended and convicted of attempted robbery. However, V had a heart condition and suffered a fatal heart attack as a direct result of the robbery. The robbers were acquitted of manslaughter, because the heart condition would have been invisible to the reasonable person.

UDAM is controversial since it leaves quite a bit of room for luck and strict liability (see Section 4.6.). Watson the burglar may well have been apprehended after a similar burglary on another elderly resident who happened to survive. Is it fair to impute the death to Watson? UDAM is therefore similar to the "thin skull" principle, according to which one "takes one's victim as one finds them." See our discussion of *Blaue* [1975] case in Section 5.2. As with other cases of strict liability, the standard response to Watson's complaint would be "You didn't have to burgle anybody!" Strict liability is to be understood as part of the deterrent value of the criminal law.

The controversy becomes more acute in the case of a "one-punch killing," such as *Mallett* [1972]. D quarrelled with his neighbour V, and punched V in the face. Falling backwards from the punch, V hit his head on a paving stone and died. As an assault, it was unlawful and dangerous. But again we have the problem with the scope of the danger: clearly there was an obvious danger of breaking V's *nose*, but there wasn't an obvious danger of V being *killed*.

Child et al (2022, p. 460) have this to say about constructive manslaughter:

> In our discussion of attempt, we conceded both (i) the impossibility of eradicating outcome luck from the criminal law, and that (ii) outcome luck could have implications for the quantum of punishment. But luck is too potent a factor in the imposition of liability for constructive manslaughter. It turns a trivial assault into a serious crime meriting a custodial sentence. Ideally there should be a clear and vivid danger that death might occur — but too often the connection between the unlawfulness and the danger is tenuous. Mallett was a trivial assault between neighbours, with no intention to use serious violence.

However, the Law Commission (2006) were happy to keep UDAM, but they advocate raising the knowledge threshold from "some injury" to "serious injury":

> 3.47. However, we are not recommending that manslaughter, in the absence of an intention to injure, should require the awareness of a risk of serious injury. This is because we believe that such a limitation would introduce excessive complexity into the law. The jury would have to be told that whilst a criminal act that causes death and which was intended by D to do some injury is manslaughter, if the criminal act was one that D was only aware might cause some injury, D could only be convicted of manslaughter if he or she was aware that it might cause serious injury.[11]

10 The low danger threshold was stipulated in the case of *Church* [1966].
11 Law Commission (2006) *Report 304: Murder, Manslaughter and Infanticide.* See https://www.lawcom.gov.uk/

Corporate manslaughter

In law, companies (corporations) are legal individuals: they can sign contracts, they can sue and be sued, and they can own property. However, there is a long-standing problem in holding a corporation criminally responsible for the death of one of its workers while carrying out her duties. And yet there were 123 workers killed in work-related accidents (mostly avoidable) in the year 2021–22.[12] This is a real problem when corporations influence and often govern so many aspects of our lives.

The traditional approach is to hold the executive director criminally responsible according to the "principle of identification," which requires the prosecution to prove that the corporation was no more than an extension of the "mind and will" of the executive director. Needless to say, before 2007 there were very few prosecutions, and these were typically small family-run businesses where the "mind and will" could be clearly identified. It was much more difficult to convict larger corporations (and they could hire better lawyers).

The situation was partly remedied with the *Health and Safety at Work Act* 1974, but contravening a regulation did not carry the same stigmatic power of the criminal law, and so Parliament continued to face pressure until the *Corporate Manslaughter and Corporate Homicide Act* was passed in 2007.[13] The CMCHA requires the prosecution to prove that the corporation had a duty of care (e.g. to its employees, or clients, or to the users of its premises), that it breached its duty, and that the breach made a substantial causal contribution to the death. The breach in question does not have to be attributable to one culpable director, but can be a general fault in the management or the organisation of the company. Importantly, the CMCHA criminalises second-order negligence: that is, attitudes and policies that would encourage employees to disregard health and safety regulations. Individual company directors remain vulnerable to a personal penalty (such as a prison sentence), but only if the gross negligence can be attributed directly to them.

Nevertheless, prosecutions under the CMCHA remain uncommon (a total of 29 since 2007), mainly because of the difficulty in proving the required negligent breach (Roper, 2022, p. 296). And a disproportionate number of convictions (86%) are still of small companies (Roper, 2022, p. 298). In addition, while the CMCHA was meant to allow a more stigmatic response to corporate manslaughter, the penalty is typically a fine. If the fine is too low, this can be predicted and absorbed as a business expense, set against the cost savings already earned by the company through its negligence; the penalty will therefore lose most of its stigmatic value. If the company is simply wound up, or if a fine is high enough to drive them out of business, this might provide some satisfaction for the victim's family, but the employees and possibly clients will be the main casualties.[14] One more problem: if the organisation in question is a public body (such as the NHS), then the fine will ultimately have to be paid by the taxpayer, from funds designed to benefit the public.

There are two more promising penalties. The first, cited in the CMCHA, is a publicity order, requiring the company to describe the events and the death, as well as the steps they are taking to improve their policies and procedures, and such a description would have to be on its website, in a local newspaper or in a trade magazine. The second penalty has been

12 Health and Safety Executive, "Health and safety statistics; key figures for Great Britain": https://www.hse.gov.uk/statistics/

13 The two crimes in the Act's title refer to the crime in England and Wales and the crime in Scotland, respectively. For our purposes we will speak only of "corporate manslaughter."

14 Typically, if a corporation is responsible for manslaughter, they may well be already in financial difficulty, and its cost-cutting efforts probably led to the negligence. So a fine could predictably ruin them.

proposed by Fisse and Braithwaite (1993): a kind of community service order. These are available to the courts in the punishment of *individual* offenders, and they could be re-purposed for corporate offenders as well. Not only would it be a visible demonstration of penance, but the particular community work could be selected for its expressive power as a kind of reparation to the individual or to his community.

Causing the death of a child or vulnerable adult

This is our first look at domestic abuse, and we will return to it later in this chapter. The offence of "causing death" is spelled out in the *Domestic Violence, Crime and Victims Act* (DVCVA) 2004. In the paradigm case, there might be a mother and a father, and their child dies through abuse or by neglect. In some cases, the mother or the father or both can be directly charged for assault or for parental neglect, but in other cases there might not be enough evidence of who did it (or of who assisted whom to do it), and both of them might have to be acquitted. So this legislation was intended to fill this gap, at least partly.

A typical case involves a father ("P") seriously injuring his child ("V") through intentional violence, and the "bystander" mother ("D") fails to try to prevent him. Section 5 reads as follows:

> (1) D is guilty of an offence if— …
>
> (c) at that time there was a significant risk of serious physical harm being caused to V by the unlawful act of [P], and
>
> (d) …
>
> (i) D was, or ought to have been, aware of the risk mentioned in paragraph (c),
>
> (ii) D failed to take such steps as he could reasonably have been expected to take to protect V from the risk, and
>
> (iii) the act occurred in circumstances of the kind that D foresaw or ought to have foreseen.

The wording of the DVCVA is interesting. The threshold of proof beyond reasonable doubt still applies when trying to find the direct cause of the death — and the Act will not help with this. If there is enough proof, P would be guilty of murder under the GBH rule or at least of manslaughter under UDAM or gross negligence. The DVCVA's novel feature is to allow the penalisation of the *non-complicit* bystander.

If we imagine a typical case: P the father abuses the child to death. D the mother is not legally complicit in the sense described in Chapter 7 — she did not intentionally assist or encourage the father to abuse anyone. As such she would normally be an innocent bystander, in the same that pedestrians watching a jewellery store heist on the High Street would not be liable for failing to prevent or to report a crime. However, given that she has an explicit duty of care to the child, then the question now becomes whether she "was, or ought to have been, aware of the risk" and "failed to take such steps." Crucially, this is a matter of negligence. Whether she did or did not foresee the circumstances, whether she was or was not aware of the risk, will be irrelevant if a reasonable person would have foreseen or been aware.

Is this fair? From the point of view of the child V, certainly. But there are other contextual factors in play. For example, D may well herself be a victim of P's physical violence, and be understandably afraid of the consequences of defying him, betraying him to the authorities, or trying to leave with the child. The occasion when the police learn of D's violence against the child is often not the first such occasion, and so it raises questions about how much the social services, or even neighbours and families, might know, and how much they should communicate their suspicions to the police themselves. Herring (2007) criticises this statute for seeking to blame negligent mothers, whereas the law should be seeking a comprehensive solution to protect mothers and their children together from violent men. In addition to Herring's concern, we could say that the DVCVA caters to an unhealthy tabloid sexism that tends impulsively to blame mothers.

A response to Herring comes in the case of *Khan (Uzuma)* [2009], where the judge stressed that an abused bystander would only be guilty under Section 5 of the DVCVA if she had failed to take *reasonable* steps to protect the child, where reasonableness would be assessed with explicit reference to the mother's circumstances and attributes.

8.3 ASSAULT

For the rest of this chapter we will be looking at non-fatal offences against the person. Again, bear in mind our rejection of the assault/battery distinction in English law — we will speak only about "assault," and when necessary we will distinguish between different kinds of assault (degrees of harm), as well as threatened assault. We are also not paying too much attention to the *degrees* of harm, as manifest in Sections 18, 20 and 47 of the *Offences Against the Person Act* (OAPA) 1861.

An obvious kind of assault is punching or hitting or kicking someone etc., with or without a weapon, and thereby causing physical and psychological harm. But assault need not be physically harmful, and can amount instead to an intrusion on one's personal space: it can involve unwelcome touching, including sexual touching. (In some cases, e.g. crowded trains that one enters freely, one cannot object to a certain amount of contact.) Assault can also include stalking and harassment, although these matters are usually dealt with under the *Protection from Harassment Act* 1997.[15]

Assault can also include reckless infection with a transmissible disease. In *Dica* [2004] D knew he was infected with HIV, and did not mention this to V before she consented to unprotected sex with him. V subsequently developed HIV too.[16]

Consent to assault

Assume D intentionally assaults a competent adult V, and V consents to the assault. When D is arrested and charged with assault, can he cite V's consent as a defence? The answer: it depends. If the assault is part of "horseplay," then yes. Such horseplay includes schoolyard fights as well as sports such as boxing. The implication is that such horseplay is not seriously

15 Before this Act, the leading case was *Ireland and Burstow* [1997]. D and V were involved in a short romantic relationship, which V ended. D was unhappy with this, and engaged in a campaign of harassment over several months. The question for the court was whether this behaviour could be classified as *harmful* in the sense of the *OAPA* 1861. The House of Lords answered the question by calling it "psychiatric harm." Importantly, the *Protection from Harassment Act* defines harassment and stalking as a conduct crime rather than a result crime — that means that the fault does not rely on the victim suffering more or less harm, psychiatric or otherwise.

16 In Chapter 9.2, we mention this case as a possible instance of deception that would vitiate the consent to sex, thereby making it both assault and rape. Such an argument would be based on the simple hypothetical: if V had known about D's infection, would she have consented? However, the Court of Appeal did not consider D's omission to comprise deception about the "nature of the act" — D was offering sexual intercourse, that is what V consented to, and that is what she got. Whether there might be unwanted *consequences* of the sex was a separate question.

harmful, and even when serious harm results, all participants had already consented to the risk of serious harm. Voluntary tattoos and piercings would also be justified by consent. One extension of the horseplay/ tattooing scenario is *Wilson* [1996], where V asked her husband D to brand his initials on her buttock with a heated knife. Even though this was genuinely harmful, and V needed hospital treatment, she was taken as having sufficiently understood the risks.

In contrast, in *Melin* [2019], D was impersonating a doctor and offering Botox injections. Two women had "consented," and suffered serious consequences, and the court found that D's impersonation had vitiated their consent. The object of their consent included the identity of the injector; that is, what they had consented to was a single package "Botox injection by a qualified doctor." Had they known that D was not a qualified doctor, they would not have consented.

So far this is basic liberalism: people should be free to do whatever they like with and to each other, as long as there is no deception or coercion. Some might not see branded buttocks as quite so attractive as Mrs Wilson did, but the point about liberalism is that each competent adult is free to seek and define their own conception of well-being.

What limits might there be, however? One set of limits has to do with certain public displays of suffering and death, as in the case of duelling and gladiatorial contests. Here the thought is that the consent of the participants is overridden by the risk of the moral debasement of the consenting spectators and of society more generally. Another limit (at least in the United Kingdom) has to do with euthanasia, where the two worries are that (i) that temporarily vulnerable (but still competent) patients will request the service without fully understanding what they are consenting to, and (ii) the onus should be on the state to offer support to vulnerable patients (including psychotherapy for depression and palliative care for the pain of terminal illness), rather than offering them the means to die.[17]

A more extreme limit is defined in the *Female Genital Mutilation Act* 2003. Although the Act is mainly designed to protect minors, it also prohibits competent adults from requesting it. There is a real question here about the small difference between some of the more exotic piercings (for example, to genitalia) on the one hand, to which one can legally consent, and adult FGM on the other hand, to which one cannot. One response to this comparison would be to say that piercings are an autonomy-*enhancing* form of (artistic) self-expression, whereas FGM is an autonomy-*denying* procedure of systematic patriarchal oppression. The paternalistic thought is that even if a competent adult woman requests FGM (even assuming that it is performed by a qualified doctor who minimises the health risks), she does not sufficiently understand how her status as a woman is being undermined in the process.

An important case here is *Brown* [1994]. A group of competent adult men were engaged in various sado-masochistic practices to which they all consented. But the House of Lords, by a narrow margin of 3 to 2, ruled out the possibility of consent as a defence. Interestingly, the events not only took place behind closed doors, but — unlike *Wilson* — nobody required any medical assistance after the fact. It is hard therefore to square this with the liberalism that informs so much else in the criminal law. In reading the judgements, one is struck by the evident distaste for the men's activities, and the choice of words is such as to invite criminalisation. As Lord Templeman famously declared (at 237): "Pleasure derived from the infliction of pain is an evil thing. Cruelty is uncivilised." But without demonstrable physical or

17 We do not have the space to discuss the hugely complicated euthanasia debate here. Suffice to say that countries such as the Netherlands and Canada believe in offering autonomous patients the choice to die (under certain conditions), while implementing safeguards to address the worries cited here.

psychological harm, and without a complaint from any of the participants themselves, it is not clear if Lord Templeman's stipulation is enough to support a general prohibition. The *Brown* judgement is reminiscent of the disgust-driven prohibition against private consensual adult homosexuality before legalisation in the *Sexual Offences Act* 1967.[18]

The spirit of the *Brown* decision was confirmed in the case of *BM* [2018]. A tattooist and body piercer was charged with causing GBH with the intent to cause GBH. In Horder's discussion (2022, p. 169), he criticises the judgement for omitting any empirical studies about what makes the putatively vulnerable clients vulnerable. Instead, surmises Horder, the Court of Appeal was motivated by disgust in response to both the practices as well as the practitioner; if a licensed middle-class doctor were to administer the same piercings, it would probably have been much less objectionable. *Brown* has also recently been incorporated into Section 71 of the *Domestic Abuse Act* 2021, entitled "Consent to serious harm for sexual gratification not a defence." The legislation was designed to deal with the recent occurrences of the "rough sex" defence: that is: V dies during sex, and D defends himself with reference to her consent to certain dangerous sexual practices such as choking. We discuss this Act in more detail below.[19]

Michelle Madden Dempsey (2013) defended the majority verdict in *Brown*. It is true that the Lords' disgust was illiberal, off-putting and irrelevant, she admits; but their point about the degradation of cruelty was important. There are times when a person should not be allowed to consent to their own degradation, because it simply cannot contribute to their well-being, regardless of their sincere search for pleasure. True consent should not only express the consenter's will at that given moment, but also her longer-term concern with her own well-being. In addition, for consent to "work," it has to be *taken* by the consentee as a reason to act, and this implies that the consentee proceeds on the basis of an indirect concern for the consenter's longer-term well-being. If the consentee merely takes the consent as permission to act on his own sadistic desires, then the consent has not "worked." "In such cases, despite B's consent, A's conduct nonetheless takes B as its victim; for, in virtue of A's sadistic explanatory reasons, B's consent failed to bear transformative normative force on the moral quality of A's conduct" (Dempsey, 2013, p. 24).

Society has a responsibility to protect its citizens from their own worst impulses, *both* as givers and takers of cruelty, however consenting the participants claim to be. The question then is whether Dempsey would propose a ban on boxing for the same reason. Liberals can still support boxing not just because of the participants' consent, but also because of its essential value as a public competitive sport (alongside other less harmful kinds), and its value as a form of self-expression — enough to counterbalance the overt cruelty.

We will return to many of these issues about consent in the next chapter, on sexual offences.

18 There was a famous debate between Lord Devlin and HLA Hart in the 1950s, Hart as the liberal, and Devlin as the "legal moralist," supporting society's right to prohibit practices that society deemed immoral. See the Stanford Encyclopedia of Philosophy entry on "The Limits of Law": https://plato.stanford.edu/entries/law-limits/

19 In its wide-ranging consultations, the drafters of the *Domestic Abuse Act* 2021 received detailed evidence of the rough sex defence from the campaign group "We Can't Consent to This": https://wecantconsenttothis.uk/.

For example, in *Broadhurst* [2019], D cited V's consent to rough sex as a defence against his GBH-rule murder charge — although in the end he pleaded guilty to gross negligence manslaughter for failing to summon medical assistance once she had started bleeding to death.

In his discussion of the new Act, David Ormerod (2021, p. 425) is sceptical about the effect of this provision, since D will still be able to claim that he lacked sufficient intent to cause GBH (thus avoiding the GBH rule), or that he did not sufficiently envisage any risk of harm arising (thus avoiding UDAM), given V's consent. (And usually we only have D's assertion that V consented.)

8.4 DOMESTIC ABUSE

In the remainder of this chapter we're going to look at domestic abuse, followed by the particular case of abusing someone so much as to drive them to suicide.

For much of this book we have been looking at discrete offences: one individual harms another individual on a single occasion. The antecedent relationship between them is normally not relevant. However fair and appropriate this paradigm might be for the majority of offences, including sexual offences, it fails to capture the particular kinds of wrong that make up domestic abuse.

For this reason alone the recent *Domestic Abuse Act* 2021 is to be welcomed. The Act has a commendably subtle and wide-ranging definition of abuse in Section 1.[20]

> (3) Behaviour is "abusive" if it consists of any of the following —
>
> (a) physical or sexual abuse; (b) violent or threatening behaviour; (c) controlling or coercive behaviour; (d) economic abuse (see subsection (4)); (e) psychological, emotional or other abuse;
>
> and it does not matter whether the behaviour consists of a single incident or a course of conduct.
>
> (4) "Economic abuse" means any behaviour that has a substantial adverse effect on B's ability to —
>
> (a) acquire, use or maintain money or other property, or (b) obtain goods or services.
>
> (5) For the purposes of this Act [D]'s behaviour may be behaviour "towards" [V] despite the fact that it consists of conduct directed at another person (for example, [V]'s child).[21]

We do not have the space to do justice to the legal complexity here, since it concerns other areas of the law (e.g. family law, housing law, mental health law) as well as other organs of the state (e.g. social services, healthcare, education). So we limit ourselves to a few philosophical points. To make things manageable, we're going to focus on the domestic abuse committed by a man against a woman, both cohabitees, and taking place within a long-term physically intimate relationship, and against a background of widespread patriarchal norms.[22]

Domestic abuse is challenging to investigate and to prosecute, in that so much of it takes place in private, without third-party testimony, and too often the case collapses into "his word against hers," falling well short of proof beyond a reasonable doubt. In addition, the relationship may be quite impenetrable to outsiders, and so it is too easy for outsiders to say

20 Already the wider concept of "domestic abuse" is better than narrower "domestic violence," as in the *Domestic Violence, Crime and Victims Act* 2004. The *Domestic Abuse Act* also includes the "controlling or coercive behaviour" first introduced in Section 76 of the *Serious Crime Act* 2015.

21 An "overarching factsheet" describing the new 2021 measures is available at the following website: https://www.gov.uk/government/publications/domestic-abuse-bill-2020-factsheets/domestic-abuse-bill-2020-overarching-factsheet

22 We feel entitled to focus the discussion in this way because the great majority of cases involve males abusing females. Of course some women abuse their heterosexual male partners, and abuse also takes place between homosexual couples (although without the same gender-based power dynamic), and we certainly do not mean to downplay this. Abuse also takes place between non-intimate friends or roommates, between non-cohabitating intimate couples; there is the distinct phenomenon of "elder abuse"; and there is the evil of child abuse. We do not have space to examine all these to the proper depth, since that would require much nuanced sociological and psychological discussion, including an understanding of how social services work, both in theory and in practice.

that it is none of their business, or to blame the victim for remaining in the incomprehensible relationship.

The central problem of conceptualising domestic abuse has to do with the *extended two-fold domestic context.* Let us explain. We say "two-fold domestic" because "domestic" has a spatial meaning and a relational meaning. First, the spatial meaning has to do with the *home.* A home is not just a building or a flat, it is a refuge. It is the place where I prepare myself to go off to fight the good fight in the world; it is the place where I retreat when things go wrong in the world. It is the place where I sleep and recover my strength and tend my wounds. It is the place where I keep my personal possessions, where I can plan and fantasise and reminisce. It is the place where I can relax, where I can remove the masks and the performances from the day and just be myself. It is the place that I decorate in ways that express my identity. Finally, it is the place where I can forbid entry to all but the closest friends and family members.

All these richer meanings of the home are intensified when two people decide to share it, as well as share their sexual life, and this increases the vulnerability of both. When the man abuses the woman in the home, its psychological effect, its impact on the woman's life, is horribly magnified by all the above sources of meaning that make it her home. If the abuse persists, she will soon have to contemplate leaving her home, perhaps with limited realistic alternatives (perhaps exacerbated by a lack of independent sources of income); and she will have to contemplate abandoning the huge emotional investment she made in the place.

Second, the *relational* meaning of "domestic" has to do with the couple's long-term intimate relationship. At some point in this relationship, if not now, there was trust and love, enough for them to move in together and be an "item," to think in the first-person plural, to plan for an indefinite future together, to help each other with all the travails "out there." Like the physical space, the intimate relationship was also a refuge. So when the abuse comes from the intimate partner of all people, its effect is compounded by the sense of personal betrayal and humiliation, and by the transformation of the previously loving partner into a stranger full of contempt, callousness and possibly violence.

Third, we described the domestic context as "extended," and this has to do with the essential existence of the relationship — and of the abuse — through time. At several junctures in this book, we have pointed out how the law treats offences as discrete occurrences: did D commit this offence against V on this occasion? Did he do it intentionally or recklessly? Does he have any excuses or justifications? D's antecedent relationship to V is usually irrelevant. However, when it comes to understanding one instance of abuse, its full meaning is often only evident within the context of the particular on-going relationship between D and V. Indeed, the one instance of abuse might not be very serious on its own; its seriousness may lie precisely in its repetition, in the accumulation of the wrong over time. In the extreme, the abuser might not need any violence at all, might not need to explicitly threaten violence, because the victim now "knows her place." This extended aspect of domestic abuse prompted the legislation prohibiting "controlling or coercive behaviour," while recognising that such control might indeed be exerted without violence or even threats of violence. The control might be ultimately psychological, combined with control over the victim's access to money and to social contacts. But central to such control is its extension through time.

There is a question about the *mens rea* of the systematic abuser. The first abusive encounter may require a particularly high dose of anger and ill will in order to overcome the natural reluctance to harm a person one previously cared about. With time and the normalisation of the abuse, the meaning of the *mens rea* might be slowly transformed in either direction. On the one hand, each new assault compounds the evil of the first, and makes the abuser even more deserving of forcible restraint and punishment for the total quantum of abuse. On the other hand, the normalisation might actually *reduce* the amount of ill will required to overcome any inhibitions, to the point where the control (or even violence) has become casual, and the man rationalises it by describing it as "the way our marriage works." As such, as Tadros points out (2005, p. 216), if the criminal law investigates a single case of late-relationship "casual" or "routine" assault without enquiring into context, it might find a *mens rea* that was not particularly culpable, indeed a *mens rea* that might even alternate with moments of genuine tenderness and remorse (remorse understood in the abuser's terms, of course).

Because of the opacity to outsiders, it is hard to investigate and prosecute domestic abuse, especially when the victim herself is unwilling to cooperate with any investigation, and unwilling to complain against her partner.[23] Moreover, the relentless and systematic nature of much domestic abuse can slowly wear down the victim's will, not only to undermine the options of resistance and realistic escape plans, but also to the point of bleak resignation, under the spirit of "better the devil you know." There are various technical terms that have crept from the psychotherapeutic literature into popular culture to capture this: learned helplessness, adaptive preferences, and the "battered woman syndrome."[24]

The "why doesn't she leave?" question is complicated and often insensitive, since it implies V's consent at *some* level — not to the abuse as such, but to the whole situation, which may remain less bad than other risky and hard-to-imagine alternative futures. Very often she doesn't leave — because she doesn't have enough money to set up a new life; because she thinks it would be a much worse option for the children; because he would come and find her anyway and there would be consequences; because her local community would not believe her, or would blame her; or because she just doesn't have the strength.[25]

Abusing someone to the point of suicide

Now consider *Dhaliwal* [2006]. A husband D had verbally and emotionally abused his wife V for many years. One day V commits suicide. Clearly D's abuse had made things a lot worse for V, but could we say that D *caused* V's suicide? Here we're picking up a discussion from Chapter 5 on causation.

In the end the Court of Appeal held that there was not enough evidence of such a causal link. There were two problems with the prosecution case. (i) The prosecution tried to claim that the *most recent* act of abuse had caused the psychological injury, and that the injury had led to the suicide. But the court found this implausible. It would have been more appropriate (and a better strategy) to claim that the *cumulative* abuse, over many years, had caused the psychological injury. Or at least that the years of abuse had been a relevant condition that made the most recent abuse the "last straw." However, the accumulation of offences goes against the "discrete act" approach of most criminal law. (ii) The prosecution tried to describe V's

23 In the United States there is a lively debate about the policy of "mandatory arrest." This would allow the police, with enough evidence, to arrest a suspected abuser without waiting for the victim to complain or even testify. The question is whether this is enough to protect the victim, or whether (i) it risks paternalistic interference with the wife's autonomy and privacy, (ii) and it risks making the situation worse for the victim in the future. A softer form of "mandatory arrest" would be a "mandatory risk assessment," i.e. with or without the consent of the victim. See Leisenring (2008) for discussion of the American context.

24 "Battered person syndrome" is in the International Classification of Diseases (ICD) (9th vol.), but is not in the Diagnostic and Statistical Manual (DSM) of Mental Disorders (5th edition). Those psychiatrists guided by the latter tend to describe the phenomenon as a kind of post-traumatic stress disorder. The Canadian Supreme Court recognised "battered woman syndrome" in the case of *R v Lavallee* [1990]. One extreme outcome of extended domestic abuse was *R v Ahluwalia* [1993], where a wife killed her abusive husband in his sleep. In Chapter 10, on defences, we ask what defences might be available to Ahluwalia.

25 The Covid pandemic made the situation a good deal worse for domestic abuse, with intimate partners trapped indoors, often with the additional stresses of home-schooling and job losses.

psychological injury, and yet the court deemed that it was not an injury that would be recognised by *psychiatrists*, and therefore could not constitute "bodily harm" in the meaning of the *OAPA* 1861.

Stannard (2010, p. 534) has highlighted the absurdity: if I give someone a slight push and it unexpectedly kills them, that is manslaughter, but if I hound them to their death by a sustained course of psychological and emotional abuse it is not.

Part of the problem with suicide is metaphysical, though: insofar as the wife was still a competent adult despite her psychological injury, she remained free to act or not act on certain reasons. There were intelligible reasons for her to be unhappy; the same reasons might have motivated her to run away. But suicide is a special case, since it is stubbornly, horrifyingly *opaque*: it is hard to imagine scenarios where the reasons "add up" to leave the desperate agent with the thought that she has no alternative.

That's part of what makes the experience of the suicide victim's family so awful. Perhaps a captured spy would have an overwhelming reason to commit "rational" suicide as the only way to avoid torture and betrayal. Perhaps a person with a painful terminal illness would have an overwhelming reason to commit suicide to avoid further suffering and indignity. But short of those two exceptions, suicide is rarely rational like other decisions because an essential presupposition of a rational decision is that the decision-maker will survive and thereby *benefit* from the decision (or at least come to know whether it was the right decision or not). And a natural response for the victim's family is to say "There must have been other options."[26]

Horder and McGowan (2006, p. 1043) argue that it would have been better for the *Dhaliwal* prosecution to seek gross negligence manslaughter rather than UDAM. This would start with the husband's clear duty of care to his wife, and his clear breach of the duty of care. This would have two key advantages:

> First, ... the grossness of negligent mistreatment of a spouse or partner is quite naturally regarded as a matter of degree, in which the cumulative nature of the effects is of central relevance. By way of contrast, the aggregation of the effects of individual offences against the person, so that the whole can be said to be greater than the sum of the parts, while possible, is an exceptional or unusual way to view such offences. Secondly, the grossness of mistreatment of a spouse or partner is not confined to the impact of specific non-fatal offences against her. It can include all forms of mistreatment including, for example, violence towards children of the family, or the imposition of degrading living conditions on the victim or on her family. (p. 1045) [27]

Munro and Aitkin (2018, p. 737) argue that criminal law might be able to move on from the conceptual limits with which it dealt with *Dhaliwal*, precisely because of three important developments. (i) The 2017 case of a man (Nicholas Allen) who launched a six-month campaign of threats and harassment against his ex-partner to the point where she committed suicide. He was found guilty of UDAM;[28] (ii) The offence of coercive and controlling behaviour, with its explicit focus on the longer-term act description (even if Munro and Aitkin lament the continuing focus on the abuser rather than on the abused); (iii) The World Health Organisation's new category of "Complex Post-Traumatic Stress Disorder" in its International Statistical Classification of Diseases and Related Health Problems (ICD), which came into effect in

26 On the question of the rationality of suicide, see Cowley (2006).

27 More recently, Lodge (2020) is more optimistic about using UDAM in the context of *Dhaliwal*, and argues that under the principle of fair labelling, it better captures the defendant's abusive intentions.

28 See: https://www.theguardian.com/uk-news/2017/jul/28/stalker-jailed-manslaughter-former-partner-killed-herself-nicholas-allen-justene-reece

2022.[29] Munro and Aitkin acknowledge a certain risk of "pathologising" the victim's response to sustained abuse rather than seeing it as a *normal* response to a sustained threat against psychological health. However, they are optimistic that the new category will allow psychiatric recognition of the effects of abuse to ground an UDAM charge.

Finally, a more recent case of "driving" someone to suicide is *Wallace* [2018] albeit not as a result of abuse. D and V were in an intimate relationship, and V announced his intention to leave. In a jealous fury, D poured acid on V's face while he slept. In addition to gross disfigurement, V was severely paralysed and in constant pain. He returned to his native Belgium, where he eventually requested and was given lawful euthanasia. The legal question is whether D caused V's death, and if so, whether this was a case of the GBH rule resulting in a murder charge or of UDAM resulting in a manslaughter charge. The original jury found D guilty of murder, but the Court of Appeal ordered a retrial, at which the jury acquitted D of both murder and manslaughter. This seems right. As Simester (2019) emphasised, it was the Belgian doctor who was the one who (lawfully) killed V; the doctor made a free, deliberate and informed act to accept V's request, and this broke the chain of causation and committed the original acid-pouring to legal history. However, D was still given a life sentence (with a minimum term of 12 years) for "throwing a corrosive fluid with intent to do GBH," in accordance with the *OAPA* 1861, Section 29.

If V had simply committed suicide, D's counsel accepted that it might have been possible to describe D as causing the death; although even here V could still be described as himself making a free, deliberate and informed decision to kill himself, in the same way as in *Kennedy (No. 2)* [2007], V was found to have made the free, deliberate and informed decision to inject the drug (and die from an overdose) that D had provided him (as we saw in Chapter 5 on causation). And while there might be an argument in *Kennedy (No. 2)* that V was not fully free because of his pre-injection addiction, and that D was fully aware of both the addiction and the risk of overdose and death, this would not apply in *Wallace*.

However, the *Wallace* case remains troubling; there is a sense that the offence of "throwing fluid" does not "add up" to the horrifying consequences on V. Although D only intended to disfigure and could not predict the paralysis and the pain, her guiding intention was clearly to *ruin his life*. Regardless of whether he eventually requested euthanasia, committed suicide on his own, or continued living, she surely succeeded. And yet English law is only able to capture consequences such as physical and psychological wounds or harm, and these make no essential reference to V's life. The implication is that it is *up to V* to come to terms with the wounds and remake his life accordingly, as the victim of any natural catastrophe has to do. So no, it would be wrong to say that in *Wallace* D "drove V to suicide"; but at the same time D did try to ruin his life, and she succeeded. Although this consideration was reflected in her eventual sentence, her offence did not capture enough of what she did to V.

29 See: https://www.who.int/standards/classifications/classification-of-diseases

CHAPTER 9

SEXUAL OFFENCES

This chapter marks the second of two chapters on particular areas of UK criminal law. One advantage of this area is that all the relevant offences have been brought together into a single statute — the *Sexual Offences Act* 2003 (henceforth the SOA 2003) — and so there is a much clearer starting place and focus than with, say, recklessness or complicity. In addition, the statute is interesting because it is recent enough to address contemporary issues, but also old enough to have generated a fair body of academic commentary and case law about its application.

Although the SOA 2003 defines a number of sexual offences, starting with rape, in this chapter we will generally focus on *sexual assault*, for a number of reasons. First, this act description is broader than rape. Second, we want to avoid the strongly emotive associations of the word rape (and the word "rapist"), in order to focus on the philosophical issues, and especially the problem of defining consent. Third, we are impressed by the authors of the Canadian Criminal Code, who abandoned "rape" for a general offence of "sexual assault."[1] Partly this has to do with avoiding the stigma of the word in the victim's self-understanding, partly it has to do with juries' occasional reluctance to convict defendants of something as stigmatic as rape, especially under the influence of classist and racist prejudices.[2]

We will take a generic schema of a male perpetrator (D) and a female victim (V), while acknowledging that assaults can take place between anybody of either gender. The chosen genders are partly for clarity in the use of pronouns, as elsewhere in this book, but also to reflect the statistically overwhelming number of cases of male-on-female sexual assaults. Given the low reporting and conviction rates, given the widespread pervasive influence of patriarchal norms (and the overlap with underreported male-on-female abuse, as described in the last chapter), we feel that male-on-female sexual assault deserves greater priority.[3] One last point about our terminology: some object to the word "victim" in the context of sexual assault, since it connotes helpless passivity; "survivor" would be preferable. We agree, but again, for the sake of consistency, we will stay with "victim" and "V," merely as a label to distinguish her from D the Defendant.

The SOA 2003 is a huge piece of legislation, with many complicated rules, and we don't have the space to discuss most of them. For example, there are important rules about children, but we consider these mainly a matter for psychologists and paediatricians and social workers rather than philosophers. We're also not going to discuss sex work and pornography, since this is a complicated social problem that would require a better understanding of social policy.

1 Section 271 of the *Canadian Criminal Code*. Section 272 describes sexual assault with a weapon, or via threats to a third party, or involving bodily harm. Section 273 then describes other forms of aggravated sexual assault, such as disfigurement or a threat to the life of V.

2 One notorious "nice man from a good family" was Brock Allen Turner in California, who was awarded a mere six-month sentence (of which he only served three months) for the rape of an unconscious woman. One of the judges argued explicitly that it would be unfair to stigmatise him as a "rapist."
See: https://en.wikipedia.org/wiki/People_v._Turner

3 See Barr and Topping (2021) "Fewer than one in 60 rape cases lead to charge in England and Wales." *The Guardian*. https://www.theguardian.com/society/2021/may/23/fewer-than-one-in-60-cases-lead-to-charge-in-england-and-wales

DOI: 10.4324/9781003351887-9

9.1 WHY SEXUAL ASSAULT IS A SPECIAL KIND OF OFFENCE

In choosing to focus on "sexual assault," this might give the impression that we are talking about just another kind of assault, something that could have been included in the list of assaults described in the *Offences Against the Person Act* 1861. However, we have to realise right away that the sexual element transforms the contact into something very different, since it invokes so many deep social meanings associated with sex (as well as invoking widespread misogynistic tropes). Unlike ordinary assault, sexual assault may not even involve much physical injury. So it was right to codify sexual assault alongside other sexual offences in new legislation.

Philosophically, the most challenging aspect of sexual assault has to do with the central role of the mental states of V and D: does V consent to the sexual contact, and does D reliably know that V is consenting? With most other crimes, and with most assaults — if D punches V or steals V's handbag — the *prima facie* wrongness and harm is immediately visible to witnesses without knowing anything about the mental states of those involved. Of course, the picture might be more complicated, but the prima facie wrongness is a good starting point for the police investigation and criminal trial. Some cases of sexual assault, those involving sheer physical force, are equally obvious in their wrongness. However it is important to recognise more insidious kinds of sexual assault, using threats or deception, and the SOA tries to recognise and define these. If D threatens V with physical violence unless she assents to his sexual assault, and she assents, a bystander might not notice anything untoward.[4]

In the last sentence, we deliberately used the word "assent." This word does not actually appear in the SOA, which uses "consent" throughout, and this leads to problems, as we will see. A victim assents merely by saying "yes," or even by not protesting or resisting — and this can be for lots of reasons, including a reasonable fear of credible threats. But of course assent is not consent; by definition, consent requires sufficient freedom (to refuse) and sufficient information (about what exactly V is consenting to, and with whom). In this way, it is similar to the control and understanding criteria for moral responsibility.

Sexual assault is special partly because it is a circumstance crime, as distinct from a result crime and a conduct crime, and this raises special complications. A result crime (such as murder) requires a describable result: in most cases, only when the dead body is discovered can a murder investigation be launched. A conduct crime (such as dangerous driving) involves certain objectively describable conduct (e.g. as captured on CCTV footage), and does not depend on any harmful results from such conduct. In contrast to both, a circumstance crime involves conduct and perhaps a result, neither of which are intrinsically wrong, but which are *made* wrong by the presence of a particular circumstance. One example of a circumstance crime is "handling stolen goods," described by Section 22 of the *Theft Act* 1968. There is nothing intrinsically wrong with you privately exchanging this television for my money (absent coercion or deception). But the transaction is *made* criminal by the television's "stolen-ness," even if the transaction does not in itself increase the harm suffered by the television's true owner.

4 Herring and Dempsey (2007) argue against this default presumption of moral neutrality. Compared to all other forms of intercorporeal exchange between humans, sex is strikingly intimate and invasive; as such, they say, it should be presumed wrongful unless and until there is subsequent evidence of V's consent — in the same way that physical assault is presumed wrongful. This would create a much stronger onus on the defendant to prove that the victim in fact consented. Indeed, Herring and Dempsey argue that sex is perhaps worse than punching, precisely because of the greater risks of psychological harm and humiliation, the risks of unwanted pregnancy and disease, and the potential for reinforcing the misogyny of the defendant and his male peers.

What are the circumstances that turn the touching into the offence of sexual assault? Let us quote from the SOA Section 3(1):

A person (A) commits an offence if—

(a) he intentionally touches another person (B),
(b) the touching is sexual,
(c) B does not consent to the touching, and
(d) A does not reasonably believe that B consents.

So rather than a positive circumstance such as "stolen-ness," we have a negative circumstance, the lack of consent. And in addition, we have a negative description of D's mental state. This makes things complicated, not only in terms of sufficient evidence during a trial, but also philosophically.

We're going to discuss the philosophical problem of consent in the next section. Before we do so, we have to say more about what makes sexual offences special: the fact that they draw part of their particular wrongfulness, indeed, part of their particular horror for the victim, from the wider contextual backdrop comprising the meanings of consensual sexual intimacy in our lives. We already mentioned the idea of a contextual backdrop in our discussion of domestic abuse in Section 8.5: the particular wrongness of the abuse is amplified precisely because of its semantic locus within the home and in the intimate relationship.

For many of us, sexually intimate relationships are central to our lives, and to the meanings of our lives. Some of these relationships lead to the creation of children, some do not, but many people choose to live with a person after discovering their mutual sexual interest and compatibility. In such a context, consent to sex is part of a larger consent to the close presence of the other person in their life. Because sexual assault physically resembles consensual sexual contact, the assault results in a kind of mockery of the victim's inner life. In contrast, being physically assaulted by a drunken stranger in a bar is physically unpleasant and painful and possibly debilitating, but it does not "reach" nearly as far into the victim's inner life. Sexual assault, even without physical injury (perhaps *especially* without physical injury), strikes at the foundation of the victim's identity and integrity.

The obverse of this mockery is the distinct kind of humiliation associated with being publicly known as a sexual assault victim; with having the details of the event first investigated by the police, and then discussed in the courtroom; with being persistently questioned about one's clothing or one's sexual history by an aggressive defence barrister. All these processes invoke ugly prejudices about ideal femininity and the various ways that women can "fall." There is a conceptual link not only to the domestic abuse discussed in the last chapter, but to more general patterns of gender discrimination in the workplace, to cat-calling in public spaces, to the sexist representation of women in culture and media, and to a sense of aggrieved entitlement among socially disempowered men. When a sexual assaulter is acquitted, it is very easy for the victim to see it as a victory for much larger forces aligned against her.

In bringing sexual offences together into a single Act, there was also an attempt to improve the investigation and prosecution processes. While there are many advantages to being judged by a jury of one's peers rather than by judges drawn from a narrow segment of the population, there is a real risk that the jury will harbour the same sexist prejudices found in wider society.[5]

5 See, e.g. Thomas (2020).

The most obvious example of this is the assumption that a woman who flirts, who gets drunk, who wears a low-cut dress, or who is believed (truly or falsely) to be promiscuous, is somehow "asking for it," that is, signalling an over-arching consent that would be "reasonably" taken by the perpetrator as overriding any later protest.[6] In the event of third-party testimony or other evidence to resolve the "he-said-she-said" stalemate in court (beyond reasonable doubt), both male and female jury members may end up lamenting that "boys will be boys," and that a "sensible" girl should be the one to take precautions against misunderstandings. Alternatively, they might be inclined to believe D's claim that he was merely engaged in romantic "pursuit" and "seduction," and not at all taking ruthless advantage of V's youth and inexperience.[7] There are real questions about how to reform the investigation and trial processes to bring justice to more victims of sexual offences; without such reform, so many victims simply refuse to report the offences at all.

9.2 V'S CONSENT AND D'S BELIEF

Consent plays a central role in the SOA's definitions of the offences. The case of overwhelming physical force involves the clear absence of consent, and so this is legally and philosophically unproblematic. Similarly, the case where V is unconscious or incompetent and therefore unable to grant consent should also be unproblematic (although as we shall see, the SOA 2003 is not as clear as it should be on this point).

Let's look again at the two circumstances in SOA Section 3(1): V does not consent, and D does not reasonably believe that V consents. The subsequent clause (2) is also important: "Whether a belief is reasonable is to be determined having regard to all the circumstances, including any steps A has taken to ascertain whether B consents." The reasonable belief requirement is quite stringent. It means that if V's lack of consent is on display (by utterance or gesture) to a degree sufficient to be understood by a reasonable person, then D cannot seriously declare later that he thought that V was consenting. (Remember that *earlier* manifest consent can be revoked at any time, of course.)

D's later claim (in response to the police investigation) that he thought V was consenting might not be an attempt to deceive the police; it probably reflects his own *self*-deception. After all, presumably most sexual assaults do not involve D acting under the description of "sexual assault" (as in "I want to *sexually assault* this woman"). Most sexual assaults involve D,

6 The "asking for it" response is also to be seen in discussion of image-based sexual abuse, often known as "revenge porn." This has been criminalised by Section 33 of the *Criminal Justice and Courts Act* 2015. Horsey and Rackley (2018) argue against the term "revenge porn," (i) because it downplays the harm caused, and (ii) the term focuses too much on the arousal of the consumer. Instead, they prefer the term "image-based sexual abuse," in order to draw attention to the cruel motivations of the image disseminator, and to the conceptual link with more familiar forms of physical sexual abuse, against the same permissive patriarchal background. For more detailed discussion see McGlynn, Rackley, & Houghton (2017).

7 Even a dry legal academic paper can involve outrageous statements, such as Hyman Gross in 2007. One really has to wonder what century the author is living in. (We hope the outrageousness is self-evident!):

> In the absence of any indication of an objection it is in the nature of normal sexual activity to proceed without requiring assurances that no objection exists. Indeed, requiring such assurance could be off-putting, even fatally disconcerting. Moreover, it is not uncommon for women to express reluctance initially and then to decide to have sex. There are good reasons why they may have changed their minds. Perhaps feelings that were lacking may have been aroused. Or a woman may have been interested but was not disposed to say yes without first being accorded the compliment and comfort of the man's importuning. (p. 221)

driven by sexual desire, reassuring himself of her consent, perhaps with a supporting story that her "no" was conveniently part of an elaborate courting ritual or role-play ("playing hard to get").

This requirement on D is "objectivist," since it invokes what a reasonable person would believe, and it therefore makes D's failure a kind of negligence. Recall our discussion of Adomako the anaesthetist from Chapter 4 on negligence. The important thing is that the court was not interested in any of the reasons that he might have offered for not noticing the tube — all that was relevant was his failure to do so. Similarly with sexual assault. D might adduce any number of reasons why he genuinely failed to correctly understand V's non-consent: maybe D had been socialised by peers and by pornography into uncritical acceptance of certain misogynistic tropes; maybe he was overwhelmed by his lust for sexual gratification (or for power or revenge); maybe he was encouraged by V's earlier behaviour which seemed so guilelessly friendly in his friendless world — all of this is irrelevant; all we are left with, legally, is his failure to notice what could and should have been noticed.

At first glance, the objectivist standard might seem overly harsh, for all the reasons discussed in Chapter 3. It might be tempting to argue for a subjectivist standard, as in ordinary "Cunningham" recklessness, where the defendant at least has to be aware of the risk and then intentionally disregard it. The controversial case of *Morgan* [1975] reveals the problems with subjectivism. D1 was married to V. After an evening of drinking with three friends (D2, D3, D4), he invited them back to his place to have sex with his wife. He assured them that she was "kinky," that her likely protests would only be for show, and that they could presume that she was consenting. The three friends raped V, one after another, and then D1 raped V as well. The Crown Court convicted the three friends of rape. (Notoriously, at the time, a husband could not legally rape his wife, and so D1 was convicted of aiding and abetting the three other rapes.[8]) The House of Lords rejected the appeal, but confirmed the theoretical possibility that if the defendants had *sincerely* — even if unreasonably — believed that V was consenting, then this would amount to a valid defence. It's just that in this case, the defendants did not sincerely believe in V's consent.

So the SOA clearly rejects *Morgan*. In line with our discussion in this chapter so far, we would support the objectivism because (i) sexual activity is sufficiently unlike ordinary activities, and therefore the practice of giving and recognising hints and signals from ordinary life is less reliable; (ii) the harm, and the risk of harm, to sexual integrity is perhaps less obvious than other kinds of harms and so requires additional deterrence, and (iii) the risk of misinterpretation and self-deception are higher in the sexual context because sexual urges are stronger than, say, greed. As Chan and Simester (2011, p. 392–393) put it:

> one reason why it is acceptable to criminalize negligence with respect to non-consensual sex, as many jurisdictions have, is that matters of consent are so closely bound up with the very nature of sexual intercourse that those engaging in sex are, implicitly, on notice that questions of consent are in play. The context is so intimate that alertness to the will of one's partner can be expected of every responsible actor, and a failure to exhibit such alertness is itself grounds for condemnation.

Despite this laudable intention to offer greater protection, two problems remain. The first is that standards of objective reasonableness still allow too much room for sexist juries to agree with D that e.g. V's clothing and flirtatious behaviour could be "reasonably" interpreted as

8 This was called the "marital rape exemption." The idea is that upon marriage, a woman thereby consented to sex with her husband *at any time of his choosing*. Equally shamefully, the exemption was revoked only in 1991, and only through the case of *R v R* rather than by legislation.

advance consent. Here one can only hope that prejudices will change with greater public discussion on the subject, or else that procedural safeguards can be introduced into jury trials.[9]

Second, a problem with any objective *mens rea* requirement is that it does not allow for certain individual weaknesses or difficulties, and can therefore be unfair. For example, if D is a sexually inexperienced 19-year-old, or is on the autistic spectrum (but still competent), and fuelled by social media misrepresentations, he might not have the necessary skills to "read" social situations correctly, to draw reasonable inferences, and to control his impulses. However, in response to this possibility, the objectivist would insist that in this context V's interests are more important than D's interests, precisely because of her initial disadvantage with respect to patriarchal norms.

The SOA's definition of consent

The *Sexual Offences Act* 2003 devotes three sections to "Consent": 74, 75 and 76. In discussing these we will be drawing from Tadros (2006). Section 74 starts with a suspiciously terse definition: "a person consents if he agrees by choice, and has the freedom and capacity to make that choice." Unfortunately, the section merely defines a difficult concept by reference to four other difficult concepts! After all, "freedom and capacity" would seem otiose, for the very concept of "consent" *already* presupposes sufficient freedom and capacity. A person lacking the freedom to not-X can perhaps assent to X but not consent to X; a person lacking capacity because e.g. they are unconscious, cannot assent or consent at all. A person lacking capacity because they are 12 years old or because they have severe learning difficulties can assent but cannot legally consent, since they do not understand enough of what they are assenting to.[10]

Similarly, the concept of "choice" does not seem to add much to the meaning of "consent." It might be rhetorically important to have the word "choice" there, with its connotations of activity and autonomy, to supplement "consent." After all, another noxious trope is the woman as "gatekeeper," passively accepting or rejecting the suitor's urges. "Choice" allows women a more active expression of their own desires. The word "choice" is also useful for different kinds of coercion scenarios: when D threatens V with violence unless she has sex with him, then this might look like V is "free" to weigh the two options, where in fact it is more natural to say that she "had no choice" — and therefore it was sexual assault. This

9 One example of a procedural safeguard is the "rape shield" law, which forbids the defence from introducing evidence of V's sexual history, and from cross-examining V about it in court. Section 276(1) of the Canadian *Criminal Code* states:

> evidence that the complainant has engaged in sexual activity, whether with the accused or with any other person, is not admissible to support an inference that, by reason of the sexual nature of that activity, the complainant (a) is more likely to have consented to the sexual activity that forms the subject-matter of the charge; or (b) is less worthy of belief.

Although the Section 41 of the UK *Youth Justice and Criminal Evidence Act* 1999 offers some restrictions, it has not been enough. In 2023, the UK Government asked the Law Commission to propose new legislation. See Banerjee (2023) "'Legal Revolution: In UK, rape victims' sexual history not to be included as evidence," *Firstpost.com*.

https://www.firstpost.com/world/legal-revolution-in-uk-rape-victims-sexual-history-not-to-be-included-as-evidence-12636192.html

10 There is a difficult question about the degree to which severe learning difficulties can undermine consent to sexual relations. On the one hand is a real risk of sexual exploitation by unscrupulous caregivers; on the other is the risk of denying the mentally handicapped a right to some kind of sexual autonomy. For the moment, I will assume the law's main task is to protect them against exploitation.

would usefully distinguish it from the case of an enticement, where D offers a promotion to his employee V in exchange for sex; here she does have a choice, and if she went with her ambition or greed it would not be sexual assault.[11]

Finally, the concept of "agreeing" in Section 74 is not much help in distinguishing assent from consent, since both can be described as an agreement, depending on whether the focus is the outward display or the internal mental state. Insofar as an outward display is required, however, how unambiguous does it have to be? In contract law, there are clear rules for outward display, most notably with the convention of physically signing a document. And yet normal consensual sexual relations are rarely "negotiated" so explicitly. The reference to "any steps D has taken to ascertain whether V consents" might perhaps be useful in borderline cases, but one can imagine D sincerely believing that no such steps would be necessary, and this brings us back to a cognitive failure "at one remove."[12]

One last comment before we look at the remaining two consent clauses of the SOA. The Act's focus on consent echoes the focus in academic discussions of sexual offences, as well as various popular initiatives such as "consent training" in universities and schools. All that might seem a laudable and obvious direction for political activism and reform. The problem with focusing on consent is that it focuses attention squarely on the victim, on her gate-keeping role, and away from men and boys. In most other offence descriptions, attention is focused on the defendant, on his *mens rea*, on his defences. Compare: with the traditional defence of provocation, attention was focused on whether the victim provoked the defendant; for this reason, English law renamed the defence as "Loss of Control" — see Section 10.5.

So any policy of "consent training" requires equal if not greater attention to men and boys about the simple wrongness of sexual assault. This could be achieved by focusing less on consent and more on what it means to respect and to disrespect someone. After all, the wrongness of sexual assault is surely much deeper than the mere infringement of the victim's consent; it has to do with failing to respect the victim as another, equal human being. Considers the analogy with theft: there it is very much the thief who *does* something bad, regardless of the victim's behaviour. Yes, it would be foolish of me to leave my bike out unlocked on the street overnight, and I should not really be surprised when it is not there in the morning. But that does not change anything about the clear wrong that has just taken place, nor does it change anything about the clear focus of the ensuing police investigation.

9.3 SOA SECTION 75: COERCION AND INCAPACITY

Despite these justified concerns about the focus on consent, we will continue with that focus precisely because of its central role in the SOA 2003. Clearly Parliament recognised the vagueness of Section 74, and so laid out a number of more specific scenarios of consent vitiation in Sections 75 and 76. Section 75 begins as follows:

11 The situation would become more complicated if she would need the money to look after dependants. This might produce a *situation* that is coercive, even if the D does not coerce her — although of course D might know about her dependants and exploit the coercive situation. Legally, this would probably still not be sexual assault, however.

12 The concept of "agreement" in contract law allows for the recognition of "unequal bargaining power" despite bilateral assent, and therefore for the legal possibility of an "unconscionable contract" that can be ruled invalid because of its grossly one-sided terms. So *if* the courts wanted to take the contractual interpretation of "agreement" further, this might provide greater protection for V.

(1) If in proceedings for an offence to which this section applies it is proved —
 (a) that the defendant did the relevant act [e.g. the sexual assault]
 (b) that any of the circumstances specified in subsection (2) existed, and
 (c) that the defendant knew that those circumstances existed,

the complainant is to be taken not to have consented to the relevant act … and the defendant is to be taken not to have reasonably believed that the complainant consented …

The ellipses are important, and we will discuss them in a moment. Subsection (2) then lists a number of different circumstances, including the following:

(d) the complainant was asleep or otherwise unconscious at the time of the relevant act;
(e) because of the complainant's physical disability, the complainant would not have been able at the time of the relevant act to communicate to the defendant whether the complainant consented;[13]
(f) any person had administered to or caused to be taken by the complainant, without the complainant's consent, a substance which, having regard to when it was administered or taken, was capable of causing or enabling the complainant to be stupefied or overpowered at the time of the relevant act.[14]

There are two significant conceptual problems with this part of the SOA, as Tadros (2006, p. 525) explains. With respect to unconsciousness and incompetence, we already saw the redundancy of Section 74 defining consent in terms of "freedom" and "capacity." Here in Section 75, we see an additional redundancy of spelling out that being asleep, stupefied, or unable to communicate will vitiate consent. Can anyone really be surprised by this? It's one thing to spell things out clearly; but this is actually worse than redundancy. Such circumstances, the Section 75 title tells us, amount to no more than "evidential *presumptions* about consent." An evidential presumption means that one can presume something unless and until the presentation of sufficient counter-evidence. But surely if V is asleep and D has sex with her, that is sexual assault *by definition*; it is not merely *evidence* of sexual assault, evidence which is in principle "rebuttable." This is where the Section (1) ellipses come in: "unless sufficient evidence is adduced to raise an issue as to whether [V] consented." What possible evidence does this clause have in mind? Are the drafters imagining a situation where the woman leaves a note next to her sleeping body, with the words "I hereby consent to your having sex with my sleeping body"?

Again, there are at least four types of sexual assault: when V is physically overpowered, when V is unconscious or incompetent, when V is coerced and when V is deceived. The rest of Section 75 covers coercion and threats. Unlike the first two types, the most important feature

13 Two notes here. The description refers to a complainant with a physical disability, not an intellectual one. The latter are covered by the SOA Sections 30–44, which open with the subtitle "Offences against a person with a mental disorder impeding choice." Another class of people with insufficient competence would be minors, and these are covered by the SOA Sections 5–15, with the sub-title "Rape and other offences against children under 13," and then in Sections 47–51, "Sexual exploitation of children."

14 This clause is alarming, because it only captures the clandestine administration of stupefiers *by* D or a third party. Such stupefiers clearly vitiate consent, but why does the clause omit V's voluntary consumption of stupefiers? If we take the robust definition of consent from Section 1 and Section 74, then V might surely have voluntarily consumed enough to vitiate consent. Is voluntary stupefaction to be understood as a kind of contributory recklessness? (This is a concept from tort law: if a driver accidently injures a jay-walker, the jay-walker may be eligible for less compensation for the injury because her recklessness contributed something to the collision.)

here is V's *assent*. She is not overpowered and she is not incompetent: she reluctantly assents. The problem is then to assess the different degrees of reluctance in different contexts, in order to determine which of them hinder the interpretative transition from assent to consent. Subsection (2) lists some of the relevant circumstances:

(a) any person was, at the time of the relevant act or immediately before it began, using violence against the complainant or causing the complainant to fear that immediate violence would be used against him;

(b) [... as in (a), but ...] against another person;

These cases are relatively straightforward. V assents to sex out of fear of violence to herself or to another person. But the same two worries here apply as in Section 74 and in the Section 75 incompetence provisions: one would assume that a "fear of immediate violence" would be enough to vitiate consent *by definition*, rather than being mere evidence for vitiated consent.[15] What possible counter-evidence does the legislator have in mind? A woman who seriously claims that she fears immediate violence *and yet* consents to sex, because that's the sort of kinky stuff she likes? Is that a serious and common enough possibility that it is worth diluting the condemnatory force of the section by waiting for the defence counsel to gather the counter-evidence?[16]

But there is a larger concern here; this section does not cover certain complexities of coercion where we would intuitively feel that assent did not amount to consent. Consider four scenarios that reveal such complexities.

(i) The notorious "Texas condom case." In 1993, a man, armed with a knife, broke into a woman's flat in the middle of the night, and demanded sexual intercourse. The woman assented. Fearing the possibility of pregnancy or sexual disease, she offered him a condom, asked him to wear it, and he did. The man was later apprehended, and a Grand Jury refused to indict him because, they felt, the victim's request that he use a condom was evidence of sufficient consent and not fear.[17]

(ii) In the case of *C v R* [2012], a man was engaging in regular sexual relations with his adult step-daughter, who regularly assented. However, further investigation revealed a long-standing process of systematic grooming and domination in the years before the trial, enough to undermine her autonomy and choice, even when she was legally competent in other contexts of her life. This might not involve fear of immediate violence *now*, but there had probably been some kind of fear and submission at an earlier, more vulnerable age, and this assent became habitual. Even if C was ultimately charged on the basis of other provisions in the SOA, it would have been good to outline this kind of scenario explicitly in Section 75.

15 The next clause in the list states: "(c) the complainant was, and the defendant was not, unlawfully detained at the time of the relevant act." Again, the power differential between D and V (and V's reasonable fear of consequences) is surely such as to vitiate any assent that V might offer to D's sexual proposal.

16 There might be some rare cases of consensual sado-masochistic sex that could involve a genuine fear of and desire for immediate violence. We saw (Section 8.4.) how the House of Lords rejected the defence of consent in the sado-masochistic case of *Brown* [1994]. And we saw (Section 8.5.) the rejection of the "rough sex defence" for manslaughter in Section 72 of the *Domestic Abuse Act* 2021. Given this trend, the "victim consent" defence would presumably not be available here.

17 See: "Man is convicted of rape in case involving condom," *The New York Times*, 14 May 1993: https://www.nytimes.com/1993/05/14/us/man-is-convicted-of-rape-in-case-involving-condom.html

(iii) The *Serious Crime Act* 2015, Section 76, introduced the offence of "coercive control."[18] This recognised the possibility of systematic coercion that does not rely on the explicit threat of *physical* violence. In some cases, it would suffice for the abuser to create an atmosphere of sufficient intimidation to vitiate his partner's consent. In other cases, the abuser could bring systematic psychological pressure (including financial control, restriction of social contacts, constant surveillance) to bear against the victim, over a period long enough to undermine the victim's freedom to refuse sex on a given occasion. She might simply be lulled into "her role."

(iv) In footnote 11, we described the case of an ambitious woman who agreed to sex with her boss in exchange for a promotion: this would be an offer, to be taken or left, and so would not be sexual assault. In contrast, consider the employer who threatens to fire his employee unless she has sex with him. Imagine if it was a time and area of high unemployment, or if she was an illegal immigrant. If she assented, the employer would probably be liable under contract and employment law, but could he also be guilty of sexual assault? Probably not, but that seems a defect.[19]

9.4 SOA SECTION 76: DECEPTION

In this scenario, instead of the victim's consent being vitiated by her lack of sufficient *freedom*, it is vitiated by her lack of sufficient *understanding*. Section 76 describes two relatively narrow deception scenarios, and as before we will be suggesting that the Section fails to accommodate other kinds of deception that we would intuitively consider sexual assault.

The classic case of (non-sexual) deception concerns a common object of a transaction. The used-car salesman assures me that *this* car is well worth the £10,000 he is asking for it, although he knows that it is not. Since I am not an expert on cars, I trust him and pay the money.[20] With sexual activity, the two descriptions apply to the activity: what exactly does the woman think she is doing (description A)? What exactly does the man think he is doing (description B)? She may assent under description A, without any implied consent under description B. Section 76 of the SOA reads as follows:

(1) If in proceedings for an offence to which this section applies it is proved that the defendant did the relevant act and that any of the circumstances specified in subsection (2) existed, it is to be conclusively presumed —

(a) that the complainant did not consent to the relevant act, and

(b) that the defendant did not believe that the complainant consented to the relevant act.

18 Section (4) runs as follows:

> (4) A's behaviour has a "serious effect" on B if — (a) it causes B to fear, on at least two occasions, that violence will be used against B, or (b) it causes B serious alarm or distress which has a substantial adverse effect on B's usual day-to-day activities.

19 This last scenario raises the larger question of whether poverty can vitiate consent in a sexual situation, and whether some sex workers are not entirely free to avoid sex. However, consider the very sad case of *Kirk* [2008], where a homeless 13-year-old assented to sex with her uncle in exchange for money to buy food. The Court of Appeal upheld his conviction for rape. This case seems exceptional, however.

20 The law has undergone a long development from *caveat emptor* (let the buyer beware) in the late nineteenth century, to *caveat venditor* (let the seller beware) under Sections 13–15 of the *Sale of Goods Act* 1979. So perhaps I would be in a strong legal position to recover my money if and when I discover the swindle.

(2) The circumstances are that —
  (a) the defendant intentionally deceived the complainant as to the *nature or purpose* of the relevant act;
  (b) the defendant intentionally induced the complainant to consent to the relevant act by *impersonating* a person known personally to the complainant. [*italics added*]

So we're looking at the two types of circumstances in (2).

The "nature and purpose" clause

The classic common law sexual assault case involving deception about the "nature and purpose" is *Williams* [1923]. A singing teacher persuaded his naïve 16-year-old student to assent to sexual intercourse by passing it off as a "special treatment" to improve her singing. Here, the victim was deceived about the very thing that was taking place. That seems clear enough.

More challenging is the case of *Linaker* [1994].[21] D agreed to pay V (a sex worker) for sex, they had sex, and then D absconded without paying. This was clearly a case of fraud, but was it also unconsented sexual assault? We can bring in the "counterfactual test" here: if V had known that D would not pay, would she have consented to the sex? Clearly not. The court, however, decided that there was no deception about the nature or purpose of the act itself: D asked for sexual intercourse, V understood what that was, she could have refused, and they duly had sexual intercourse. D had simply failed to keep his side of the bargain, and for that he was culpable.

However, Herring (2005) argues that the sex worker did not in fact consent to "sex" but to something quite different: "sex-for-money." The money was part of the meaning of the act to which she consented. Imagine that V has a boyfriend. With the boyfriend, she simply has "sex," i.e. without money. Even if the physical movements are similar, the meaning of the movements are entirely different when the financial motivation is absent. So when Linekar ran off without paying, the "sex-for-money" effectively became simple "sex," and V had *not* consented to that; so she was deceived about the "nature and purpose" of the act, and therefore this should have been sexual assault. In addition, Linekar had no money with him, had no intention to pay, and knew that the prostitute would not have sex with him if he admitted his intention ahead of time. The sex worker would have reason to consider herself not only robbed, but violated.[22]

Even if we accept that *Linekar* was decided correctly, there have been some inconsistent applications of Section 76 in the recent case law. In *Dica* [2004] D had HIV, but did not mention this to V before she consented to sex. V subsequently developed HIV. The court declared that V was not deceived about the nature or purpose of the act, and so it was not sexual assault. Instead, it was treated as intentional assault occasioning (non-sexual) bodily harm under the *Offences Against the Person Act* 1861.[23] In *Lawrance* [2020], D was sexually fertile, but claimed to have had a vasectomy in order to enjoy unprotected intercourse with V. Again, the

21 This was prior to the SOA 2003, but the common law had essentially the same account of deception vitiating consent.

22 Herring accepts that it might be too strong to describe Linekar as having committed "rape" or even "sexual assault," so he proposes a new and lesser offence of "obtaining sex through deception." Section 3 of the *Sexual Offences Act* 1956 described an offence of "procuring another to have sex by means of false pretences or false representations." See Gibson (2020).

23 In Canada, the fraudulent concealment of HIV-positive status vitiates consent if there was a "realistic possibility of transmission." The act becomes sexual assault, aggravated through endangerment to life, even if the disease is not transmitted. See the Canadian Supreme Court case of *Maribor* 2012 SCC 47.

Court of Appeal declared that this was not deception about the nature and purpose of the sex, and therefore was not sexual assault. So far, so consistent.

However, *Lawrance* should be compared to *Assange* [2011] who lied about his intention to use a condom, but then, unbeknown to V, refrained from putting it on (so-called "stealthing"); and to *R(F)* [2014], where D lied about the intention to withdraw before ejaculating. In both cases the courts considered the deception sufficient to vitiate consent, thereby making them acts of rape. In *Assange*, presumably the court would agree that V consented to a particular act, "sex with a condom," and that is not what she got. Perhaps the court would argue that the condom is something directly visible, unlike (at the moment of intercourse) Linekar's money and Dica's infection. But even so, the risk of unwanted pregnancy for Assange's and R(F)'s victims were exactly the same as the consequences for Lawrance's victim.

The impersonation clause

The "impersonation" clause (2)(b) is a reference to cases such as *Elbekkay* [1995], where D intentionally impersonated V's boyfriend in the dark in order to have sex with her. Again, the key is to look at the description of an action. Here the SOA was designed to recognise that V was not consenting to "sex" but to "sex-with-my-boyfriend"; the identity of the other person was essential to the activity. V did not just desire the sex, she desired the boyfriend, the specific and irreplaceable person with whom she had a longer-term intimate relationship. If V had known that D was not her boyfriend, she almost certainly would not have consented to sex — and D knew this and deceived her about it. (She might have consented to sex with D in very different circumstances, but that would not be relevant to what happened in *these* circumstances.)

The points about the act description and the counterfactual non-consent could in principle be applied more broadly than to the explicitly narrow circumstances of the impersonated boyfriend. Herring (2005) goes on to ask the following rhetorical questions. What if D exploits his physical resemblance to a famous celebrity? What if D claims that he is very wealthy and V has sex with him precisely under that assumption? What if D lies about his feelings ("I love you") or his intentions ("I want to marry you")? What if D lies about his criminal record or about his membership in a far-right political organisation?[24] These are not covered by the impersonation clause. In each case, Herring argues, we can imagine a situation where (i) the relevant fact, if known by V in advance, would be a sexual deal-breaker for V, and where (ii) D knows that it would be a deal-breaker for V, and so (iii) D lies in order to obtain sex with V. It is important that the "deal" be on V's conditions, regardless of whether others consider V "unreasonable." The question then is whether some of these deception cases are sufficiently close to *Elbekkay* to criminalise D's behaviour (and if not as sexual assault, then at least as "procuring another to have sex by means of false pretences").

Hyman Gross (2007), in defence of the narrow reading of Section 76, offered two responses to Herring's arguments, which we now summarise, together with summaries of Herring's (2007) own response to the responses. This will conclude the chapter.

1. Gross: While it is *immoral* to lie for sex in the above ways, it would be too heavy-handed to make it *criminal*. (Compare: adultery is usually harmful and immoral, but

24 In *Monica* [2018], D was an undercover police officer posing as an environmental activist. He began a sexual relationship with V, a "fellow" activist. When D's identity was revealed, the DPP refused to launch criminal proceedings against D, and V unsuccessfully filed for judicial review of the DPP's decision.

it is not and should not be criminal.) This is because the law, in general, should non-intrusively allow people to learn from their mistakes, in a spirit of *caveat emptor* (let the buyer beware), here modified to *caveat amator*, let the lover beware. Gross asks (pp. 224–225): "Is the criminal law needed to protect women against the disappointments and humiliations that are a consequence of their bad judgment, their gullibility, or their too trusting nature?" (i) Part of the problem is evidential — it would be very difficult for a court to reliably determine D's and V's states of mind, let alone the relevant counter-factuals; (ii) Gross is also assuming that sexual deception is *hurtful* but not especially *harmful*, at least when compared to other harms the law seeks to prevent.

In response, Herring reminds us that "we should take V as we find her," together with the particular vulnerabilities that might result in real harm from sexual deception. We should also avoid blaming the victim for her "bad judgement" and "gullibility," and instead focus on the wrong of D's intentional sexual deception.

2. Gross: D's pre-coital assurances are logically distinct from the coitus. V must *first* decide whether to believe the assurances, and *second* whether to consent to the coitus. The first decision requires a mature scepticism, with which all of us should evaluate any claims of strangers. The second decision should be based only on V's full understanding of what sex involves; if she decides to consent to the sex, this entails consent to the risk that D might have been lying in his prior assurances.

In response, Herring would stress the conceptual link between the two decisions, based on V's particular understanding of the link. When D lies about his intention to marry V, then V is consenting not to "sex" but to "sex with my future husband" — that is the relevant description *to her*, as important as the identity of V's sexual partner was in *Elbekkay*. Of course, some women do not place such a high premium on marriage and do not link sex so explicitly to marriage, and that's fine. But some women do, and it is the individual woman's values that are the most relevant here. If the man does not like a woman's values, he can and should walk away.

CHAPTER 10

DEFENCES

This will be a longer chapter, with a lot going on. But of course it's key to understanding the central problem of responsibility. To start off, recall the three components of the trial described in the Introduction. The prosecution has to prove that (i) D performed the actus reus, and (ii) with a certain mens rea; (iii) if that is established, then D will have the opportunity to claim a defence. This chapter will look at some of the things that D can say in her defence, which qualify her responsibility for the actus reus in various ways. The law recognises a number of defences, and they involve pointing out relevant features about the situation or about the defendant that might not have been evident at first. Once D raises a defence, and supports it with some evidence, then the prosecution will normally have the new task of proving beyond a reasonable doubt that she did *not* have that defence.[1]

Before we begin, we have to say a bit about "capacity" and its lack. A person "is competent" or "has capacity" if she can understand enough of the world, and of herself in that world, and has enough control of herself, to be held responsible in the full sense of the word. The police might arrest a person and begin investigating whether she performed the actus reus with a certain mens rea, but discover that she lacks capacity, and is therefore "unfit to stand trial." In such a case she might be formally handed over to mental health services for further assessment and processing, and she might leave the criminal justice system. Alternatively, a person might be considered fit to stand trial, but during the trial, she pleads "not guilty by reason of insanity." This effectively splits the trial into two stages, the first to ascertain whether she did it, and the second to ascertain whether in fact she was/is insane.

So unfitness and insanity are the biggest defences of all. Indeed, it might not be quite right to call them defences but rather *exemptions* (following Antony Duff). For the defendant to deploy a defence presupposes that she is sufficiently competent to engage in the defence-deploying practice, itself part of the larger practices of giving and taking reasons, and of being held responsible and taking responsibility. If the defendant lacks capacity, the problem is not only that (i) she cannot sufficiently understand the trial *as a trial* (i.e. that *she* is "on trial"): she cannot sufficiently understand what it means to be held responsible for something she did in the past (where she might not be able to remember why she acted), or she cannot sufficiently understand what it means to have harmed someone. In addition, (ii) she cannot be *punished* in the full sense of the word — she can only be *managed* and *processed*; for society is only justified in punishing the defendant if it can in principle send her a message about her actions and about the transgression of the relevant social values, and if the defendant is capable in principle of understanding — and ideally accepting — that punitive message. (We discuss punishment in the next chapter.)

In our book we're not planning to discuss capacity or insanity much, precisely because it would require a lot of complicated psychiatric and psychological detail, which would take us too far away from the philosophical discussion. The psychopaths and serial killers of the television detective dramas are actually not very interesting in philosophical terms. (However, there is a defence of "diminished responsibility" which we will talk about later in this chapter, in Section 10.7.)

1 The word "defence" is a little confusing, since the *defendant* and her *defence* barristers have already been defending their account throughout the trial, even before they raise a "defence." And to make it even more confusing, one of the defences the defendant can raise is self-defence.

DOI: 10.4324/9781003351887-10

For our purposes, we're going to divide this chapter into *justifications* (Part A) and *excuses* (Part B), and consider the main examples of each. This is more of a philosophical distinction, and does not have much systematic impact in the practice of law — law students normally just learn the different definitions and criteria of the different defences. It's not a hard and fast distinction, either, since some defences might have elements of both. But philosophically, justifications and excuses work in very different ways — both in the criminal court as well as in ordinary life. The distinction is also legally relevant in that justification is taken as all-or-nothing; if the defendant is found to have been justified, then she will be acquitted. In contrast, excuses lie on a scale. Some excuses will only partly reduce culpability, while others might eliminate it.[2]

10.1 PREAMBLE: EXCUSES AND JUSTIFICATIONS

Let's recall the moral responsibility paradigm from the Introduction, and especially the assumptions behind holding someone responsible (i.e. blaming them). When I blame you for a harmful consequence X, then I am already assuming:

1. You caused the consequence X and it was harmful (the causal condition)
2. You sufficiently *understood* that (i) you were causing X, and that (ii) X is harmful (the understanding or knowledge condition)
3. You were sufficiently *free* to refrain from causing X (the control or freedom condition).

In the trial, we have already established that the defendant committed the actus reus (X), and that she did it with sufficient mens rea. At this stage, she may now offer an excuse, where the excuse comprises a denial (in full or in part) of either the understanding condition or the control condition:

a) Despite appearances I did not actually *understand* that I was causing X (or that X was harmful); or
b) Despite appearances I was not actually sufficiently *free* to refrain from causing X.

Take the denial of the understanding condition. Perhaps the most common excuse in everyday life is the honest misunderstanding: "I'm so sorry, I thought that was my pen." Notice that even in the case of an honest misunderstanding as a sufficient excuse to turn away blame, there is still a moral obligation to return the pen and to apologise! (There might also be a moral obligation to offer the victim some kind of compensation e.g. if the victim, lacking a pen, had to buy one.)

On the other hand, while it is true that I genuinely did not understand what I was doing, and am therefore not "first-order" culpable, I might nevertheless be "second-order" culpable. This distinction between orders is familiar from our discussion of "prior fault" in Chapter 4 on negligence. I accept that you genuinely thought that it was your pen, but I blame you for being hasty and careless: if you had looked more closely, you would have surely seen that it was not your pen. Here the locus of blame is not the intention behind the harm caused (since there was no intention), but rather the defective character trait that avoidably led to the harm. Perhaps the blame can be corroborated with reference to past behaviour patterns: "You're

2 See Dsouza (2017) for a very detailed discussion of defences.

always so hasty and careless." So in shifting the locus of blame, your excuse reduces, but does not remove, the culpability behind the harm caused. In the same language of orders, perhaps you could then offer a second-order excuse: "I'm sorry, I was careless because I'm going through a messy divorce and I've got a lot on my mind."

In terms of excuses denying the *control* condition, there are two main types, which will be discussed in Part B. According to the first, my freedom was constrained by a very strong emotion: "What you did made me so angry I couldn't help myself." So in the specific context of anger leading to homicide, the defendant would claim the excuse of "Loss of Control." However, this only applies in response to a murder charge. The idea is that D would normally be fully able to control herself, but the particular circumstances resulted in such a strong emotion that she intentionally killed V.

According to the second type of excuse invoking the control condition, my freedom was constrained by a credible threat from a third party (i.e. I intentionally caused harm but I was acting under *duress*). One paradigm is the bank teller intentionally handing over the bank's money to the robber (thereby intentionally assisting the robbery) because of the robber's credible threat of imminently shooting her if she refuses. Technically the teller was still free to obey or disobey the robber's commands, but it would not be reasonable to expect the teller to risk her life for the sake of the bank's money (i.e. she could plausibly say that she "had no choice.")

Throughout, the important thing about excuses is that we all agree that the action was harmful and that I should not have done it. However, in offering an excuse I am claiming that I am not as culpable as you initially thought I was. Again, there is nothing uniquely *criminal* about any of this: we offer and accept excuses in all kinds of ordinary situations. It is a central part of the moral education of children, both at home and at school. (Think about how children "try out" certain imaginative excuses to avoid blame: "Teddy said it was all right"!) While there may be borderline situations where two people can reasonably disagree about how strong or how relevant X was as an excuse, there will be paradigm situations that ground the norms of excuse-giving and excuse-accepting in social discourse. It is on the basis of these shared intuitive norms that we can then criticise the criminal law for being e.g. too lenient or too demanding in a particular context.

So much for excuses. *Justifications* (also known as "permissions") work differently. Instead of saying "I intentionally caused X, I know X is bad, but I'm not fully responsible for it," I say "I intentionally caused X, I know X is bad, but I had a good reason to do it, and so all things considered in my situation, it was better that I caused X." As a paradigm, you are about to walk across the road, and I pull you back violently. You look at me angrily: "What the hell are you doing?" And I point at the speeding car that you had not seen. There are actually two justifications here: first, I *was* justified in pulling you back; second, in explaining why I pulled you back, I justified it to you. Once you understand the justification, then ideally you accept it, and you thank me. Given the options available to me in the situation (to pull you back, to not pull you back), I did the right thing. Sometimes this is called the all-things-considered right thing.

Justification compares a narrow and broad description of what happened: my intentional action seemed to you like an "unprovoked unconsented pull" (narrow), but when I explained and pointed out the car, you discovered that the action was in fact a "pull *in order to* save you by the best means I could see" (broad). The "in order to" is a crucial part of the description of the action; and my *intention* also included the "in order to." I was motivated directly by my concern for your welfare. Although I pulled you without your consent, I presumed that the threat to your health or life was severe enough, and later evident enough, that you would be relieved and grateful for the intervention, and that you would grant me, as it were, "retroactive" consent. Retroactive consent is not so mysterious: if I am unconscious on the road, the ambulance driver does not wait for my consent before taking me to the hospital; and I am sure glad she did not wait. All of this is based on mutual concern for the other's welfare, and mutual knowledge of what is and is not generally conducive to the other's welfare.

As with excuses, there are shared norms of proportionality and relevance governing justifications, depending on context. It is clearly acceptable for me to miss our planned social meeting in order to take my sick mother to the hospital; "my mother's immediate medical needs" are pretty high on the list of reasons anybody can offer for breaking a promise. But there will be some close calls, and room for intractable disagreement. Am I justified in missing our social meeting because I'm watching the big game on the telly, and it's going to extra time? It depends. You might accept that live football is a very important part of my life, and you have to accept the occasional promise-breaking as the "price" of our friendship. Or you might be annoyed, since you consider football a matter of mere pleasure, not comparable to the importance of keeping promises to friends. Sometimes the meaning of my promise-breaking (and the attitude it implies to the promisee) can be retroactively changed by my efforts to make it up to you later. The meaning of the promise-breaking will also depend on past promise-breakings, and this time might just be the last straw.[3]

PART A: JUSTIFICATIONS

So an excuse maintains that the act was wrong, but reduces or eliminates the responsibility/culpability of the defendant; a justification declares that the act was, all things considered, right (or at least permissible), and therefore the defendant has actually done nothing wrong/illegal. As we will see, there are some legal defences that might function as either an excuse or as a justification, depending on the circumstances. For the moment, we will start with the clearest and most famous justification.

10.2 SELF-DEFENCE

Of all the defences, this one has probably received the most philosophical attention.[4] Consider the paradigm case of a street mugging. The aggressor is V. (This sounds counter-intuitive, but he's the one who ends up the victim!) V threatens D with serious violence unless D hands over her purse. (As before, the genders are merely to allow efficient use of pronouns.) The threatened violence is imminent, and the threat is credible. D knows she probably cannot outrun V, the street is deserted, and there is not enough time to call the police. D reaches into her

3 That is not to say that friendships are entirely self-defined: in order to call any relationship a *friendship*, it still has to be governed by certain recognisable behavioural norms, e.g. norms of demonstrated affection and loyalty. If I consistently break my promises to you, you and others would be justified in wondering whether I really was your friend, as I claim.

4 The relevant legal category here is wider: it includes the defence of another person (especially an intimate), the defence of property, and even the defence of law (i.e. any action designed to prevent another from breaking the law). For simplicity, we will focus mainly on self-defence in this chapter. The wider category is used in Section 76 of the *Criminal Justice and Immigration Act* 2008. The American *Model Penal Code* (MPC) has an even wider scope. Deadly force is never permitted, "unless the actor believes that such force is necessary to protect himself against death, serious bodily harm, kidnapping or sexual intercourse compelled by force or threat" (Section 3.04). This may sound vague, but it is supplemented by several pages of guidance for commonly-occurring scenarios (Sections 3.04–3.08).

One famous philosophical article on self-defence is Thomson (1991). An important book-length treatment is Uniacke (1994). For a book-length treatment of the law surrounding self-defence, see Leverick (2006).

purse and pulls out a knife. V lunges at D, and D stabs him in the stomach. V collapses to the ground. D calls the emergency services, not only for an ambulance to rescue V, but also to summon the police to explain what happened. While she waits for them to arrive, V bleeds to death.

Prima facie D has intentionally committed GBH against V, and upon V's death this would be a prima facie case of murder under the "GBH rule" (see Section 8.1). All claims of self-defence need to be carefully investigated, not only because of the seriousness of any fatality, but also because many genuine *murderers*, once apprehended, will probably claim self-defence to conceal their crime.

Any justification requires a move from the narrow to the wide description of the act. The narrow description reads: "D killed V intentionally"; the wide description, the description under which D claims she was acting, reads: "D killed V as the last resort, as a proportionate response to a credible threat of serious imminent violence." In other words, D is not merely *killing* V, she is *killing-V-in-self-defence*; all those hyphens are meant to irreducibly qualify the intention that drove the act. If D's self-defence claim succeeds, then the intentional killing has been justified, the killing was permissible "all things considered," the apparent crime turns out not to be a crime, and the defendant is acquitted.

Let us look more closely at the four conditions. The first two overlap, so we will consider them together. But there is sometimes overlap among other pairs of conditions too.

(i) *The threat was credible*
(ii) *The threatened harm was serious and imminent.*

In our mugging example, it might seem that D would have little problem reliably recognising the credibility of the threat and the imminence of the threatened harm. But strictly speaking, D can never be absolutely sure about the reality and the severity of the threat until V has launched the attack; (or perhaps, to use the language of the *Criminal Attempts Act* 1981, until V had taken steps that were "more than merely preparatory.") And yet for a D who is already in a weaker position, waiting that long might be disastrous, so she needs to pre-empt the attack.[5] But if the pre-emptive strike is too far in advance of a threat that is too distant (and/or too imprecise), then it will lose its justification. In addition, D might be unreasonably paranoid, defined as a condition involving precisely the unconscious exaggeration of the threatened harm.

Here's the interesting thing, however. In English law, D's beliefs about the credibility of the threat and the imminence of the threatened harm must be sincere but do not need to be *reasonable*. As the lawyers say, it is a "subjective test" of D's beliefs. D is judged on the facts as she sincerely believes them to be. (This makes self-defence fundamentally different from duress in English law, since duress requires D's beliefs about the threat to be reasonable — see Part B of this chapter.)

The effect of this is to bring some instances of self-defence closer to an excuse rather than a justification. If D is paranoid and overreacts, then it might be that she does not do the right thing, all things considered: her action is wrong, but understandable, given the mistaken beliefs under which she reacted. The classic case here would be the homeowner who

5 There is a parallel debate in just war theory, which concerns the conditions where it is justifiable for a *country* to wage military war. The paradigm condition is in self-defence, but sometimes pre-emption is morally permitted for a weaker party. The classic example of justifiable pre-emption might be the Israeli airstrike on the Egyptian airfields in the 1967 "six-day" war, once Israeli intelligence had confirmed imminent invasion plans by several Arab neighbours.

interrupts a burglar in the middle of the night. The burglar may have no plan to use violence, and just wants to get away. And yet because it is the middle of the night, because the homeowner has no experience with violence, and because of the additional vulnerability due to the threat taking place in her own home (normally her place of safety), she misjudges the risk of violence, and fatally (and disproportionately) shoots him.[6]

(iii) *The lethal response was proportionate to the threat.*

We saw above that the beliefs about the nature and imminence of the threatened harm need not be reasonable. In contrast, *given those beliefs*, then D's judgement about the proportionality of her response *does* have to be reasonable. Section 76(3) of the *Criminal Justice and Immigration Act* 2008 states: "The question whether the degree of force used by D was reasonable in the circumstances is to be decided by reference to the circumstances as D believed them to be …" So in our mugging example, V was unarmed when he approached D, but she genuinely believed that if she refused to give him her purse, that he would use his fists and superior strength to cause her serious bodily harm. Whether his behaviour reasonably justified her fearful belief is not relevant. Given her fear, she reasonably judged the knife stabbing to be a proportionate response to defend herself — and she had the presence of mind to aim at his stomach rather than at his chest, thereby confirming her intention to incapacitate rather than to kill. (She also confirmed her original intention by calling the emergency services as soon as she was out of danger.)[7]

However, the permitted subjectivity of the beliefs about the severity and imminence on the one hand, and the required objectivity (reasonability) of the belief in the proportionality on the other, do not lend themselves to a clear boundary. Padfield (2016, p. 147) says that the situation is exacerbated by the binary nature of the defence: either the self-defence is accepted as *entirely* legitimate and the defendant acquitted, or it is entirely rejected, and the defendant faces a murder charge. Would there not be room, Padfield asks, to take disproportionate force as grounds for a partial *reduction* rather than an elimination of culpability, thereby reducing the charge from murder to manslaughter? This would align it better with duress, which does allow degrees.[8]

(iv) *The lethal response was the last resort (a.k.a. it was "necessary")*

We prefer the term "last resort" so as to avoid confusion with the defence of necessity (discussed in the next section). This condition places a duty on D to (i) escape if possible and/or (ii) call for official protection if possible. Only if neither of these are possible is she then entitled to reach for lethal force. The last resort condition is qualified by the "Castle principle" — "a man's

6 Notice that in the interrupted burglary case, the homeowner has to sincerely believe that the harm has been threatened against *her person*; if she were merely trying to stop the burglar from stealing *her property*, then the fatal attack would be disproportionate (i.e. personal injuries are usually more serious than theft).

One famous interrupted burglary case was that of Tony Martin in 1999. Martin lived alone in a farmhouse. After a string of burglaries, he acquired a shotgun (illegally). The next time he was woken up by burglars, he came downstairs, shot at them in the dark without warning, and then shot at them twice more as they tried to get out of a ground floor window. One of them died at the scene. Martin claimed self-defence and defence of property, but his response was judged disproportionate, especially since the wounds were in the *backs* of the burglars. He was convicted of murder, later reduced to manslaughter on the grounds of diminished responsibility supported by psychiatric testimony. He ended up serving three years in prison, but garnered a lot of sympathy in the media.

7 D's narrative is also plausible since D and V appear to have been strangers, and there is no obvious way that D could have benefited from V's death.

8 As we will see in our discussion of the Loss of Control defence in Part B, the *Coroners and Justice Act* 2009 has a section (subsection 55(3)) that allows one to strike while in fear of one's life, and if successful, this defence would reduce murder to manslaughter.

home is his castle" — according to which there is no obligation to try to escape the aggressor if D is attacked in her home. Again, however, the belief in the fact of the "last resort" has to be reasonable — the law wants to instil an essential reluctance to use force. If the defendant has an unreasonable belief that e.g. the police are useless and that she therefore has to take the law into her own hands, that should not justify force. On the other hand, if her personal experience with the police has been demonstrably worse than that which a normal citizen would be entitled to expect (e.g. because of institutional police racism), this might permit her to reasonably ignore the "last resort" principle. Once again, however, there is room for conceptual confusion. For if I am permitted subjective paranoia in my estimate of the credibility and imminence of the threatened harm, then the appearance and scale of the threat might already be partly constituted by my (unreasonable) belief that I cannot run away or call the police; moreover, my rising panic will also lead me to underestimate my own escape options.[9]

The moral underpinnings of self-defence

There is a moral problem at the heart of self-defence. Assume the aggressor V is genuinely intent on killing D; D successfully defends herself by killing V while fulfilling the four conditions. Intuitively D seems justified. But if the situation is such that one person must die and one can live, why exactly should V die when morally, D and V are equal, and have an equal right to life? The standard answer has to do with V knowingly and voluntarily *forfeiting* her right to life *by* attacking D with intent.[10] This is to be contrasted with duress, where the law refuses to allow duress to function as an excuse in murder cases. In other words, when T threatens me with death unless I kill V, then I am supposed to accept my death over that of the innocent V, precisely because V has not forfeited his right to life.[11]

One problem for this forfeiture account is generated by "innocent aggressors." If an insane person credibly threatens me with serious injury or death, then legally, she cannot be guilty of murder since she does not understand what she is doing or she is subject to irresistible impulses. As such she has not voluntarily forfeited her right to life, and her right remains equal to mine.

10.3 NECESSITY

The necessity defence is a bit odd. First, we have to warn against two possible confusions: (i) acting "under necessity" does not mean acting under coercion from outside, or acting under compulsion from inside: I am still free to choose. It's just that there is only one option that I

9 In *Williams (Demario)* [2020], V gate-crashed a party, stabbed D in the arm, and stole his necklace. D chased and subsequently caught V, and, with others, stabbed V to death. D claimed self-defence, but this was dismissed on the grounds of D pursuing V out of the house; this made the stabbing of V an act of revenge rather than self-defence. It certainly did not look like a last resort.

10 See Uniacke (1994, Chapter 6) for a detailed discussion of "forfeiture argument." Article 2 of the European Convention on Human Rights describes everyone as having an equal right to life, but allows an exception in the case of unlawful violence:

1. Everyone's right to life shall be protected by law …
2. Deprivation of life shall not be regarded as inflicted in contravention of this Article when it results from the use of force which is no more than absolutely necessary:
   (a) in defence of any person from unlawful violence …

11 In response to the Tony Martin burglary case (see above), many people defended Martin's disproportionate shooting of the unarmed burglars precisely because they felt that voluntary trespassers had effectively forfeited *all* rights, and therefore could not complain about *any* defensive response, even if fatal.

can reasonably choose. (ii) The justificatory defence of necessity should not be confused with the "necessity condition" of self-defence, which we called the "last resort" condition, above.

But necessity is also odd because (i) it's not recognised very often, (ii) it's hard to define, and (iii) it has to be subject to strict limits to prevent some outlandish implications. But while it might not be too important legally, it is interesting philosophically in representing the ethical theory of consequentialism in action. In its crudest form, consequentialism claims that an ethically good end justifies ethically dubious means. Consequentialism sees nothing intrinsically good about promise-keeping or truth-telling, for example; if breaking a promise or telling a lie generates better consequences than the alternative, then that's what one should do. Sometimes this is phrased in terms of the lesser evil: if I cannot avoid producing evil consequences one way or the other, then I might as well choose that option that is more likely to produce less evil. And the necessity defence is based precisely on the claim that committing a crime was a lesser evil compared to the evil that was thereby averted.

A solitary hiker is lost in the remote Scottish wilderness, her phone is dead, she has miscalculated the weather and her own strength and preparations, and she finds herself exhausted, hungry, cold and wet, as daylight fades and a massive blizzard is building. Her circumstances look bleak. She continues walking, hoping vaguely to make it back to the village whence she departed, but she is not sure where it is, and she can't see very well where she is going. She comes across a cabin, but the lights are off, the door is locked, and nobody answers when she thumps on it. She is so desperate that she smashes a window, crawls inside, lights a fire, eats some of the food, and falls asleep. The next morning, the weather has cleared and she is strong enough to resume the walk down to the village, which she can now see. The cabin owner complains, and the hiker is arrested, and charged with (intentional) damage, trespassing, and theft. She readily admits all that, but claims that she "had to" break the law, in order to save herself from a serious and imminent risk to her health or even life.[12]

If the DPP drops the prosecution, or if the matter goes to trial and the court recognises the defence of necessity, then the hiker will be acquitted. In parallel to the *criminal* process, however, she may be rightfully pursued by the cottage owner through a *civil* claim. Somebody has to pay to fix the broken window and to replace the lost food, and it is perfectly fair to expect the hiker to do that. As we saw in our discussion of *Adomako* in Chapter 4 on negligence, there is nothing incoherent about these two legal processes running in parallel and even coming to different results.

The defence of necessity is subject to certain conditions. The first condition is that the defendant's assessment of the situational peril, including her belief that no alternative options exist, has to be reasonably correct — this can be checked against meteorological reports, for example. She cannot break into the cabin merely to avoid getting her designer clothes wet and muddy. A key part of the reasonable assessment, important enough to call it the second condition, has to do with her belief in the imminence and severity of the risk to her (as with the defences of self-defence and duress). An impoverished and hungry homeless person might well be in danger of dying over the next few weeks, but such a person cannot use the defence

12 It might be uncomfortable to view the law-breaking of the hiking scenario as *justified*. Instead, it might be better to see it as an *excuse*, where the hiker acted from understandable fear and desperation. In the late 1980s, the English courts developed a new defence of "duress of circumstances," which looks like necessity but was analogous to ordinary duress, one of the paradigmatic excuses. Padfield (2016, p. 137) argues that this compromise confuses more than clarifies, and should be abandoned. For the sake of clarity in this chapter, we will only speak of the justification of necessity and the excuse of duress.

There are two other famous examples of necessity in the criminal law textbooks. (i) an individual breaks the speed limit in order to get her sick friend to hospital as quickly as possible. (ii) A ship's crew is justified in throwing cargo overboard (thereby harming the cargo owner) if necessary to save the ship in a storm.

of necessity to justify burglary from a supermarket, especially given the existence of homeless shelters and food banks in larger towns. In *Southwark LBC v Williams* [1971], the Court of Appeal rejected an argument that homeless people could claim necessity to justify trespass on vacant council premises. Part of the court's reason was that the problem of homeless accommodation should be dealt with as a matter of broader public policy rather than by the courts. More generally, if necessity is construed as *no more* than a calculated lesser-evil defence, then one can imagine many modern-day Robin Hoods acquitted for putting rich people's money to better use.[13]

Medical necessity: the conjoined twins

Here's a complex and controversial example of *medical* necessity. Normally medical necessity has to do with lesser evils: the classic case is when it may be necessary to sedate an incompetent patient before providing her with beneficial treatment.[14] But the Conjoined Twins case has the unusual benefit of offering three defences (from three different judges), all three of which are problematic in this unique context. We shall follow Uniacke's (2001) useful summary of the philosophical issues.

The twins were named Jodie and Mary by the court to preserve their anonymity, and we shall follow them on this. Jodie was the larger and stronger twin. They were joined at the hips and chest in a complicated way. The question was whether to surgically separate them. According to the best prognoses, such surgery would result in the certain death of Mary, whose heart was not sufficiently developed to sustain her life. Without surgery, however, both twins would die within six months. As devout Catholics, the parents could not support a procedure that would have Mary's death as an inevitable side-effect. Nevertheless, the courts overruled the parents, the doctors performed the surgery, Mary died, and Jodie went on to lead a healthy life.[15]

The three judges argued as follows (Uniacke, 2001, pp. 208–209):

(i) Walker LJ (Lord Justice) did not see the surgery as involving a killing. This was because Mary was "doomed to die" whether or not the surgery was carried out, and therefore her interests would not need to be considered. All that mattered was the duty of the doctors to make the best effort to save Jodie's life.

(ii) The other two judges agreed that the surgery would involve the intentional killing of Mary, and therefore would require a defence, but they disagreed on the relevant defence. Ward LJ preferred self-defence. Jodie was being attacked by Mary, and threatened with likely death; it was therefore legitimate to help her defend herself by removing her attacker. Ward was famous for his highly charged language, to the point of cruelty: Mary was seen as "sucking the life-blood" of Jodie.

13 For further philosophical discussion on necessity as a defence, see Dennis (2009).

14 In *Re F (Mental Patient Sterilisation)* [1990], a 36-year-old woman with severe learning difficulties was living in a hospital. She had recently started a sexual relationship with another patient. It was judged that she would be deeply upset by pregnancy and birth. Contraception was inappropriate for various reasons, and so the hospital successfully claimed a defence of necessity for performing an unconsented sterilisation. The *Mental Health Capacity Act* 2005 now lays down conditions and guidance for such cases.

15 Their real names were Gracie and Rosie Attard, from Malta. The surviving Gracie is about 23 as this book was written. She was interviewed in this 2015 newspaper article. Culliford, G. "Never Forgotten; 'I'm not sad, I know she is with the angels' ... 15 years on from historic conjoined twins case, sister speaks." *The Sun*, 28 November 2015. There is an interesting question of what Gracie thinks about the parents' reluctance to agree to the surgery. For further discussion of the Conjoined Twins case, see Cowley (2003).

(iii) Finally, Brooke LJ reached for the defence of medical necessity. The separation surgery was the lesser evil in allowing at least one of the twins to live, again given the fact that Mary would not survive beyond six months anyway.

Uniacke rejects all three arguments, and rejects the more or less explicit assumptions that were necessary to make them work:

(i) Since *Nedrick* [1986], the concept of "murder" has included those individuals whose death was a virtually certain side-effect, and Mary was virtually certain to die from the surgery. Recall our discussion in Chapter 2 on intention, of the person who places a bomb on a cargo plane in order to destroy the cargo and claim the insurance money. She does not intend for the pilot to die, but clearly she should be held liable as a murderer, given his virtually certain death. Walker's attempt to describe Mary as "doomed to die" is irrelevant: after all, we are all doomed to die. If a 96-year-old Stage IV cancer patient has only a month to live, killing that patient now would still be murder.

(ii) It is plainly ridiculous to describe Mary as "attacking" Jodie, let alone as *choosing* to attack Jodie. Mary was born an infant, and simply exists; she was not *doing* anything at all, let alone doing it "against" Jodie. In addition, it was not *Mary* who was "sucking" anyone's life-blood, the fact was simply that blood was being shared between the two. Furthermore, Ward imagined Jodie being able to speak, and saying "Stop it, Mary, you're killing me." Uniacke imagines Mary responding: "What do you want me to stop, exactly?" (p. 212). There might be an argument in taking Mary as an innocent aggressor, against whom Jodie would be entitled to defend herself. But normal cases of innocent aggression presuppose the existence of an antecedent non-aggression situation, a situation that the law can allow the aggressed party to attempt to restore. But there was no antecedent situation here, since both twins began their lives conjoined.

(iii) The problem here is that Mary is just as much of a patient as Jodie, and the doctors have the same duty of care to her. Brooke's same lesser-evil calculation would justify doctors killing a single healthy individual in order to save five other patients by redistributing the individual's organs for transplant. Basically, consequentialism cannot accommodate anything like robust individual rights. While Ward (the second judge) might argue that Mary "deserved" to die as an aggressor, Brooke would impose on her a "duty" to sacrifice herself, which is even more questionable. But more legalistically, the greatest obstacle to the necessity justification is that necessity can never be a defence to murder.[16]

In the end, Uniacke proposes the following solution (p. 218). If Mary and Jodie could be surgically separated, and Mary immediately placed on a heart–lung machine that would sustain the flow of blood, then the two children would survive the operation, and their respective fates could be decided on *separately*. Mary could then be evaluated in terms of her new bleak

16 This was the main conclusion of the famous case of *Dudley and Stephens* (1884). Four men survived a shipwreck and found themselves in a lifeboat miles from land, and without food or water. On the eighth day, two of the men decided to kill and eat the weakest, and this allowed them to survive long enough to be rescued three days later. Their defence of necessity was rejected, and they were convicted of murder. Interestingly, however, the public outcry was such that their sentence was reduced from capital punishment to life in prison; and after six months in prison, they were released.

prognosis, the heart–lung machine could be removed as "futile" medical treatment, and she could be allowed to die from the inadequacy of her own heart. This would be an ethically routine decision, akin to many other instances of withdrawing futile treatment from dying patients. The problem with such a solution, however, is that it seems contrived. After all, why bother with the heart–lung machine stage if one already knows the treatment will be futile? Why not just let her die immediately following the surgery?

10.4 WOMEN WHO KILL THEIR ABUSIVE PARTNERS

In Section 8.5., we discussed the problem of domestic abuse. Here we want to look at a particular case of abuse that raises interesting questions about the most appropriate defence to be used. The comparison between defences will allow a useful segue between Part A and Part B of this chapter. The case in question was *Ahluwalia* [1993]. Kiranjit Ahluwalia had been married to her husband for ten years, during which she suffered systematic physical, sexual and psychological abuse. She had tried to escape the marital home on several occasions, but her husband always found her and "punished" her for it. After attacking her one evening in 1989, her husband went to bed. She fetched some petrol from the family garage, and once he was fast asleep, she poured it on him and set him alight. He was hospitalised with severe burns, and died from them some days later. The court interpreted this as straightforward murder, and she was sentenced to life in prison. Four years later (in 1993), her conviction was overturned on the grounds that she had not been made aware of the possibility of claiming diminished responsibility. She was released, and the Crown Prosecution Service declined to re-prosecute her.

The excuse of diminished responsibility involves saying that she was not in full control of her actions as a result of the years of abuse. (We discuss this in Section 10.7.) But there is a question of whether she should have been allowed to claim the justification of self-defence or the excuse of Loss of Control, and what this would have meant for our understanding of the case. McColgan (1993) compares the three defences, and argues that she should have been able to claim self-defence precisely because of her husband's credible threats of severe bodily harm. The problem, however, was that at the moment of her attack on him, her husband was sleeping, and so he did not present any threat of *imminent* harm. In addition, while he slept, she certainly had the option of physically leaving the house, and so killing him was not the "last resort."

McColgan argues that the court could have taken more account of two things. First, his superior physical strength made self-defence difficult while he was awake, and so this might justify her recourse to a pre-emptive strike while he was most vulnerable. Second, whatever her real escape options, she did not see herself has having escape options, partly because of her reasonable fear of rediscovery and reprisals from her husband, partly because of her lack of money and lack of knowledge of where to go, together with her suspicion of social services. (Besides, under the "castle principle," she could not be reasonably expected to leave her home to evade the threat.) Moreover, argues McColgan, there is an important symbol in claiming a justification (like self-defence) over an excuse. If killing her husband was justified, it means that *he* was in the wrong, and a successful defence would carry a strong condemnation of domestic abuse more generally. If the killing was merely excused, then it means that *she* was in the wrong (albeit excusably).[17]

17 Desirable as it may be to claim self-defence, Howes et al. (2021) explain why it will likely remain an ineffective legal strategy. See also Storey (2019) who explains, with reference to *Challen* [2019], why someone suffering from "coercive control" would not be able to rely on that as a defence to murder.

In fact, Ahluwalia originally tried to claim the excuse of provocation (the earlier name for Loss of Control). The central idea behind provocation is that the victim has done something so provocative as to partially excuse the defendant's murderous response. However, at the time, provocation had an imminence condition just like self-defence. Ahluwalia could not claim to have discovered any shocking new facts, and the sight of her sleeping husband could not in itself provoke new anger. (We discuss Loss of Control in Section 10.5., below.)

PART B: EXCUSES

Unlike a justification, a successful excuse means that the wrongdoing remains wrong all things considered, but the defendant's responsibility for the wrong (and therefore her culpability) is reduced, either in part or entirely. The practice of giving excuses, and the shared norms of what constitutes a good or a bad excuse, are familiar from ordinary situations.[18]

The two most important excuses are Loss of Control and duress, both of which involve a denial of the control condition for moral responsibility. We will spend the bulk of Part B on those two. At the end we will also have something to say about the excuse of diminished responsibility, which may involve denials of both the control and the understanding condition.

10.5 LOSS OF CONTROL

The basic structure of this defence runs as follows. D intentionally kills V; D is charged with murder; D claims Loss of Control — in other words, he was not fully responsible. If D is successful, then the murder charge will be changed to manslaughter (called "voluntary manslaughter"). It is only a partial defence; most likely he will still go to prison. In the United Kingdom, the defence of Loss of Control replaced the defence of "Provocation," via Section 54 of the *Coroners and Justice Act* (C&JA) 2009. Most other jurisdictions still call this defence provocation, and it has a long history in common law. For consistency, we will generally use the term Loss of Control in this section. The difference is not just cosmetic: one of the problems with provocation is precisely that it focuses attention on V and what she did to "provoke" D into killing her. In contrast, the defence of Loss of Control focuses attention squarely on D, on whether he really did lose control, and whether this response was somehow acceptable or understandable.[19]

Despite this book's focus on the UK context, we're going to start with a simplified version of the American case of *Nessler* [2003], since it presents the philosophical issues particularly clearly. D is the mother of W, aged 6. While W was at summer camp, he and others were sexually assaulted by V. Eventually V is arrested and put on trial, and D and W came to watch the trial. To D's growing horror she realises that V will probably be acquitted for lack of evidence. At the same time, V notices W, winks at him, and W breaks into tears. D, in a fit of spontaneous rage, pulls out a gun and shoots V dead. D is arrested and charged with murder, but claims Loss of Control.

18 The classic discussion of excuses is Austin (1961) "A plea for excuses." See also the detailed monograph by Horder (2004).

19 Sullivan et al. (2021) argue that it would be better to abolish the defence of Loss of Control (as well as the defence of Diminished Responsibility) because it would be easier to deal with such mitigating circumstances at the sentencing stage. However, such a proposal is blocked by the mandatory sentence for murder, and Sullivan et al. acknowledge that this policy is unlikely to change in the near future. This paper contains useful commentary on the cases invoking the Loss of Control defence since its creation in 2009.

The central idea of Loss of Control is that the anger reduced D's normal self-restraint. The anger did not lead to a complete loss of self-control, obviously, because D was still able to control her movements enough to kill V. The killing has to be committed in "hot blood": the elapsed time between the "trigger" (that's the C&JA term) and the killing is important: if it is too long and/or it involves too much preparation and planning, the more it looks like a matter of "cold-blooded" revenge or vigilantism, which is never legally justifiable.[20] In a genuine Loss of Control situation, D will be immediately regretful: she accepts that her reaction was disproportionate, that she should have left the investigation and prosecution to the proper authorities, and that what she did was "not really her." In claiming Loss of Control, she hopes to persuade the jury that (i) in all other areas of her life, she is not only law-abiding, but also has a normal amount of self-restraint and a normal control over her emotions, but that (ii) in this exceptional situation, her angry response was essentially *understandable*, something that jury members can imagine themselves doing in D's shoes. Insofar as she does not fully identify with the act, she asks that she not be held fully culpable for it.[21]

Within the context of Loss of Control (and other excuses), there is a debate between "choice theorists" and "character theorists" about the exact nature of the excuse. According to the *choice* theorist, something like anger distorted or impeded the agent's choice. This anger is seen as external to the self. Normally she would not choose to kill, but she was inclined that way by the anger. Meanwhile, the *character* theorist will see D, once provoked, as acting *out of character*: although she intentionally fired the gun, the action did not fully express who she really was. Normally a person deserves full punishment on the basis of who they are, as reliably expressed through fully intentional actions. When she partly loses control, there is less point in punishing her fully, because after the killing she will — with remorse and horror — repudiate the consequence, perhaps saying "I don't know what got into me."[22]

We have deliberately chosen a starting example with strong initial plausibility. Even here, however, there will always be an argument to abolish the defence of Loss of Control. Murder is such a serious crime that it requires the strongest of deterrent effects, lest anyone think they can try to excuse themselves by simply describing their anger. Anger (and other emotions) are precisely the sort of thing that *every* competent adult is expected to bring under control in order to participate in civil society and in personal relationships. There might be grounds for reducing the *sentence*, continues the sceptic, but not for reducing the murder charge (the label). This argument has some value, but it faces three problems: (i) it underestimates the over-stigmatic power of a murder conviction, especially for someone in our example who was otherwise law-abiding, self-controlled, and subsequently deeply regretful; (ii) in many countries a murder conviction carries a mandatory life sentence, and so there would be no room for justified leniency (as there would be with a manslaughter conviction); (iii) As Marcia Baron (2003) argues, only the defence of Loss of Control can protect certain individuals from the full consequences of their understandable reaction to a severe moral wrong — and she uses *Nessler* as just such an example.

20 In the real case, Nessler left the courtroom in order to get her gun from her car and bring it back in — and this was considered too long to consider her as acting solely on the basis of provoked anger. She was therefore sentenced for murder. (She was released after three years, however, after a successful appeal relating to jury misconduct.)

See: https://en.wikipedia.org/wiki/Ellie_Nesler

21 Sceptics about the Loss of Control defence would reject D's suggestion that her violent response was somehow "not really her" — on the contrary, surely D has revealed her propensity to violence (as a disproportionate response), and therefore merits the full force of the law to deter her from future violence after her prison sentence.

22 On the relationship of character to criminal responsibility, see Duff (1993).

Nessler is a rare type of Loss of Control case. Far more common in the history of common law is the husband who catches his wife in bed with her lover, and in a rage kills one or both of them. But this has always been controversial. The recognition of a defence of Loss of Control in such cases comes close to a "boys will be boys" indulgence of insecure possessiveness and violent jealousy. The continuing defence of provocation in many Western countries, argue critics, is strong evidence of the continuing domination of patriarchal thinking, not only among the mostly male senior judges and legislators, but also in the tabloid accounts of such killings. And as we saw, the very concept of "provocation" places the emphasis on what the wife "must have done" to provoke her poor husband; the wife was "asking for it" by being unfaithful in the first place. If one pauses to think about this, it is astounding that the defence has existed for so long to protect these violent men. The defence exists, they say, because the jury will understand the defendant's all too human weakness. But this is a troubling form of "understanding": a jury can certainly understand being angry and hurt in response to infidelity — but can one really understand *killing* in response to it? Surely that is not just disproportionate, but radically disproportionate.[23]

The UK Coroners and Justice Act (C&JA) 2009

The legislation is interesting not only for changing the name of the defence. Let's look at the definition in Section 54:

> (1) Where a person ("D") kills or is a party to the killing of another ("V"), D is not to be convicted of murder if —
> (a) D's acts and omissions in doing or being a party to the killing resulted from D's loss of self-control,
> (b) the loss of self-control had a qualifying trigger [*to be defined in Section 55*], and
> (c) a person of D's sex and age, with a normal degree of tolerance and self-restraint and in the circumstances of D, might have reacted in the same or in a similar way to D.
> (2) For the purposes of subsection (1)(a), it does not matter whether or not the Loss of Control was sudden.
> (3) In subsection (1)(c) the reference to "the circumstances of D" is a reference to all of D's circumstances other than those whose only relevance to D's conduct is that they bear on D's general capacity for tolerance or self-restraint.
> (4) Subsection (1) does not apply if, in doing or being a party to the killing, D acted in a considered desire for revenge.

There are a number of overlapping points here. First, a relatively simple point: the expansion of the timespan in subsection (2) now allows more scope for "slow-burn" or "last-straw" killings (perhaps like Nessler), rather than the traditional limitation to the spontaneous or immediate response. However, the non-sudden clause is limited by the subsequent clause: the

23 In addition to jealous husband cases, there have been other egregious examples when provocation was recognised. In the case of *Doughty* [1986], a father killed his 17-day-old son. The mother had had a difficult Caesarean section, and was told to take things easy, so the father was looking after both of them, and the baby was constantly crying. At one point he covered the baby's mouth to mute the crying, and because of his fatigue and irritation he misjudged how hard he was pressing, and the baby suffocated to death. The trial judge rejected the provocation defence because the baby's behaviour was "perfectly natural." Nevertheless, Doughty's appeal was allowed.

longer the timespan between trigger and killing, the greater the risk that the killing will be interpreted as a "considered desire for revenge," and the defence will fail.

As for subsection (1), the first thing to notice is the interesting relationship between the subjective and the objective. The jury's first task will be to determine the fact of whether D really did lose control (i.e. her subjective experience). Unfortunately the expression "Loss of Control" is not defined in the C&JA 2009. In the post-C&JA case of *Jewell* [2014], Loss of Control was defined as "the loss of the ability to act in accordance with considered judgement or a loss of normal powers of reasoning" —Jewell's claim to have lost control was rejected because of lack of evidence, and his murder conviction allowed to stand.[24]

However, not just any genuine Loss of Control will do, and here there are two *objective* safeguards: the trigger has to be the right type (Section 55 — we discuss this below), and D's response would make sense *as* a Loss of Control for someone like D. It is good that the "circumstances" clause includes the person's age, since teenagers will likely be more impulsive. It is not clear why the clause includes the person's sex. This *might* be a clumsy effort to help *Ahluwalia*-type abused women to claim a Loss of Control; but it also risks going back to the allowance made for men who are "naturally" possessive and violent.

There is a question of how broadly "in the circumstances of D" will be read, beyond sex and age, and this relates back to our discussion of reasonableness in Chapter 3 on recklessness. Subsection (3) is interesting here, since it excludes certain character traits that would affect D's *general* capacity for self-restraint. The pre-C&JA case of *Mohammed* [2005] is relevant here. D found his daughter in bed with a young man, and stabbed her 19 times. His defence of provocation was based on his devout Muslim beliefs concerning sex before marriage, but his defence was rejected, mainly on the basis of testimony from D's siblings that he was already a man of violent disposition. For the same reason *Mohammed* would not succeed in claiming Loss of Control under the C&JA. There is a more unsettling question, however. Imagine a different Mohammed, of gentle disposition, who nevertheless claimed to lose control because of the daughter's offence to his religious beliefs. Would such beliefs be taken as part of Mohammed's "circumstances" under 54(3), and his defence allowed?[25]

Section 55 then defines the "qualifying trigger."

> ... (3) This subsection applies if D's loss of self-control was attributable to D's fear of serious violence from V against D or another identified person.
>
> (4) This subsection applies if D's loss of self-control was attributable to a thing or things done or said (or both) which —
>
> (a) constituted circumstances of an extremely grave character, and
>
> (b) caused D to have a justifiable sense of being seriously wronged...
>
> (6) In determining whether a loss of self-control had a qualifying trigger —...
>
> (c) the fact that a thing done or said constituted sexual infidelity is to be disregarded.

Subsection (3) is interesting because of the overlap with self-defence (or with the defence of another). It might make more sense for D to claim self-defence out of a "fear of serious violence" since if successful, she would be fully acquitted; whereas if she claims Loss of Control,

24 For comparison, the American *Model Penal Code* s. 210.3 uses "Extreme mental and emotional disturbance" (EMED) which effectively combines provocation and diminished responsibility.

25 Child et al. (2022), p. 435 think it could be. We are more optimistic that a jury under the C&JA would reject the religiously sincere "honour-killer" as a candidate for the Loss of Control defence. Surely there is nothing in mainstream British Islam (i.e. not a radical version) that would theologically support the interpretation of pre-marital sex as "*extremely* grave," enough to *justify* a feeling of being "seriously wronged," to use the language of Section 55.

she will only have a partial defence. Still, maybe this clause was again designed with *Ahluwalia* in mind, since there is no reference to the "serious violence" being *imminent* in this clause, (and it has to be read with the explicit allowance of non-sudden Loss of Control).

What does "extremely grave" mean? This is an objective question, about the meaning of the trigger as evaluated by the jury, rather than about D's beliefs about the trigger. At first glance, this would seem to be a welcome addition, since it would allow Nesler to claim, but would presumably reject insults to insecure manhood, and would reject screaming babies (the *Doughty* case). The objectivity of the graveness is also buttressed by the requirement that D's "sense of being seriously wronged" be *justifiable*, that is, with reference to objective moral norms as evaluated by the jury. "Justifiable" is a much higher threshold than "understandable" or "excusable" and one wonders whether it might be too high. "Justifiable" also seems to pull against the "circumstances of D" clause.

Finally we have subsection 6(c), with the explicit rejection of sexual infidelity as a qualifying trigger. This is certainly to be welcomed.[26] Surprisingly, "infidelity" is not defined, either in terms of the specific activity or in terms of the kind of relationship that such activity would allegedly betray. As will be seen in the next section, there might be a problem if the infidelity is an integral element in a set of events and facts that cumulatively qualify as a trigger.[27]

Clinton

The C&JA, and especially the infidelity clause, was tested in *Clinton* [2012]. Mr. and Mrs. Clinton had lived together as husband and wife for 16 years, and had two school-age children. Things were going badly in the marriage, partly because Mr Clinton was persistently unemployed and clinically depressed.

Two weeks before the fateful day, Mrs Clinton moved to her parents in order to begin a trial separation. At one point she informed her husband that she had begun an affair. On the fateful day, Mr Clinton had been consuming alcohol and drugs, and had been searching the web for advice on how to kill himself. Mrs. Clinton came to visit in the afternoon in order to pick up some personal effects. She noticed the suicide website open on the computer, and she mocked him for lacking the "bollocks" to go through with it. When he asked her about her affair, she claimed to have slept with five different men since leaving him, and even started describing details of their sexual acts. At that point Mr. Clinton attacked her with a wooden post, and then strangled her to death. He then removed her top, lay her in various poses, photographed the body, in order to send the images to one of the men with whom she was having the affair.

When it came to trial, Clinton wanted to claim Loss of Control; but the trial judge rejected the claim on the basis of the C&JA sexual infidelity subsection. In contrast, the Court of Appeal felt that there was enough evidence of a qualifying trigger to offer the jury, and therefore ordered a re-trial. (In the end Clinton pleaded guilty to murder, and so he abandoned the defence.)

The Court of Appeal was primarily interested in V's *taunting* of D. The taunts were partly about his lack of suicidal resolve, but partly about his sexual inadequacy compared to the

26 The wording is a little strange here too: "the fact that a thing done or said constituted sexual infidelity is to be disregarded." A thing "said" could *describe* sexual infidelity, but it could surely not *constitute* it.

27 Astonishingly, Child et al. (2022, p. 437) reject the infidelity clause because they see nothing special about the marital context for claiming Loss of Control: "if the 'normal person' would have acted as D did had she found her partner having an extramarital affair, the defence ought to be available." We are not sure how they can ignore the patriarchal excesses of the provocation defence in the past.

other men. The taunting was not directly about sexual infidelity, although the comparisons made reference to the sex with other men. As such, the Court felt that the jury should have been given the chance to explore whether the taunting was sufficiently grave in character, and whether Clinton's sense of being seriously wronged was justifiable, *given* the infidelity that was an essential part of the taunting.

> where sexual infidelity is integral to and forms an essential part of the context in which to make a just evaluation whether a qualifying trigger properly falls within the ambit of subsections 55(3) and (4), the prohibition in section 55(6)(c) does not operate to exclude it.
>
> *[para 39]*

Critics of the *Clinton* appeal decision worried that sexual infidelity would henceforth be allowed in the back door, thereby allowing the possessive, insecure men to get away with murder.[28]

Two facts about *Clinton* make us question the Appeal Court decision. First, V's taunting was intentionally cruel, certainly. But did it amount to a serious *moral* wrong against Clinton? To our ear, that is what the word "justifiable" is all about. Insofar as the taunting comprised a mere insult, then it should not be a qualifying trigger. Whatever happened to the ideal of "sticks and stones may break my bones but words can never hurt me"? What's more, she had moved out and began a trial separation, so in that strict sense she could not actually be unfaithful, and this would mean his "sense of being seriously wronged" was even less justifiable.

Furthermore, we would suggest that it is important to examine Clinton's behaviour *after* the killing in order to understand more about his state of mind *during* the killing. A genuinely excusable case of provoked killing, we suggest, should be followed by horror, remorse, and a prompt call to the emergency services. Instead, Clinton undresses the body and photographs it in an effort to carry out his morbid revenge against his wife and her lover. Whatever might be said about the genuine spontaneous anger of the killing, we suggest this postmortem behaviour would seem to turn the killing into a considered desire for revenge, thereby undermining any "Loss of Control" plea.

The Loss of Control defence is still relatively new, and it will be interesting to follow the evolution of its interpretations over the next decade or so.

10.6 DURESS

This is the second major excuse that can be claimed. Let's take as a paradigm situation the bank robber (T for "threatener") who points a gun at a teller (D) and demands that she hand over the bank's money. This is a very schematic example to make the duress clear: in legal reality, the duress would be so clear that the teller would never even be charged, let alone convicted.

The threat must be clear, and the action demanded must also be clear.[29] When she hands over the cash, she is intentionally assisting T's theft and would normally be liable as an accessory. When she claims duress, what exactly is she claiming? The standard legal phrase is that,

28 Hence the ironic subtitle of Morgan's paper on the case: "Loss of self-control: Back to the good old days" (2013). For a more recent discussion, see Wu (2020).

29 In addition to the credibility and imminence conditions, there is also a condition of *specificity*, about both the nature of the threat and the action T is demanding that D perform. In *Cole* [1994], D owed money to T, and was told to find a way to pay it back "or else." D attempted to rob a bank, was arrested, and then claimed to be acting under duress. This was rejected by the Court, not only because the threatened harm was not imminent, but also because the threatened harm was not specific, nor did T ever specify what D needed to do — T didn't care, as long as he got the money. D's decision to rob the bank was his alone.

after showing reasonable steadfastness, her will was "overborne." That sounds like "overwhelmed," and maybe she was, maybe she just panicked and handed over the money. But it's important to realise that she could also have kept her sang-froid, and realised that she had no reasonable alternative but to hand over the money: it is not as if anyone expected her to risk her life for the bank. So while she was physically free to resist, she was not meaningfully free, and so can be absolved of any responsibility for intentionally assisting the robbery.

There is a question about the difference between a justification and an excuse here. If D panicked when she saw the gun, and acted out of fear, that would be an excuse. But if she calmly chose the lesser evil, this would seem to make it a justification, similar to the lost hiker breaking into the empty cabin out of "necessity." Child et al. (2022, p. 850) claim that when D's crime is *much* less serious than the threatened harm, it would be "perverse" to describe D as merely "excused," as if it was some kind of understandable weakness — she would be entirely justified. However, it is perhaps better to call it an excuse because the bank robber's initial culpability — unlike the non-culpable threat of the Scottish weather — adds a morally irreducible demand, the satisfaction of which can never plausibly be morally justified. At any rate, it makes sense to call it an excuse because of the universal familiarity with the fear of personal attack. The thought is that *anybody* could imagine doing what D did out of fear, even if this particular teller felt no fear and obeyed the robber's instructions mechanically.

But the re-description as a justification already brings in an important structural feature in the three points of the triangle: the harm threatened against D should really be greater than the harm D inflicts on V (in this case the bank), under the assumption of "reasonable steadfastness," i.e. that D is not unusually timorous (on which, see below). This is clear in this scenario because personal harm is usually considered to be more serious than property harm (especially when the harm to the bank is pretty close to "victimless" insofar as it will be absorbed by insurance policies and/or a wide number of shareholders).

Other conditions for the defence of duress are reminiscent of self-defence, and indeed of the old defence of provocation: the threat must be credible, and the threatened harm must be serious and imminent. "Imminent" does not have to be as immediate as in the bank teller scenario. In *Hudson and Taylor* [1971], two teenage girls were asked to testify against a suspect. In the days leading up to the trial, they had been repeatedly threatened by the suspect's associates. Once in the courtroom, they saw one of these associates in the audience, glaring at them: both denied they had seen anything. Later they were charged with perjury, and claimed duress because of the threat from the associates, even if the threat was of something vague and distant. On appeal, the Court recognised that threatened action need not be "imminent," but the *effect* of the fear of the threatened action could still be "present" sufficiently to "neutralise the will," as it had in this case. Importantly, the ages of the defendants, 17 and 19, were also taken into account as it added to their vulnerability.[30]

The threatened harm must be "serious," which means only serious personal injury (including rape) or death — to D, or to someone close to D.[31] This is interesting, because of

30 Interestingly, the American *Model Penal Code* leaves out the imminence condition:

> 2.09 (1) It is an affirmative defense that the actor engaged in the conduct charged to constitute an offense because he was coerced to do so by the use of, or a threat to use, unlawful force against his person or the person of another, that a person of reasonable firmness in his situation would have been unable to resist.

31 In *Hasan* [2005], para. 21(3), Lord Bingham used the formulation "somebody for whom he reasonably regarded himself as being responsible." If T threatens D's child, this might actually be more effective

course there are plenty of ways to threaten someone just as effectively as threatening their health or life: I can threaten to burn down D's shop or to spread vicious rumours on social media. With non-personal threats such as these, no duress can be claimed, and so D will be legally on her own. One might wonder, with Padfield (2016, p. 125), why duress cannot be allowed on a sliding scale of threatened actions, where the jury would look at the "severity ratio" between the harm threatened and the coerced crime to determine a degree of mitigation. Perhaps the fear is of a proliferation of duress claims, and an over-complication of the trial. In addition, threats of less than personal injury, together with the relevant ratio, can be taken into account at the sentencing stage.[32]

The most interesting contrast with self-defence concerns the reasonability of D's belief about V's threat. With self-defence, the belief may be sincere but does *not* need to be reasonable: D can be paranoid or over-sensitive. With duress, the belief has to be sincere *and* reasonable, based on the evidence available to her. One reason for this is that we want D to be *sure* about the threat before she goes off to commit a separate crime on an innocent victim; with self-defence, there is no separate crime and no other victim.

Not only must the belief in the imminence and the magnitude of the threatened harm be reasonable, but the defendant must be judged against another objective standard, a "sober person of reasonable firmness." (This expression comes from *Graham* [1982].) The reasonable firmness condition might be unfair to timorous people. In *Bowen* [1996], D was charged with fraud, but claimed to have been threatened by two men. Importantly, D had an IQ of 68, and was therefore unusually susceptible to vague and minor threats, a susceptibility exploited by the threateners (whom we can imagine later defending themselves by saying "it was only a bit of fun"). The Court deemed D's IQ irrelevant.[33] The thought is that every competent adult is expected to have acquired a reasonable firmness; this is a moral quality in principle accessible to everyone, not an intellectual quality accessible only to some. As Joshua Dressler (1989, p. 1351) puts it:

> At some point in one's life a person becomes (or should become) aware of his strengths and weaknesses. One who is (or should be) aware that he too easily accedes to others' unlawful entreaties or demands has the responsibility to attempt to strengthen his resolve; one who fails to make the effort should be held accountable even if his will is … truly overborne.

In *Bowen*, the court did allow other personal characteristics to be relevant: age, sex, serious disability and pregnancy. So it would be understandable for a young teenager to *feel* more threatened than an adult would feel by the same objective threat. The additional vulnerability associated with disability and pregnancy are obvious. As with the loss-of-control defence, however, we have another reference to D's sex, and it is not clear why this is relevant. If the thought is that women tend to be physically smaller and weaker than men, then the reference should be to the physical difference between D and T, rather than sex. By referring to sex, the

than threatening D herself, and the law can recognise this. The *Model Penal Code* 2.09(1) only speaks of "another."

32 It would be unfair to stigmatise a coerced defendant with a criminal record, even with a lenient sentence. In *Dao* [2012], the Court spelled out the compelling policy reasons for limiting duress to threats of personal injury or death, and not including, e.g. a threat of false imprisonment.

33 However, the courts have not been consistent in this. In *Antar* [2004], an 18-year-old with mild to moderate learning disabilities was charged with conspiracy to rob, and his duress defence rejected. On appeal, the court said that medical evidence of his low IQ, together with his high score on the Gudjunsson Suggestibility Scale ascertained during police interviews, should have been released to the jury, who could then have decided on duress. This is another instance where moral virtues are pushed aside by medicalisation: instead of relying on ordinary moral judgements about how much pressure someone ought to be able to resist, the medical experts are brought in to rule on the matter.

court seems to suggest that women could claim duress more often than men, and this would confirm unhealthy stereotypes.[34]

There are two important limitations to the duress excuse. First, the defendant cannot voluntarily enter into a situation which he knew (or reasonably should have known) could lead to duress, either in the short or long term; that is, he could not join a criminal gang, and then claim duress when he was threatened into committing a crime. Second, duress cannot be a defence to murder, attempted murder, or complicity to murder, and this was confirmed in *Howe* [1987]. The reason for this policy is partly because of the requirement that the threatened harm has to be worse than the coerced crime, and nothing is worse than murder. The law needs all the deterrence it can muster to prevent murder, and if citizens know that duress will not be available, this might inspire more of them to refuse the duress.[35] Another argument is that if duress provided such a defence, then a gang boss could threaten an underling into murdering a member of a rival gang member, effectively with impunity.

The denial of duress for *complicity* in murder is controversial. Before *Howe* prohibited it, *Lynch* [1975] allowed duress in such cases. In Belfast during the height of the Troubles, D was "asked" by T to drive him and three associates one night to a certain destination. D knew T as a local IRA leader, and knew of his reputation for violence, so reasonably deduced an implicit serious threat. He also had a pretty good idea of the men's plan to murder. D did as he was ordered, the men carried out the murder, and D was charged with complicity to murder, but successfully claimed duress. *Howe* [1986] then overruled *Lynch* with these memorable words by Lord Hailsham:

> I have known in my own lifetime of too many acts of heroism by ordinary human beings of no more than ordinary fortitude to regard a law as either "just or humane" which withdraws the protection of the criminal law from the innocent victim and casts the cloak of its protection upon the coward and the poltroon in the name of a "concession to human frailty."

In other words, Hailsham was claiming that Lynch had been a coward, and should have risked his own life by rejecting T's demand for complicity. This is already a harsh line, but is even harsher in the Belfast context, surely. Hailsham was essentially telling all people to be heroes, when heroism by definition is something that I cannot be blameworthy for failing to be.

The harshness of the *Howe* judgement was starkly revealed by *Wilson* [2007], where a 13-year-old boy helped his father murder their neighbour. Because the boy was over the age of criminal responsibility, he was convicted of murder, as an accessory. However, the boy had an acute fear of his father, stemming from years of violent parenting. If the boy's crime had been anything less than murder, the duress defence would have been easily recognised.[36]

34 *Branford* [2016] was a case of "indirect" duress. D was charged with conspiracy to supply controlled drugs. She claimed that her boyfriend P had asked her to carry the drugs because *he* was facing a serious threat. Her appeal was dismissed, partly on the grounds that the threat to him was vague and non-immediate, partly because she had voluntarily associated with known criminals, but mainly because she seemed to be acting more out of love for P than out of fear for P's safety. The case is interesting, nevertheless, because it allowed the possibility of an indirect threat: if T credibly threatens D's husband P with imminent death (and P had no prior involvement with T), then D might have a defence if she assisted P's crime as the only way to avoid T's threat.

35 As part of the "moral luck" theme throughout this book, Child et al. (2022, p. 852) point out a moral luck situation in this context. Imagine T threatens D with death unless he causes grievous bodily harm to V. As instructed, D carries out the GBH on V, and V ends up in hospital in critical condition. If V lives, then D can claim duress and will be acquitted; if V dies, then D cannot claim duress and he will be sentenced to the mandatory life sentence for murder. D's two radically different futures depend entirely on the luck of V's developing medical situation.

36 The Law Commission argued for allowing duress for murder. See Part 6 of its Report no. 304, *Murder, Manslaughter and Infanticide* (2006).

10.7 DIMINISHED RESPONSIBILITY

The defence of "diminished responsibility," known colloquially as "temporary insanity," can have either a cognitive or volitional aspect. Before we look at the statutory grounds, it should be said that this defence, like Loss of Control (provocation), (i) applies only to murder charges, and (ii) is only a partial defence, in that, if successful, it reduces the charge from murder to manslaughter — the defendant will probably still go to prison. So the defendant is taken as having *some* degree of understanding and control.

Section 2 of the *Homicide Act* 1957 is entitled "Persons suffering from diminished responsibility," and reads:

> (1) Where a person kills or is party to a killing of another, he shall not be convicted of murder if he was suffering from an abnormality of mental functioning which —
>
> (a) arose from a medical condition
>
> (b) substantially impaired D's ability to do one or more of the things mentioned in subsection (1A), and
>
> (c) provides an explanation for D's acts and omissions in doing or being a party to the killing.
>
> (1A) Those things are —
>
> (a) to understand the nature of D's conduct;
>
> (b) to form a rational judgment;
>
> (c) to exercise self-control.[37]

The conditions for diminished responsibility are worth laying out as a "negative" definition of moral responsibility, but also because they are relevant to our discussion of the "Loss of Control" excuse. The crucial difference between them is that diminished responsibility has to arise from a medical condition, which can only be diagnosed by a psychiatrist (i.e. not only the condition, but also the causal link to the behaviour), and so there is not much more that law or philosophy can contribute — as such we are not discussing either diminished responsibility or insanity at any length in this book.

A couple of comments on the three 1A capacities, however. The first is about D understanding what she is doing; but this is ambiguous about whether she understands the *moral aspect* of what she is doing, and, insofar as she does understand that her conduct is e.g. harmful, whether her understanding involves some kind of *appropriate moral repulsion* from the conduct or the consequences.[38] The second 1A capacity refers to the capacity to form a rational judgement, but does not specify whether the corresponding incapacity has to do with a defect of

37 It's worth just adding clause 1B, which qualifies 1A(c) as follows:

> For the purposes of subsection (1)(c), an abnormality of mental functioning provides and explanation of D's conduct if it causes, or is a significant contributory factor in causing, D to carry out that conduct.

38 In contrast, the original definition of insanity under the M'Naghten Rules of 1843 have an explicit reference to the wrongness of the act:

> to establish a defence on the ground of insanity, it must be clearly proved that, at the time of the committing of the act, the party accused was labouring under such a defect of reason, from disease of the mind, as not to know the nature and quality of the act he was doing; or if he did know it, that he did not know he was doing what was wrong.

reason, or instead from the experience of an overwhelming emotion; insofar as the diminished responsibility was due to the latter, then it overlaps significantly with the defence of Loss of Control.

The third 1A capacity — "to exercise self-control" — is controversial, and indeed has been controversial since Socrates denied the existence of *akrasia* (weakness of will) in Plato's dialogue *Protagoras.*[39] (The original M'Naghten Rules for the defence of insanity did not include any reference to self-control.) The basic problem here is about how one would test D's claim that she was unable to control herself. D's failure to understand the nature of her conduct or her failure to form a rational judgement can be corroborated by evidence of her behaviour and utterances before and after the killing. But such corroboration is much more difficult with respect to self-control. It might seem that the only effective test would be if D would experience a relevant failure of self-control in committing a crime with a police officer literally standing at her side.

39 In Plato's dialogue *Protagoras*, the character Socrates declares "No one who either knows or believes that there is another possible course of action, better than the one he is following, will ever continue on his present course" (*Protagoras* 358b–358c). In other words, if a smoker says "I really wish I could give up smoking," then Socrates would say: if you *really* wanted to give it up, you would have already done so — nobody is compelling you to smoke.

CHAPTER 11

PUNISHMENT, PARDONS AND PAROLE

Most criminal law textbooks do not include a chapter on punishment, but it is an area of rich philosophical debate.[1] There are also two large areas of the social sciences called criminology and penology, which, among other things, examine different kinds of penal systems and procedures in order to see which is the most effective at reducing the rates of various types of crime. The criminologist's data is essential for guiding police and public policy in trying to predict and reduce crime rates; the penologist's data is essential for prison reform and to improve policies for integrating the offender back into society with a minimum of recidivism. We're not going to look at the social sciences here, since we are more interested in the *meaning* and the *ethical value* of the punishment, both for the offender, and for society.

For most of this book, we have remained metaphorically in the courtroom, with occasional asides at the crime scene or in the police investigation. For this chapter, we're assuming the defendant has been investigated and tried fairly, all the evidence and testimony have been considered, all defences evaluated and the verdict given. Once found guilty beyond all reasonable doubt, the defendant becomes an "offender," and moves to the next stages of the process: sentencing (still in the courtroom), and then punishment (a fine, various kinds of community penalties, or prison).

A philosophical theory of punishment starts with the following question: how can a liberal democratic state justify deliberately harming (e.g. through incarceration) some of its citizens? Answer: because those citizens have broken the law. But so what? What exactly connects their law-breaking to the incarceration? That will concern us for the bulk of the chapter. The state has laid out some of the purposes of punishment, and we will discuss these.[2] In the last third, we will discuss the situation where the allocated punishment is cancelled (as in the case of a pardon) or reduced (as in the case of parole). If we assume that the police investigation and the court process have been thorough and fair, then it will result in an assigned punishment which will itself be fair by definition; but that would mean that anything that alters that assigned punishment would be essentially *unfair*. So what's going on with pardons and parole? It cannot simply be about some kind of justified lenience, since all the relevant factors have already been taken into consideration in the trial itself.

1 See, for example, Bennett (2008) and Canton (2019). In addition, see the entry "Legal punishment" in the *Stanford Encyclopedia of Philosophy*.

2 The *Criminal Justice Act* 2003, Section 142 lists the purposes of punishment:

Any court dealing with an offender in respect of his offence must have regard to the following purposes of sentencing —

(a) the punishment of offenders,
(b) the reduction of crime (including its reduction by deterrence),
(c) the reform and rehabilitation of offenders,
(d) the protection of the public, and
(e) the making of reparation by offenders to persons affected by their offences.

It is also worth looking at the *Sentencing Council for England and Wales*. The Council, to quote the homepage, "promotes greater consistency in sentencing, whilst maintaining the independence of the judiciary. The Council produces guidelines on sentencing for the judiciary and criminal justice professionals and aims to increase public understanding of sentencing."
https://www.sentencingcouncil.org.uk/

DOI: 10.4324/9781003351887-11

11.1 INSTITUTIONS, RULES AND PUNISHMENT

To understand what punishment is, we first have to understand what an institution is, and this will take us into one area of "jurisprudence" — the nature of law. There are lots of institutions: universities, companies, football clubs, restaurants, churches, choirs, families ... and of course the state itself. All of these institutions have rules that restrict the autonomy of their members in various ways: indeed, we could say that each institution is partly constituted by its rules. That is, most rules are justified with reference to the institution's fundamental values (or to the purpose of the institution, why it was established, whom it serves, etc.).

Institutions also have hierarchies, with certain members having the authority to discipline other members when they break the rules, together with the authority to recruit and expel members — notice that they have the *authority*, granted to them by the institution, rather than merely the *power* to discipline. That's an important distinction: power is always arbitrary. The more that a rule restricts members' autonomy, then (i) the greater the justification required (always with reference to the institutional values), (ii) the greater the threat required to maximise compliance, and (iii) the greater the visible "follow-through" required against the non-compliant (with the ultimate sanction being expulsion). As the Lord Chief Justice of England said in 1924, justice must not only be done, it must be seen to be done.[3]

Think about a simple rule which most readers of this book will be familiar with: the prohibition of plagiarism in a university. Plagiarism is prohibited because it undermines the whole purpose of the university as a place of honest competition and fair assessment in learning desirable knowledge and skills. It is a constitutive rule: a university that does not have an explicit prohibition of plagiarism would simply not be a university. This prohibition is not some arbitrary restriction articulating the current university president's dislikes; just as a student who plagiarises is not guilty of personally offending the university president. Rather, she offends against the institution and is punished by the institution *for* breaking the rule. Every student, upon accepting their offer of a place at the university, is taken to have tacitly consented to the rules that define that institution, and therefore to have tacitly consented (in advance) to being disciplined upon breaking those rules.

Notice that there are two ways of consenting to the rules: prudentially and morally. The difference can be brought out by considering three punished plagiarisers.[4]

- A: the software is getting much too good, it's not worth the risk, I'm not going to plagiarise again.
- B: I got caught this time because I was foolish; next time I will have to be more clever.
- C: I cheated, and getting a zero on my course is no more than I deserve; I am ashamed, and I won't do it again.

Prudential or instrumental consent is about self-interest. Both A and B are worried about their self-interest, but they reach different conclusions about the risks and the benefits. Insofar as they were only concerned about their self-interest, they have not been *punished* in the full moral sense of the term: instead, they have been *managed*, and their risk–benefit calculations have simply been disrupted. For them, the rules are not moral obstacles, but practical obstacles.

3 Lord Hewart in *Sussex Justices* [1924].
4 This is an adaptation of an example by Peter Winch (1972), and more generally this chapter is indebted to Winch's approach. For a recent discussion, see Reid (2020).

Only C has been punished in the sense that she has been brought to see the wrongness of the plagiarism, and she feels appropriate shame.

The institution obviously has to design its rules for the self-interested, but its penalties must be intelligible as punishment for ethically sensitive rule-breakers. A consequentialist would not be too interested in the different kinds of offenders, as long as the rules managed to reduce the amount of plagiarism.

We have laboured this analogy with university rules because the readers of this book will probably have more direct experience with university rules, with the temptation to break those rules, and with suffering the penalties for breaking the rules, than with criminal laws. The word "experience" is key here. To fully understand a rule is partly to *feel* the way that it guides one's behaviour, consciously or subconsciously; and to *fear* the punishment for breaking the rule.

Once we understand the institutional basis of all punishment, then criminal punishment it is much more familiar. And so we move from the university to the state, to ask: how can a democratic state justify punishing offenders? Because the legislature (with its democratic authority) has passed laws expressing the values of the state; and laws have to be enforced (unenforced laws are merely recommendations). So law-breakers need to be punished if the laws are to work as rules.

Essential to the enforcement of the laws is that (i) the main laws have to be relatively accessible to the citizens (at the very least, the state education system has to inform them); (ii) laws have to make basic sense to the citizens as expressions of the state's values; (iii) citizens can only be punished on the basis of breaking pre-existing published laws; (iv) the penalties for breaking the laws are basically familiar, in order for the law to fulfil its deterrence function; (v) as a result of all these conditions, it should be relatively easy for the citizen to live her life, and to know that she can live her life, within the limits of the law.

The vast majority of a state's laws are administrative and regulatory, and invisible to the ordinary citizen — she will only bump up against them once she is working in a regulated company, for example. In a book about criminal law, we're only looking at a very small selection of laws, but most criminal laws should be intelligible as extensions of the moral rules that we learn as children. And part of learning these moral rules requires punishment from parents and teachers. In this sense, the children, once adults, should be "primed" to understand the basic prohibitions of the criminal law and the purpose of the punishment for infringements of such prohibitions. The only difference is that the state has taken on the authority to punish. This is another version of the paradoxical thought, outlined in the Introduction, that every crime is actually committed against the state; strictly speaking, the human being who is the victim of crime is no more than a witness. It is the state that investigates the crime, tries the defendant, and punishes the offender — and prohibits any actions of private vengeance from the victim. Traditionally, this understanding has often led the state to neglect the victim of crime.[5]

Note one important limitation in the following discussion: a child of 9 or under cannot *legally* commit a crime because she is below the age of "criminal responsibility." Of course, she can factually cause lots of changes in the world, but it is assumed that she lacks sufficient freedom and understanding to be fairly held responsible and punished by the state for breaking

5 In the United Kingdom there is a government website (https://www.gov.uk/get-support-as-a-victim-of-crime), and certain compensation schemes (https://www.gov.uk/browse/justice/compensation-victim-support), but these do not seem to be working very well. See Topping A. "Justice system failing victims, says commissioner for England and Wales." *The Guardian*, 21 July 2021.

its laws. England and Wales are unusual in having such a low age of criminal responsibility; most Western countries set the age at 12, or even 14.[6]

11.2 THEORIES OF PUNISHMENT

A word about the larger theoretical structures: within the broad field of political philosophy, we are discussing *punitive* justice. This is to be distinguished from *distributive* justice (which is about taxing and redistributing through welfare) and *corrective* justice (where e.g. tort law governs compensation for damages). Punitive justice is guided by two ideals. First, the criminal trial is designed to find out *exactly* how guilty the defendant is; second, the criminal justice system is designed to assign *exactly* the punishment that the defendant deserves. Although it is easy to be sceptical about these ideals in the real world, they are still crucial in shaping the design of the institutions and in shaping our assessment of their success.

Traditionally there are two theories (or families of theories) to justify punishment: retributivist and consequentialist. Suffice to say that both theories can be deployed in different contexts, and sometimes this produces tensions, even contradictions. Real legal systems invoke a loose hybrid between the theories, leaning one way or the other in different contexts or at different times.

- Retributivism focuses on *individual desert*; the offender committed crime X and therefore she simply deserves punishment Y.[7]
- Consequentialism focuses on the best *consequences for society*; the offender committed crime X, and punishment Y is most appropriate (in length and type) to reform or to deter the individual's re-offending and to deter offending by others, all as a trade-off against the financial cost of punishment.

The main argumentative move behind retributivism is to see the crime and the punishment as conceptually related across time. This conceptual relation is sometimes captured in the word "thereby." When a citizen contemplates committing a certain crime, she *thereby* worries about the future punishment if she gets caught. If I learn that Smith is being punished now (fairly), I *thereby* start to wonder what Smith is being punished for. When I myself am in prison (fairly), and dwell on my discomforts, I *thereby* think about the crime I committed in the past: for I know that I am not here by accident of fate, just as I am not here because the state merely wants to assert its power over me, I am here because of the crime I chose to commit.

The retributivist can describe the conceptual link in different metaphors:

- the offender's crime disrupts the moral equilibrium, and the state has to restore the moral equilibrium by punishing the offender;
- the offender has taken advantage of the state's trust in order to enrich herself, and now she has to repay her "debt";

6 In a notorious case from 1993, two 10-year-olds were convicted of murdering 2-year-old James Bulger in Bootle, near Liverpool. At the time of writing (July 2023), a bill is currently in Parliament that would raise the age of criminal responsibility to 12. (See: https://bills.parliament.uk/bills/2613).

7 There is a philosophical debate about conflicts between different desert "bases." Imagine I am watching my sister competing in an athletic race. (i) I might say she deserves to win, because she has trained so hard; or (ii) because she has overcome so many obstacles to get this far, or (iii) because she really really wants to win, and it would make her so happy; or (iv) because it would be great publicity for our town if she won … On the other hand, (v) within athletics only the fastest runner deserves to win!

- the offender has forfeited the moral innocence with which she came into the world, and now has to "earn" it back in order to rejoin the moral community.
- the criminal is a gambler. By choosing to participate in the "crime game," she has consented to the rules, and consented to the possible punishment if she gets caught.

If we take some of these metaphors further, not only do they justify the infliction of punishment on the reluctant offender, but they also explain why the offender *needs* to be punished, and why the morally mature offender might even recognise this. Not only does the community benefit from the offender being punished, but the offender herself benefits. In Dostoyevsky's *Crime and Punishment*, the whole story turns on Raskolnikov's crushing guilt for his murders, and his belated recognition that he has to confess and go to prison in order to save his soul.

This idea of a "need for punishment" starts with the child's moral education. Good parents do not punish rule-breaking in order to inspire fearful compliance; they punish in order to teach the children about the moral reality of the potential harm arising from the broken rule. Ideally, the child will internalise and understand the rules of morality so that she can reliably comply even when the threat of punishment is removed. Putting a toddler on the "naughty step" (e.g. for stealing from her sibling) is about teaching the toddler to feel the moral wrongness of the stealing, and to imagine the theft from the victim's point of view. We will return to this idea of moral education when we look at Jean Hampton's theory in the next section.

We said the retributivist sees a conceptual connection between the crime and the punishment (see, for example, von Hirsch, 1993). This also applies to the intuition that the punishment should "fit" the crime. This fit entails a number of things. First of all, that it is absolutely forbidden to "punish" the innocent. We have put "punish" in scare quotes because conceptually the innocent *cannot* be punished in the full sense of punishment; they can of course be thrown in prison on the basis of faked evidence. Consider the notorious case of the "Birmingham Six." Two bombs exploded in two pubs in Birmingham in 1975, and the IRA claimed responsibility. The police were not making much headway in their investigation, but they had picked up six Irish labourers near the pubs, and so they prosecuted them on the basis of fabricated evidence. The retributivist would condemn such a move out of hand. The consequentialist might not: look at the good consequences first, she will say. The families of the bomb victims felt satisfied by the apparently efficient police work. The British public, made nervous by the bombs, were now reassured. Although the IRA would of course know that the labourers had been framed, other potential terrorists might well be deterred by a new fear of the English police. (It took 16 years before the injustice was discovered, the sentences quashed, and compensation paid out.) [8]

The second thing that follows from the punishment fitting the crime is the idea of a ladder of punishments lined up alongside a ladder of crimes, rising from least to most severe. At the bottom will be something like graffiti, at the top will be murder. At the bottom will be formal cautions, rising to fines, then to community punishments, until we reach imprisonment, which will increase in the number of years and restrictions, right through to the mandatory life sentence for murder.[9] In response to such a scale, the consequentialist will tend to allow

8 A more sophisticated consequentialist will be worried about the bad consequences of the truth leaking out, as it did eventually. But the point is that even the more sophisticated consequentialist has nothing in principle against framing the innocent if the risk-benefit comparisons justify it.

9 Note that a "life sentence" does not usually mean life in prison. Upon sentencing, the offender will learn of her "minimum term" which she will serve in prison, and this is usually 15 years, although it can be longer for offences aggravated in various ways. See Schedule 21 of the *Sentencing Act 2021*.

exceptions and make adjustments based on a trade-off between costs and crime rates. The consequentialist cannot in principle object to draconian punishments for graffiti damage, as is the case in Singapore (so long as the costs of such draconian punishment do not exceed the costs of cleaning up the graffiti).[10]

The third thing that follows from punishment fitting the crime is that the retributivist will oppose discretionary parole. If the state has calculated, on the basis of the severity scale, that offender D deserves five years in prison, then D should be imprisoned for five years; not a day less, not a day more. Whether she behaves well or badly in prison is irrelevant. Whether she is repentant or resentful is irrelevant. In contrast, the consequentialist will ask: what's the point of keeping the repentant, well-behaving offender in prison at such a cost, especially if we can reliably predict that she presents no danger to society? This is a more plausible argument, and we will return to it in the section on parole, below.

The central thought behind consequentialism in all areas of ethics runs as follows: Whenever I face two options here and now, I should choose the option most likely to generate the best overall consequences (i.e. with the probability "multiplied" by the quality). Quality can be measured in all sorts of ways, with the most plausible criterion in public policy debates having to do with best interests or welfare. And it's right for governments to be concerned with using their limited tax revenues to maximise the welfare of the greatest number of citizens. When it comes to penal policy, the main criterion is public safety, as measured by crime statistics, and especially recidivism statistics. To ask whether a penal policy "works" is mainly to ask whether offenders are choosing not to re-offend; but that is obviously part of larger questions, not only about police investigative budgets, but also about the social welfare system, and whether certain citizens have enough opportunities and support to "go straight."

When consequentialist penologists calculate the best sentence for a given crime, they will balance the costs against the measurable deterrence, and they will tweak these calculations regularly as the new data comes in.[11] Imagine there are two offenders, with similar criminal records, who have been found guilty of the same crime. One of them is clearly repentant at the trial, the other not. The retributivist will tend to say that they deserve the same sentence for the same crime. The consequentialist may well suggest that the repentant offender has already "got the message" and therefore does not need as long a sentence as the non-repentant offender.[12]

After that minimum term, a parole board will consider (i) her behaviour in prison, (ii) the danger she poses to the public, and — related to the first two criteria — her remorse and understanding. (We discuss parole later in this chapter.) She may then be released, although she will be "on licence" for the rest of her life. She may be subject to varying restrictions, such as wearing an electronic tag. And if she commits any new offence, however small, she may be imprisoned once again.

10 The relevant legislation is the Singapore *Vandalism Act* 1966.

11 See Walker & Walker (1991); According to the website Statista, in 2021, the cost of housing one prisoner in a UK prison for one year was £48,000, but this cost is rising:

https://www.statista.com/statistics/1202172/cost-per-prisoner-england-and-wales/

Of course the financial cost is only one kind of cost. On the one hand, prison is bad enough to act as a deterrent. On the other hand, prison brutalises prisoners, and so makes some of them *more* likely to re-offend after release. In addition, prison is the ideal location to meet other offenders, to learn skills and information from them, and to form new alliances and make new plans. For all these reasons, many penologists argue in favour of different kinds of non-custodial punishments, such as house arrest, curfews, tagging, alongside fines and unpaid work in the community. This is an on-going debate, and we cannot summarise it here. For the purposes of this chapter, we are largely taking "punishment" to mean imprisonment.

12 One strand of consequentialism focuses on *rehabilitation*. The thought is not only that the citizens need to be deterred from offending and re-offending, the offenders also need help changing their characters. After all, deterrence policies presuppose not only an actor who is rational, that is, who can correctly assess risks and costs, but also an actor who has enough strength of will to act on her conclusions about her best interests. Many citizens lack such strength of will, and end up in prison again and again. Rehabilitation

Moral education

An ambitious justification for punishment is Jean Hampton's "moral education theory" (1984), which combines elements of both retributivism and consequentialism. Punishment is justified insofar as it *morally educates* the offender. This is still consequentialist in that the proof of the pudding will be in lower crime rates; but it is retributivist in its emphasis on the offender's understanding rather than prudential cost/benefit calculations.

Hampton's starting point is the family and the school, where children are morally educated. Both institutions use punishment as a normal part of the educational process. The small child does not yet understand the wrongness of what she did, or the suffering of the victim, and so she has to learn to feel the wrongness through punishment combined with parental/teacher disapproval. Throughout, it is crucial for the parent/teacher to explain why exactly the child is being punished, in order to justify it *to the child*. Ideally, the child will come to understand something of the overarching moral order that is the non-arbitrary source of the punishment. Without such an explanation pointing at intelligible moral reasons, without the socialisation and internalisation of the rules, the child will merely resent the power while biding her time and seeking rule-evading opportunities to satisfy her desires.

Much the same process takes place at the level of the state, argues Hampton. Most offenders are not children, but adults who remain ignorant of some important moral truths; her theory could thus be described as Socratic, in the sense that Socrates saw ignorance as the root of all evil. Moral education involves bringing the offender to see the moral wrongness of what she has done, typically through some reference to the suffering she directly caused to her victim.[13] If successful, the offender will feel genuine remorse, and this remorse will counteract any temptation to re-offend.

Moral (re-)education is important to distinguish from deterrence and rehabilitation, *even if* the desirable consequence (the reduction in recidivism) is the same. On the one hand, the rationally deterred offender is induced to make new risk–benefit calculations, but will gladly re-offend when her calculations support it, and may lack the necessary strength of will to avoid short-term temptation and peer pressure. On the other hand, the rehabilitated offender does not necessarily understand the wrongness of the offence either, for she has just been "reprogrammed" to turn away from crime. In contrast, the moral education approach to punishment respects the moral autonomy of the offender by treating them as essentially educable. In addition, the moral education approach differs from the pure retributivist in that the latter bases punishment *merely* on the offence, whether or not the offender understands the punishment as a moral response to the offence. In contrast to all three, the morally re-educated offender will be glad to have been punished because it brought her the education she needed to restore her own deepened moral understanding.

Hampton acknowledges that there are limits to the state's attempts to morally educate, especially among older, hardened offenders. Once education efforts have failed (however such failure is to be characterised and evaluated), then the state will have to fall back on deterrence and rehabilitation.

---

efforts can use a range of psychological techniques to strengthen the will, reduce impulsiveness, control emotions, and improve longer-term planning.

13 One practical application of this approach is in "restorative justice" programmes, such as this one in Northern Ireland: https://www.crjireland.org/. And here is an American one: http://www.rjpmidcoast.org/. The idea is especially to take morally immature teenagers (convicted of e.g. burglary) and to bring them into face-to-face contact with their victims. We think it's fair to say that the results of such initiatives have been uneven.

The death penalty

We cannot have a chapter on punishment without briefly discussing the death penalty.[14] But the debate over the death penalty is a curious one: for in all countries of the Western world — bar one — there *is* no real political debate. One after another, all the Western countries — bar one — abandoned it between the middle and the end of the twentieth century. So there is something disingenuous about, e.g. having an earnest philosophical debate on the subject in a British university debating club, when there is no realistic prospect of the death penalty being brought back in Britain. Whenever a serial killer or a child murderer is caught, then there will be a public outcry sufficient to shift the opinion polls toward reinstatement, but this outcry has never been strong or persistent enough to push Parliamentarians to respond. It is tempting to see this as a matter of moral progress, and to see Western societies — bar one — as having made moral progress.

Of course, the one Western exception is the United States, or at least 31 of the 50 American states, and so a genuine debate continues in that country (or at least in those states), much to the bafflement of other Western observers. The arguments for and against the death penalty mirror the arguments already described in the previous sections, and are not worth expounding in more detail. Suffice to say that the retributivist argument has an extra piquancy from the Biblical "Talon law": an eye for an eye and a tooth for a tooth. Even though law-makers do not demand Talonic retribution for other crimes (e.g. rapists are not to be raped), even though it seems paradoxical for the state to kill someone to show that killing is wrong, the death penalty appeals to a basic primitive response, and one can well imagine the victim's family demanding that the state respect their primitive response. The same primitive response underpins the attractive vigilante justice of the Western film genre.

Earlier in the chapter, we described retributivism in terms of the conceptual link between crime and punishment. Supporters of the death penalty would claim the same conceptual link. And yet most people in the Western world would claim that the conceptually linked Talonic urge, while understandable, has to be overcome in the spirit of civilisation overcoming barbarism.

The central problem with trying to justify the death penalty is that it is hard to classify it as *punishment* in the full sense of the word. For to punish someone is to impose harsh treatment on them, which they are meant to *suffer through*, and ideally from which they are meant to learn — learn either in the sense of revising their risk–benefit calculations, or in the sense of moral education. When the offender is executed, there is no further room for suffering, no room for future deterrence, let alone for shame or repentance, or for moral education. In executing the offender we have simply given up on them.

The death penalty advocate might say, first, that the experience of being on death row before the execution is itself part of the punishment, part of what they suffer through, and it is the place where they — ideally — come to understand that they morally deserve death, in a manner that could appeal to both the retributivist and the moral educationalist. It is only the awareness of imminent and certain death that finally brings home to the offender the seriousness of what she has done. Alternatively, the death penalty advocate might say that the offender's crime is *so* serious as to reveal that they have voluntarily abandoned the moral community, and thereby forfeited any right to the hope and respect that would lead to Hampton's re-educative attempts. The death penalty is therefore not so much a punishment so much as the final recognition of the offender's chosen abandonment.[15]

14 For a review, see Hood and Hoyle (2015).

15 There is a question of the threshold of seriousness. Should it be simple murder, or at least a second murder? Or a murder aggravated by sexual assault or racism, or by the victim's status as a police officer or a child?

Death penalty advocates often reach for extreme cases such as Nazi war criminals: surely we can all agree that at least such criminals deserve to die? We hesitate to discuss this argument, since we are sensitive to the unfortunate tendency among English-language philosophers of wheeling in the caricature "Nazi" to nudge the reader's intuitions without any sensitivity to historical realities. Despite such hesitation, it is instructive to listen to the words and the tone of senior Nazi Adolf Eichmann on trial in Jerusalem in 1961.[16] Eichmann sticks to his obvious defence, that he was only obeying orders, that he was merely a cog in a machine, and that he was not responsible for the fate of the Jews after they reached the destinations to which he sent them. Whether or not he believed his own defence, he was well aware of his own fate, as if he shrugged and said "All right, you caught me, you're stronger now, go ahead and kill me." In other words, despite the sheer number of witnesses testifying about the death camps, it's almost certain that he did not accept his guilt, did not accept the trial's authority, and did not accept the *moral* appropriateness of the death sentence. It was no more than "victor's justice," not justice at all. Insofar as this is the case, then at a fundamental level the trial failed; and as "punishment" the execution could not succeed either. In Eichmann's own eyes, he died as an obedient soldier, not a criminal (and his last words expressed this fact). Perhaps this was inevitable, given the sheer amount of self-deception required to function as a high-ranking Nazi bureaucrat in the first place, and then to hold on to the various comforting narratives after the war as he rebuilt his ordinary life. But one can't help thinking that the execution was *too soon*, precisely because it prevented anything like understanding from ever taking root.[17]

In contrast to Eichmann, Albert Speer, Hitler's Minister of Armaments and War Production from 1943, was sentenced at Nuremburg to 20 years' imprisonment for his collusion in a vast system of slave labour. (He denied any knowledge of the Holocaust, and was believed at Nuremberg.)[18] During his prison years, he wrote three autobiographies that come close to articulating some kind of remorse. There is some debate about how sincere the autobiographies were, and the degree to which they were twisted by self-deception or by calculation; but either way it is at least arguable that Speer was punished "more" than Eichmann (although perhaps never enough) simply by being kept alive for a longer time in prison (effectively in solitary confinement, since the other Nazi convicts did not talk to him), but also because after release he was accessible to further discussion about the nature of his moral failure. To give him credit, Speer continued to give many interviews from his release in 1966 right through to his death in 1979. Again, we can be cynical and say that he was polishing his legacy; but we can also appreciate that he resisted the temptation to just disappear into his own private interests and hobbies, as most ex-Nazis did.

11.3 PARDONS

Before discussing pardons, we have to briefly distinguish three concepts that are often conflated and used interchangeably, but which should be defined precisely for our philosophical

16 As head of the Reich Security Head Office Section IV B4 in the latter part of World War II, Eichmann was in charge of the logistics of mass deportation of Jews from across Europe to the death camps of Poland. After the war, Eichmann fled to Argentina, where he was located and kidnapped by a secret Israeli commando in 1960. He was tried in Jerusalem for "Crimes against the Jewish people," found guilty, and executed in 1962. The most famous account of the trial is perhaps Hannah Arendt (1964), where she coined the expression "the banality of evil."

17 Eichmann did not repent. But even when the imminent execution brings about repentance as the death penalty advocate hopes, questions remain. Tim Robbins's 1995 film *Dead Man Walking* is about a murderer who undergoes a transformative remorse as he nears the execution date. Now if the remorse is genuine, that could be an argument for keeping him alive in order to prolong his suffering, rather than giving him an easy way out.

18 The full extent of Speer's knowledge and lies during the Nuremberg trials were documented in Sereny (1995).

purposes: forgiveness, mercy and pardons. First of all, forgiveness is essentially *interpersonal*: typically, one individual victim forgives the individual who harmed her. This has nothing to do with the law, and nothing to do with institutions like the state. A victim will face the question of whether to forgive her attacker or not; this is entirely her decision, and it will have no bearing on whether the state decides to prosecute the attacker or not. Again, this is because the attack was committed not against the victim but against the state. It is also perfectly possible for a victim to forgive her attacker, while at the same time — persuaded by Hampton's moral education theory of punishment — to support the state's efforts to prosecute, sentence and imprison the attacker.[19]

In contrast, mercy is essentially institutional, like punishment.[20] In criminal law, mercy is usually internal to the trial process, and might take various forms. It might comprise a willingness to give the defendant the benefit of the doubt when interpreting vague evidence or testimony. It might comprise a prosecutor's reluctance to keep digging for further evidence. It might comprise a jury's increased sympathy for the defendant's defence. Finally, it might comprise the judge's leaning toward lenience when considering the range of available punishments. Importantly, mercy might also make reference to the defendant's *life*, beyond the circumstances that contributed to her culpability. For example, the defendant might have serious health issues that would be exacerbated by prison; she might be a sole breadwinner whose dependants would suffer if her earning power were restricted; she might be a reckless driver who had caused the death of her own child as a fellow passenger, who had clearly "suffered enough," and therefore no longer deserved a prison sentence.

There is a question about the relationship between mercy and justice. On some occasions, the merciful decision or interpretation might come *closer* to justice, precisely in taking account of more particulars; on other occasions, it might arguably challenge *criminal* justice by bringing in relevant considerations of a *broader* justice.

Like mercy, a pardon is also institutional, but it comes *after* the trial. The defendant has been duly tried and sentenced, with due regard for mitigating circumstances. In purely procedural terms, justice has spoken. As such, a pardon — from the country's president, for example — would be essentially *unjust*. But we should distinguish three kinds of pardons.

(i) The first is perhaps the most common but philosophically uninteresting: a pardon that is no more than a blatant political reward for past partisan support, as US Presidents tend to do on their last day in office.

(ii) Not strictly a pardon, but a more efficient way of correcting an injustice relevant to culpability. Some new evidence might have come to light, for example, and it is easier

19 There is an interesting debate about whether forgiveness should be *conditional* or not; in other words, whether the victim should wait for the attacker to fulfil some conditions before forgiving him: the obvious condition would be repentance, perhaps manifest in an apology, an offer of compensation, a commitment not to do it again. The thought is that the attacker has to "earn" forgiveness; if the victim forgives without such conditions, then she risks denigrating herself and sending a message of condoning the wrong. In response, those in favour of an "unconditional" forgiveness (possibly including Christians) would say that the conditionalist account is too "transactional." Genuine forgiveness, in accordance with its etymology, has to be like a gift, essentially unearned. It is only when the attacker is unrepentant that forgiveness amounts to real moral work. See Garrard and McNaughton (2014).

20 It is true that an individual can judge another individual mercifully. Bennett (2004) imagines having a racist grandfather, who is not a thug but merely inherited his racism during his upbringing. As a result of being merciful, Bennett imagines withholding criticism of his grandfather's racism. But he notes that such restraint actually contains a denigrating message, that the grandfather is too old to have an honest moral conversation.

to grant a pardon than to resubmit the evidence to a newly-convened court that would quash the earlier verdict, and cleanse the criminal record.[21]

(iii) This is the most controversial. It is neither blatantly political, nor is it corrective, but it challenges the criminal justice with reference to the broader injustice of the offender being punished. One reason for the pardon might have to do with new circumstances arising during the punishment that reduce the severity of the original crime. For example, in 1977 President Jimmy Carter pardoned over 200,000 Vietnam draft dodgers once the public view of the war had changed, and in 2022, the British government issued pardons for all abolished same-sex crimes.[22]

11.4 PAROLE

Almost all offenders, once sentenced, will in principle be eligible for discretionary early release from prison, often called parole. Like a pardon, discretionary parole is essentially controversial since it seems to undermine the result of a fair trial. And whenever an offender, out early on parole, re-offends, this always hits the headlines of the right-wing press as evidence that the government of the day is "soft on crime."[23]

As already mentioned, the obvious justification for parole has to do with money, especially in a country (like the United States and the United Kingdom) with prisons that are already overcrowded. Letting a safe prisoner out early saves money, and prisoners behaving well (i.e. fulfilling a condition for parole) are easier and cheaper to supervise. But there is also a strong case for "rewarding" the offender's genuine repentance. "Reward" is in scare quotes because many offenders may of course feign repentance in order to get the reward, and we have to assume that the experienced and expertly-trained parole officers can distinguish the genuine from the feigned.

Parole still carries restrictions: there might be an electronic tag, a curfew, and a duty to report to the parole officer regularly. As such it is better to describe parole as a change in the mode of punishment rather than as early release. Any infringement of the parole conditions, or any association with criminal activity, is likely to result in immediate re-incarceration. As a merely different mode of punishment, most debates about parole policy could be shifted over to the penologists to adjust the times and conditions based on empirical data.

As we saw, the two main theories of punishment have different views on parole. The retributivist will say that the quantum of punishment determined at the fair trial is what the offender deserves and is what she should get, regardless of her post-trial change of heart or good behaviour. The consequentialist would want to discuss risks and benefits and costs with

21 In 1952, Derek Bentley (aged 19) assisted Christopher Craig (aged 16) in the night-time burglary of a factory. After the police arrived, Craig shot a policeman dead. Craig was convicted of murder, but was spared the death penalty because of his age. As his accessory, Bentley was sentenced to death, and hanged in 1953. Already at the time of the trial, there were doubts about Bentley's mental capacity, doubts about Bentley's alleged complicity, and doubts about how the judge presented the facts to the jury. After a campaign by Bentley's family lasting several decades, he was formally *pardoned* in 1993, and eventually in 1998 his conviction was *quashed*. The symbolism of the pardon was not enough to rescue Bentley's name.

22 On the draft dodgers, see: https://www.history.com/this-day-in-history/president-carter-pardons-draft-dodgers

On same-sex crimes, see: https://www.gov.uk/government/news/historical-convictions-for-same-sex-sexual-activity-to-be-wiped

23 In 2023 the BBC made a fascinating documentary series, featuring real cases of real offenders coming before real parole boards: www.bbc.co.uk/programmes/m001jfsn

the penologist and the parole board psychologist in order to determine the "right" moment for early release. In the 1960s this process was guided by a rehabilitative ideal, but since then the parole board's task has changed. Now the board deliberates about whether to delay release: the offender is given an indeterminate sentence and is only considered for release once they have served all of their minimum term. And before they can order release, the parole board must be "satisfied that it is no longer necessary for the protection of the public that the prisoner should be confined" (see 28(6)(b) of the *Crime (Sentences) Act* 1997). They also decide on the re-release for those who have been recalled to prison after their automatic release (often at the half-way point in the sentence).

Hampton's moral education theory of punishment would seem to support parole for the newly "educated." In fact, however, she argues against parole, for two reasons:

> Because it is difficult to be sure that a seemingly repentant criminal is truly repentant, and thus because a policy of suspending or shortening sentences for those who seem repentant to the authorities could easily lead the criminal to fake repentance before a court or a parole board, the moral education theorist would be very reluctant to endorse such a policy.
>
> Moreover, it might well be the case that, prior to or during sentencing, a criminal's experience of repentance is produced in large part by the expectation of receiving the full punishment, so that the state's subsequent failure to inflict it could lead to a weakening of the criminal's renunciation of the action. Like a bad but repentant child who will conclude, if he is not punished by his parents, that his action must not have been so bad, the repentant criminal might well need to experience his complete sentence in order to "learn his lesson" effectively.
>
> (*Hampton,* 1984, pp. 233–234)

To add to Hampton's first point. In addition to the risk of parole boards being deceived by skilled performers, there is also a risk of parole boards being prejudiced (i) against working class or minority prisoners and their insufficient "fluency" in the language of remorse, and (ii) in favour of middle-class offenders who have a stable home to return to, where they will be supported in their parole conditions. To compensate for these luck factors, a parole board might be instructed to ignore the offender's pre-crime life and likely post-release family situation, and concentrate only on their prison behaviour, i.e. the place where offenders have some modicum of control and can therefore earn the right to parole.

This point about the modicum of control goes further. Behaving well as a response to the parole incentive gives prisoners something *to do* in prison, some way of thinking to structure their experience, and some reason to refuse the temptations of despair and distraction. "Good behaviour" may include training schemes and work projects, all of which will enrich the prison experience, and improve her post-prison opportunities. Even if she only *pretends* to do good, the thought is that some of this pretending might rub off on her character by the time she gets out. In contrast, if "five years" really means five years, as the retributivists and Hampton demand,[24] then she might as well switch off for those five years, merely enduring, while seeking illicit opportunities for pleasure and excitement, and without any need for uncomfortable thoughts about guilt. In summary, bad people need some opportunities for choice and agency and some grounds for hope if they are to improve at all.[25]

24 We are simplifying slightly here. Retributivists might not have a problem with five years meaning (i) two and a half years inside and (ii) two and a half years on license in the community — if that is what the judge, supported by the sentencing council, has decided is appropriate: it is the *discretionary* nature of early release which troubles them.

25 Bell (2022) offers another way to think about parole. What we have been discussing in this chapter she calls "beneficent mercy," and is grounded in the recognition of imperfection in individual human beings.

11.5 THE QUESTION OF CHARACTER

We have been discussing pardons and paroles, which are ways of reducing the trial-determined sentence. In this final section, we examine two policies pointing in the opposite direction: toward longer sentences, on the basis of certain character traits. The idea of a prisoner repenting (or undergoing a moral re-education) raises questions of character and about judgements of character. We have mentioned character on several occasions before, and we have said that it should not normally be relevant to criminal law. After all, the trial is structured by the three stages of questioning: did the defendant do it? Did she do it intentionally or recklessly? Did she have a defence? It should not matter what sort of character she has, just as it should not matter what her class and race and lifestyle is. Some of her character, just like some of her biography, will inevitably seep into the courtroom, and the defence lawyer and judge both have to watch out for this. There is always a risk of the jury liking or not liking the defendant, and allowing this to influence their deliberation in borderline evaluations. Similarly, the defendant's criminal record should really be kept secret during the trial, precisely to avoid steering the jury away from any benefit of the doubt they might be otherwise inclined to give.[26]

A controversial exception to the above tradition can be seen where there are mandatory sentences, or increased sentences, for repeat offenders. A dramatic example is the "three strikes" policy in California, but there are similar mandatory minima in England and Wales. The basic idea is simple. On the first "strike," the punishment will fit the crime, as normal. So too on the second strike. But if she commits the same crime a *third* time, then she has revealed herself to be a "hardened" criminal (that's the character judgement) who cannot understand the risk–benefit calculations in the normal language of deterrence. As such, the penalty for a thrice-committed crime has to be pushed up drastically, enough to "help" her understand the language of deterrence. It is as if the defendant is being punished for all three offences at once, but also punished for her stubborn character. By calling the offender "hardened," we are not yet giving up on her, we are simply adjusting our consequentialist calculations.

Another controversial exception involves the violent offender, the sex offender, and especially the paedophile. The thought is that most criminals are driven by simple greed, and are therefore amenable to deterrence, if the experts get the calculations right. In contrast, the sex offender may be like a drug addict, driven by forces not entirely in his rational control, and may be undeterred both before apprehension and after release. There is then a question of whether the public will *ever* be safe in the presence of such an offender after release. And yet, in theory the sex offender is duly tried and sentenced, serves his time, and has to be released. If no parole is involved, then no parole conditions are involved, and so the sex offender should in principle be *completely* released. After all, his debt is paid, his slate wiped clean, and society's moral equilibrium restored. If there were grounds for declaring him insane, then he could be detained as a threat to the public, but most sex offenders are perfectly sane, and therefore, in theory, should be allowed to resume their status as free citizens.

In contrast, "critical mercy" involves justified lenience, grounded in a recognition of the imperfection in human institutions and social rules.

26 The traditional irrelevance of character in the English law was dramatically changed by Section 98 ff. of the *Criminal Justice Act* 2003, which explicitly allows character evidence to be introduced for or against the defendant, as well as allows the defendant to introduce character evidence for or against another witness. Again, no defendant is convicted solely on the basis of "bad character"; but such evidence might be enough to nudge a borderline case one way or the other. Nevertheless, a judge can still rule a particular piece of evidence inadmissible.

And yet, because of the particular vulnerability of his previous victims, because of the non-rational aspect of his drives, he might well be required to wear a tag, or to live in a place a certain distance from schools, or to avoid proximity to certain friends and partners, as well as to other known ex-convicts. But how far should this go? If his tag surveillance discovers him in flirtatious conversation with a new acquaintance, should that acquaintance be informed about his past? Should his new neighbours be informed, and given the right to veto his move into their apartment block? This is a discussion topic that is still very much "live."[27]

CONCLUSION

This chapter has made a bit of room for philosophical discussion, while avoiding the huge quantities of social scientific research about punishment.[28] The ideal should be an on-going dialogue between philosophers and social scientists in the development of penal policy. It is too easy for philosophers to condescendingly reject the social scientific data on the grounds that the social scientists do not understand fully what their concepts mean; and it is too easy for the social scientists condescendingly to reject the philosophical discussions on the grounds that they are not supported by data.

Otherwise, this chapter brings the book to a close. We hope to have inspired curiosity in a number of directions for future enquiry. For those who want to pursue some of these difficult issues further, please consult the very first footnote in the Introduction for some important work in the philosophy of criminal law. Philosophy students, now more comfortable with the terminology, would also be encouraged to consult one of the many textbooks on criminal law designed for law students. Again we have to remind the reader of just how selective we have been in our choice of topics — we are a long way from a comprehensive introduction to the criminal law of the United Kingdom. But our hope is that all the topics will at least be familiar to ordinary citizens from within their ordinary lives, and that they will be better able to orient themselves in public debates about criminal policies, as well as to better appreciate the newspaper reports of individuals who have fallen foul of the law.

27 In England, the supervision of dangerous offenders includes MAPPA supervision: Multi-agency public protection arrangements. Here are the guidelines:
https://www.gov.uk/government/publications/multi-agency-public-protection-arrangements-mappa-guidance

28 Canton (2017) has a good introductory survey of the social scientific approaches.

BIBLIOGRAPHY

Alexander, L., & Ferzan, K. K. (2009). *Crime and culpability: A theory of criminal law*. Cambridge: Cambridge University Press.

Anscombe, G. E. M. (1957). *Intention*. Cambridge: Harvard University Press.

Arendt, H., & Kroh, J. (1964). *Eichmann in Jerusalem*. New York: Viking Press.

Auchmuty, L. (Eds.). (2018). *Great debates in gender and law*. Palgrave.

Austin, J. L. (1961). A plea for excuses. *Philosophical Papers*. Oxford: Clarendon.

Baron, M. (2003). Killing in the heat of passion. In Calhoun (Ed.), *Setting the moral compass: Essays by women philosophers*. Oxford: Oxford University Press.

Bell, K. (2022). Critical mercy in criminal law. *Law and Philosophy* [Published on-line first on 14 November 2022].

Bennett, C. (2004). The limits of mercy. *Ratio*, *17*(1), 1–11.

Bennett, C. (2008). *The apology ritual: A philosophical theory of punishment*. Cambridge: Cambridge University Press.

Bratman, M. (1981). Intention and means-end reasoning. *The Philosophical Review*, *90*(2), 252–265.

Campbell, J. (1982). Conditional intention. *Legal Studies*, *2*(1), 77–97.

Canton, R. (2017). *Why punish? An introduction to the philosophy of punishment*. Bloomsbury.

Chan, W., & Simester, A. P. (2011). Four functions of mens rea. *The Cambridge Law Journal*, *70*(2), 381–396.

Chau, P. (2018). Punishment and bad upbringing. *Criminal Justice Ethics*, *37*(2), 103–121.

Child, J. (2017). Understanding ulterior mens rea: Future conduct intention is conditional intention. *Cambridge Law Journal*, *76*(2), 311–336.

Child, J., Simester, A., Spencer, J., Stark, F., & Virgo, G. (2022). *Simester and Sullivan's criminal law: Theory and doctrine* (8th edn.). Hart.

Cowley, C. (2003). The conjoined twins and the limits of rationality in applied ethics. *Bioethics*, *17*(1), 69–88.

Cowley, C. (2006). Suicide is neither rational nor irrational. *Ethical Theory and Moral Practice*, *9*(5), 495–504.

Cowley, C. (2015). "Thank God I failed" – How much does a failed murder attempt transform the agent? *Ethical Perspectives*, *22*(4), 523–545.

Cowley, C. (2019a). Complicity and rape. *The Journal of Criminal Law*, *83*(1), 30–38.

Cowley, C. (2019b). *Jogee*, parasitic accessorial liability and conditional intention. In B. Krebs (Ed.), *Accessorial liability after Jogee*. Hart.

Cowley, C. (2020). Reckless enabling. *Criminal Law and Philosophy*, *14*(1), 51–67.

Cowley, C. (2024, Forthcoming). Apologising for negligence. In Matheson (Ed.), *The Nature and Ethics of Apology*. OUP.

Davidson, D. (1963). Actions, reasons, and causes. *Journal of Philosophy*, *60*(23), 685–700.

Deigh, J., & Dolinko, D. (2011). *Handbook of the philosophy of criminal law*. Oxford: Oxford University Press.

Delgado, R. (1985). 'Rotten Social Background': Should the law recognize a defense of severe environmental deprivation? *Law and Inequality*, *3*(1), 9–90.

Dempsey, M. (2013). Victimless conduct and the *Volenti* maxim: How consent works'. *Criminal Law and Philosophy*, *7*(1), 11–27.

Dempsey, M., & Herring, J. (2007). Why sexual penetration requires justification. *Oxford Journal of Legal Studies*, *27*(3), 467–491.

Dennis, I. H. (2009). On necessity as a defence to crime: Possibilities, problems and the limits of justification and excuse. *Criminal Law and Philosophy*, *3*(1), 29–49.

Dimock, S. (2008). Reasonable women in the law. *Critical Review of International Social and Political Philosophy, 11*(2), 153–175.
Dolinko, D. (2014). *The theoretical and philosophical foundations of criminal law*. Routledge.
Donnelly-Lazarov, B. (2017). Intention in criminal law: The challenge from non-observational knowledge. *Ratio Juris, 30*(4), 451–470.
Dressler, J. (1989). Exegesis of the law of duress: Justifying the excuse and searching for its proper limits. *Southern California Law Review, 62*, 1331.
Dressler, J. (1999). Some brief thoughts, (mostly negative) about "Bad Samaritan" laws. *Santa Clara Law Review, 40*, 971.
Dsouza, M. (2017). *Rationale-based defences in criminal law*. Bloomsbury Publishing.
Dubber, M., & Hörnle, T. (Eds.). (2014). *The Oxford handbook of criminal law*. Oxford: OUP.
Duff, A. (1990). *Intention, agency and criminal liability: Philosophy of action and the criminal law*. Basil Blackwell.
Duff, A. (1993). Choice, character, and criminal liability. *Law and Philosophy, 12*(4), 345–383.
Duff, A. (1997). *Criminal attempts*. Oxford: Clarendon Press.
Duff, A. (1998). *Philosophy and the Criminal Law; principle and critique*. Cambridge: Cambridge University Press.
Duff, A. (2007). *Answering for Crime; Responsibility and Liability in the Criminal Law*. Oxford: Hart Publishing.
Duff, A., & Green, S. (2013). *Philosophical foundations of criminal law*. Oxford: OUP.
Fisse, B., & Braithwaite, J. (1993). *Corporations, crime and accountability*. Cambridge: Cambridge University Press.
Flanders, C., & Hoskins, Z. (2016). *The new philosophy of criminal law*. Rowman & Littlefield.
Frankfurt, H. (2008). Inadvertence and moral responsibility. *The Amherst Lectures in Philosophy, 3*. 1–15, Available at: www.amherstlecture.org/
Garrard, E., & McNaughton, D. (2014). *Forgiveness*. Routledge.
Gibson, M. (2020). Deceptive sexual relations: A theory of criminal liability. *Oxford Journal of Legal Studies, 40*(1), 82–109.
Goff, L. (1987). The mental element in the crime of murder. *Israel Law Review, 22*(1), 1–36.
Goldberg, J. C., & Zipursky, B. C. (2006). Tort law and moral luck. *Cornell Law Review, 92*, 1123.
Greenberg, A. (2021). Why criminal responsibility for negligence cannot be indirect. *The Cambridge Law Journal, 80*(3), 489–514.
Gross, H. (2007). Rape, moralism, and human rights. *Criminal Law Review, 3*, 220–227.
Hampton, J. (1984). The moral education theory of punishment. *Philosophy & Public Affairs, 13*(3), 208–238.
Hart, H. L. A. (1968). Negligence, mens rea, and criminal responsibility. Reprinted in H. L. A. Hart (Ed.), *Punishment and responsibility*. Oxford: Clarendon.
Hart, H. L. A., & Honoré, T. (1959). *Causation in the law*. Oxford: Oxford University Press.
Herring, J. (2005). Mistaken sex. *Criminal Law Review*, July, 511–524.
Herring, J. (2007). Human rights and rape: A reply to Hyman Gross. *Criminal Law Review, 3*, 228–231.
Herring, J. (2007). Familial homicide, failure to protect and domestic violence: Who's the victim? *Criminal Law Review, (December)*, 923-933.
Herring, J. (2020). *Great debates in criminal law*. 4th ed., Palgrave.
Hood, R., & Hoyle, C. (2015). *The Death Penalty: A worldwide perspective* (5th edn.). Oxford: Oxford University Press.
Horder, J. (2004). *Excusing crime*. Oxford: Oxford University Press.
Horder, J. (2022). *Ashworth's principles of criminal law* (10th edn.). Oxford: Oxford University Press.
Horder, J., & McGowan, L. (2006). Manslaughter by causing another's suicide. *Criminal Law Review*, 1035–1046.
Horsey, K., & Rackley, E. (2018). Tort law. In Auchmuty (Ed.), *Great debates in gender and law*. Palgrave.

Howes, S. K., Williams, K. S., & Wistrich, H. (2021). Women who kill: Why self-defence rarely works for women who kill their abuser. *Criminal Law Review*, *11*, 945–957.

Hunter, R., McGlynn, C., & Rackley, E. (Eds.). (2010). *Feminist judgments: From theory to practice.* London: Hart Publishing.

Hurd, H. M. (1996). The moral magic of consent. *Legal Theory*, *2*(2), 121–146.

Hurd, H. M. (2014). Finding no fault with negligence. In Oberdiek (Ed.), *Philosophical foundations of the law of torts.* Oxford: Oxford University Press.

Kadish, S. H. (1985). Complicity, cause and blame: A study in the interpretation of doctrine. *California Law Review*, *73*(2), 323.

Kotiswaran, P. (2014). Feminist approaches to criminal law. In Dubber & Hörnle (Eds.), *The Oxford handbook of criminal law.* Oxford: Oxford University Press.

Krebs, B. (2015). Mens rea in joint enterprise: A role for endorsement? *Cambridge Law Journal*, *74*(3), 480–504.

Krebs, B. (2019). *Accessorial liability after Jogee.* Oxford: Hart Publishing.

Kutz, C. (2000). *Complicity: Ethics and law for a collective age.* Cambridge: Cambridge University Press.

Kutz, C. (2007). Causeless complicity. *Criminal Law and Philosophy*, *1*(3), 289–305.

Laird, K. (2021). Gross negligence manslaughter: R. v Rebelo (Bernard). *Criminal Law Review*, *12*, 1075–107.

Lepora, C., & Goodin, R. E. (2013). *On Complicity and Compromise.* Oxford: Oxford University Press.

Le Sage, L., & De Ruyter, D. (2008). Criminal parental responsibility: Blaming parents on the basis of their duty to control versus their duty to morally educate their children. *Educational Philosophy and Theory*, *40*(6), 789–802.

Leisenring, A. (2008). Controversies surrounding mandatory arrest policies and the police response to intimate partner violence. *Sociology Compass*, *2*(2), 451–466.

Leverick, F. (2006). *Killing in self-defence.* Oxford: Oxford University Press.

Lodge, A. (2020). Domestic abuse, suicide and liability for manslaughter: In pursuit of justice for victims. *The Journal of Criminal Law*, *84*(4), 273–292.

MacIntyre, A. (1984). *After virtue: A study in moral theory.* South Bend: University of Notre Dame Press.

Mackie, J. (1974). *The cement of the universe.* Oxford: Clarendon.

McColgan, A. (1993). In defence of battered women who kill. *Oxford Journal of Legal Studies*, *13*(4), 508–529.

McGlynn, C., Rackley, E., & Houghton, R. (2017). Beyond 'revenge porn': The continuum of image-based sexual abuse. *Feminist Legal Studies*, *25*(1), 25–46.

Mellema, G. (2016). *Complicity and moral accountability.* University of Notre Dame Press.

Moore, M. S. (2009). *Causation and responsibility: An essay in law, morals, and metaphysics.* Oxford: Oxford University Press.

Moore, M. S. (2010). *Placing blame: A theory of the criminal law.* Oxford University Press.

Morgan, C. (2013). Loss of self-control: Back to the good old days. *The Journal of Criminal Law*, *77*(2), 119–135.

Munro, V., & Aiken, R. (2018). Adding insult to injury? The Criminal Law's response to domestic abuse-related suicide in England and Wales. *Criminal Law Review*, *9*, 732–741.

Nagel, T. (1979). Moral luck. In *Mortal questions.* Canto.

Ormerod, D. (2021). The domestic abuse bill 2021. *Criminal Law Review*, *6*, 423–426.

Ormerod, D., & Laird, K. (2021). *Smith and Hogan's criminal law* (16th edn.). Oxford: Oxford University Press.

Padfield, N. (1989). Exploring a quagmire: Insanity and automatism. *Cambridge Law Journal*, *48*(3), 354–357.

Padfield, N. (2016). *Criminal law* (10th edn.). Oxford: Oxford University Press.

Pedain, A. (2003). Intention and the terrorist example. *Criminal Law Review*, September, 579–593.

Reed, A., & Bohlander, M. (2016). *Participation in crime: Domestic and comparative perspectives.* Routledge.

Reid, L. (2020). Winch on punishment: Contested concepts, justification, and primitive reactions. In Campbell & Reid (Eds.), *Ethics, society and politics: Themes from the philosophy of Peter Winch.* Berlin: Springer.

Roper, V. (2022). The Corporate Manslaughter and Corporate Homicide Act 2007: A re-evaluation 10 years on from the first case. *Criminal Law Review*, (4), 290–306.

Rubin, G. (2003). New light on *Steane's case. The Journal of Legal History*, *24*(2), 143–164.

Sereny, G. (1995). *Albert Speer: His battle with truth.* Picador.

Shiffrin, S. (2017). The moral neglect of negligence. *Oxford Studies in Political Philosophy*, *3*, 197–228.

Shute, S., & Simester, A. P. (Eds.). (2002). *Criminal law theory: Doctrines of the general part.* Oxford: Oxford University Press.

Simester, A. P. (2013). A disintegrated theory of culpability. *The sanctity of life and the criminal law – The legacy of Glanville Williams, Baker and Horder* (eds) Cambridge: Cambridge University Press.

Simester, A. P., & Sullivan, G. R. (2019). Causing euthanasia. *Law Quarterly Review*, *135*, 21–27.

Simons, K. W. (2002). Dimensions of negligence in criminal and tort law. *Theoretical Inquiries in Law*, *3*(2), 2–54.

Smith, J. (1997). Criminal liability of accessories: Law and law reform. *Law Quarterly Review*, *113*, 453–467.

Stannard, J. (2010). Sticks, stones and words: Emotional harm and the English criminal law. *Journal of Criminal Law*, *74*(6), 533–540.

Stark, F. (2016). *Culpable carelessness: Recklessness and negligence in the criminal law.* Cambridge: Cambridge University Press.

Storey, T. (2019). Coercive control: An offence but not a defence: *R v Challen* [2019]. EWCA Crim 916, Court of Appeal. *The Journal of Criminal Law*, *83*(6), 513–515.

Sullivan, G. R., Crombag, H. S., & Child, J. J. (2021). Loss of control in the appeal courts. *Northern Ireland Legal Quarterly*, *72*(2), 200–223.

Tadros, V. (2005). *Criminal responsibility.* Oxford: Oxford University Press.

Tadros, V. (2006). Rape without consent. *Oxford Journal of Legal Studies*, *26*(3), 515–543.

Thomas, C. (2020). The 21st century jury: Contempt, bias and the impact of jury service. *Criminal Law Review*, *11*, 987–1011.

Thomson, J. J. (1991). Self-defense. *Philosophy and Public Affairs*, *20*(4), 283–310.

Uniacke, S. (1994). *Permissible killing: The self-defence justification of homicide.* Cambridge: Cambridge University Press.

Uniacke, S. (2001). Was Mary's death murder? *Medical Law Review*, *9*(3), 208–220.

Von Hirsch. (1993). *Censure and sanctions.* Oxford: Clarendon.

Waldron, J. (1997). Moments of carelessness and massive loss. In Oberdiek (Ed.), *The philosophical foundations of tort law.* Oxford: Oxford University Press.

Walker, N., & Walker, N. (1991). *Why punish?* (Vol. 107). Oxford: Oxford University Press.

Williams, B. (1981). Moral luck. *Moral luck.* Cambridge: Cambridge University Press.

Williams, G. (1987). Oblique intention. *Cambridge Law Journal*, *46*(3), 417–438.

Wilson, W. (2002). *Central issues in criminal theory.* Hart.

Winch, P. (1972). Ethical reward and punishment. *Ethics and action.* Abingdon: Routledge and Kegan Paul.

Wu, A. (2020). Going full circle: Gender and the 'loss of control' defence under the Coroners and Justice Act 2009. *Rule of Law Journal*, *1*(1). 46–54.

Yaffe, G. (2010). *Attempts: In the philosophy of action and the criminal law.* Oxford: Oxford University Press.

CASES CITED

A. THE UNITED KINGDOM

The formal titles of many of these cases have the official title of "R v. Smith" (i.e. Regina or Rex vs. Smith), but we have omitted this to allow easy alphabetical ordering. The exception is when the defendant is named by only an initial, as in "R v. G" or "Re F." For further details about any case, put the full reference into Google, and you should find handy summaries offered by websites like "Law Teacher." For the full text of the judgement, visit the British and Irish Legal Information Institute (https://www.bailii.org/) and type in the case name and year, or use the Westlaw and LexisNexis databases (available for free through most University subscriptions). Supreme Court decisions are available here: https://www.supremecourt.uk / decided-cases/index .html

B. OUTSIDE THE UNITED KINGDOM

INDEX

For Product Safety Concerns and Information please contact our EU
representative GPSR@taylorandfrancis.com
Taylor & Francis Verlag GmbH, Kaufingerstraße 24, 80331 München, Germany

www.ingramcontent.com/pod-product-compliance
Ingram Content Group UK Ltd.
Pitfield, Milton Keynes, MK11 3LW, UK
UKHW020002200926
475702UK00015B/2430

* 9 7 8 1 0 3 2 3 9 8 9 6 9 *